# THE PURSUIT OF INTIMACY

# THE PURSUIT OF INTIMACY

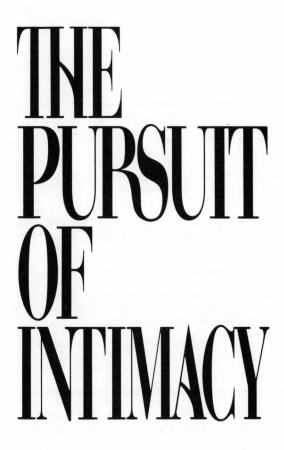

David and Teresa Ferguson
Chris and Holly Thurman
*with* Carole Gift Page

A
JANET
THOMA
BOOK

Thomas Nelson Publishers
Nashville

Published in Nashville, Tennessee, by Janet Thoma Books, a division of Thomas Nelson, Inc., Publishers, and distributed in Canada by Word Communications, Ltd., Richmond, British Columbia, and in the United Kingdom by Word (UK), Ltd., Milton Keynes, England.

Except where indicated, Scripture quotations are from THE NEW KING JAMES VERSION of the Bible. Copyright © 1979, 1980, 1982, Thomas Nelson, Inc., Publishers.

Quotations indicated KJV are from the King James Version.

Quotations marked NASB are from THE NEW AMERICAN STANDARD BIBLE, copyright © 1960, 1962, 1963, 1968, 1971, 1972, 1973, 1975, 1977 by The Lockman Foundation and are used by permission.

Clients' names and the details of their stories have been changed, fictionalized, and intermingled to protect their identities.

**Library of Congress Cataloging-in-Publication Data**

The pursuit of intimacy / by David and Teresa Ferguson, Chris and
  Holly Thurman, with Carole Gift Page.
      p.    cm.
    ISBN 0-8407-7794-9
    1. Marriage—Religious aspects—Christianity.   2. Intimacy
(Psychology)—Religious aspects—Christianity.   I. Ferguson, David,
1947-   .
BV835.P87   1993
241'.63—dc20                                                    93-19621
                                                                    CIP

Printed in the United States of America.

1234567—97 96 95 94 93

All we've come to know and experience concerning intimacy is because of God who has made Himself available to us in Christ.

> "For the crooked man is an abomination to the LORD;/But He is *intimate* with the upright."
>
> Proverbs 3:32 NASB

It's to Him and His divinely ordained human relationships—marriage, family, and the church—that we offer this book desiring

> "to impart to you not only the gospel of God but also our own lives, because you had become very dear to us."
>
> I Thessalonians 2:8-9 NASB

David and Teresa Ferguson          Chris and Holly Thurman

# Contents

# Acknowledgments

As you'll soon encounter in this work, our conviction is that we yearn for intimacy with our Creator and through meaningful relationships in our lives. It's with heartfelt gratitude that we express our thanks to so many "meaningful others" who have touched us deeply along our marriage journey.

To our families and children who endured, supported, and accepted us.

To the Garzas, Bouldins, and Olivers who early on befriended and loved us.

To the O'Chesters, Daileys, and Zamorskys who believe in us, encourage us, and care.

To the McCoys, Evans, and Walters who let us be real and share with us a common vision for marriage.

Special thanks to Janet Thoma for her vision, expertise—and most of all, for her belief in us. Finally, to Carole Gift Page for her endless creative contributions in making Intimacy Therapy "come alive."

—David and Teresa Ferguson

Our greatest debt of thanks in writing this book is to God. He has been so gracious in helping us to weather the difficult storms that are part of everyone's marriage. That we are even writing a book on marital intimacy is only because of what God has lovingly taught us over the twelve years we have been married. God, we will never be able to thank you enough for caring about our marriage like you do and for helping us to mature in our pursuit of intimacy.

We also owe a huge debt of thanks to our writing partners and friends, David and Teresa Ferguson. They have graciously allowed us to be a part of their lives and their ministry to hurting couples. We have learned so much from them about marital intimacy, both from what they have taught us and by just watching their union as a couple. David and Teresa, thank you for loving us and showing us what God's design for marriage looks like in word and deed.

Our thanks also go to the couples who have been our close friends over the years. While we won't mention you by name (to protect the guilty), you know who you are and how much you mean to us. Your love for us has meant so much, and we have grown as a result of your friendship. Thank you for being such an encouragement to us.

Finally, our heartfelt thanks to Thomas Nelson Publishers. They have been wonderful, as usual, to work with during the writing of this book. Special thanks to Janet Thoma for her invaluable guidance as this book took shape and to Carole Gift Page for her editorial genius. Your special talents and abilities have made all the difference in the world in how this book turned out.

—Chris and Holly Thurman

# THE PURSUIT OF INTIMACY

# WHAT FALLING IN LOVE WAS MEANT TO BE

# CHAPTER 1

# Marriage Intimacy: Elusive Dream or Obtainable Reality?

*There are many objects of great value to man
which cannot be attained by unconnected individuals,
but must be attained, if attained at all, by association.*
Daniel Webster
Pittsburgh address of 1833

IT'S A FACT.

We need one another.

It's not good to be alone.

As social beings, we need to establish positive, deep relationships in order to live satisfying lives.

It all adds up to intimacy.

Everybody wants it, but most folks haven't the slightest idea what it is. Fewer still have any inkling how to achieve it. The authors began their marriages as ignorant of true intimacy as anyone else. Take David and Teresa Ferguson's experience, for instance. Their first date was a "Coke date"—that's what they called them in the sixties. Actually, it was more of a "jail date." You see, David had this great idea. "I decided Teresa and I would go to the county jail to visit one of my friends who was locked up there. This guy's greatest aspiration in life was to be in every county jail in Texas at least once. He actually had a map on his closet door with pushpins to show the jails he'd already been in. So that's how my romance with Teresa began—the two of us going to jail to see my buddy.

"A few months later, at the ripe old age of sixteen, Teresa and I were married, not so much out of love as out of rebellion. We told our parents, 'If you don't let us get married, we'll run up to Kansas and get married anyway.' We figured if we got married our parents would never bother us again and we wouldn't have anyone telling us what to do."

Right.

Now Teresa often tells engaged couples, "There were tears at our wedding, but they weren't tears of joy." She and David began their relationship as husband and wife without their parents' blessing. They were just two young rebels without the slightest idea what marriage was all about.

On their wedding night they went to a local hotel, and the next morning David's buddy Stanley showed up and wanted him to go play pool. Teresa was still asleep so he figured, *Why not?* Off they went down the block to the local pool hall. When Teresa awoke, she was alone and had no idea where David had gone. She didn't even have money for the hotel bill. So, fighting panic and disappointment, she dressed and walked home, wondering, *Has David bailed out on me already?*

Teresa's feeling of abandonment would replay itself countless times throughout their marriage, but the first seeds of distrust and insecurity were planted that morning.

"During our first three years of marriage, we never set up housekeeping on our own; we merely played house," David remembers. "We lived together during our first year while I finished high school and started junior college. During the summers we swapped back and forth, living first with her parents, then with my parents. Even when our daughter, Terri, came along, we couldn't afford to establish a home together. In fact, the only thing we did right in those early days was stay in school.

"When I went off to the University of Texas in Austin, Teresa and the baby would stay with me until our money ran out, then they would move back home. We would see one another on holidays and during the summers. In fact, Teresa often complained that she couldn't even find me. It wasn't hard to figure out why. One semester I lived in my car down by the river. I even had a roommate, a guy named Wayne. He slept in the backseat. We kept our belongings in the trunk. I'd wear my sweatshirt for a week then turn it inside out and wear it another week. That's how I lived—a vagabond lifestyle my wife couldn't appreciate.

"Our third year of marriage was the charm. That's the year Teresa and I were forced to come to grips with what it meant to be a family living together through thick and thin. That year Teresa and Terri joined me at the university and Teresa discovered, to her dismay, that I had continued my single lifestyle. I had my studies, my routine was set, and I'd established my identity with all my single friends. There was little room in my schedule or my life for Teresa and our little daughter.

"The truth is, Teresa and I endured eight to ten years of disaster before our marriage got on the right track. During those years we hurt each other deeply again and again. One day I came right out and asked Teresa if she loved me. She said, 'I don't know. I just feel emotionally numb.'

"Five years into our marriage I established a personal relationship with Christ, and three years later Teresa made the same commitment. Our lives started changing; we began to grow spiritually and emotionally. But our faith didn't automatically 'fix' our relationship. Our hurts were too numerous, and they were so deep-rooted God had to get our attention before He could begin to work on the wounds one by one. In a slow, painstaking process He started healing the hurts in our marriage so we could share real intimacy and become one—the way we were meant to be from the beginning."

Married for more than thirty years now, David and Teresa have invested most of their adult lives in marriage and family issues. As founders of the Center for Marriage and Family Intimacy, they share with thousands of couples every year, rejoicing with them as Intimacy Therapy makes a positive impact on their relationships. David also maintains a marriage and family counseling practice through the Minirth-Meier Clinic in Austin, Texas.

What is intimacy? you may be wondering. The word *intimate* comes from the Latin word *intimus*, which means "innermost." Intimacy is that wordless gnawing of the soul for emotional and spiritual connectedness with our Creator and other human beings. We've all experienced that hunger—yet it's as hard to define as physical hunger. Most of us never attempt to put words around the concept; instead, we respond instinctively to the neediness we feel. We try in a hundred different ways to fill our empty emotional cup and satisfy our deepest yearnings. We want someone to know us thoroughly and accept us unconditionally. We want love that covers a multitude of sins. We want to know that someone else appreciates our uniqueness and understands our needs. We want to be reassured we're not alone.

From a cultural perspective, E. H. Erikson defines intimacy as "the capacity to commit [one]self to concrete affiliations and partnerships and to develop the ethical strength to abide by such commitments, even though they may call for significant sacrifices and compromises."[1]

Psychologists have evolved their own list of defining features for intimacy: openness, honesty, mutual self-disclosure, caring, warmth, protecting, helping, being devoted to each other, mutually attentive, mutually committed, surrendering control, dropping defenses, becoming emotionally attached, and feeling distressed when separation occurs.[2]

## EXPECTING MARRIAGE TO MEET OUR NEEDS

Most of us enter marriage expecting it to meet our needs. Not only that, we expect it to happen automatically, spontaneously. *If he loves me, he'll make me happy. If she's the right one for me, she should fulfill all my dreams. If we love each other, nothing else matters. Once we're married, we'll live happily ever after.*

You know. We know. It doesn't work that way.

Today, perhaps more than in any previous generation, there is a preoccupation with love and relationships, with finding acceptance and boosting self-esteem, with discovering the secrets of emotional bonding to another human being. And yet never before have people felt so isolated, alienated, and alone.

Why aren't we connecting with one another in a satisfying way?

Why isn't marriage providing the emotional haven it once offered? Why isn't the family the sanctuary for hurting hearts it once was?

What's gone wrong?

For one thing, we're listening to the wrong voices these days because we have few good role models. We—especially the young— watch the silver screen and the small screen for examples of what relationships should be. We—especially the young—listen to the lyrics of MTV music videos to form our ideas of what love and romance are all about. For a couple of generations we've bought into the cynical, twisted attitude of the entertainment industry that marriage and family are somehow passé, if not downright destructive. While glorifying rugged individualism and personal rights, the entertainment media promote lust instead of love, sex instead of sharing, and violence instead of vulnerability. In movies and TV, marriage is rarely represented except in negative terms; families are portrayed as broken, fragmented, disturbed, or dysfunctional. Love between married couples doesn't seem to exist.

Michael Medved, co-host of the PBS TV show "Sneak Previews" and author of *Hollywood vs. America,* confirms that the traditional family has received surprisingly harsh treatment from today's movie moguls. "Take a look, for example, at the [1991] Oscars," he suggests. "Five very fine actors were nominated for best actor of the year. Three of them portrayed murderous psychos: Robert De Niro in *Cape Fear,* Warren Beatty in *Bugsy,* and Anthony Hopkins in *The Silence of the Lambs* (this last a delightful family film about two serial killers—one eats and the other skins his victims). A fourth actor, Robin Williams, was nominated for playing a delusional homeless psycho in *The Fisher King.* The most wholesome character was Nick Nolte's, a good old-fashioned manic-depressive-suicidal neurotic in *The Prince of Tides.*"

Medved goes on to say, "Did you ever notice how few movies there are about happily married people? There are very few movies about married people at all, but those that are made tend to portray marriage as a disaster, as a dangerous situation, as a battleground— with a long series of murderous marriage movies. . . . The message is that marriage is outmoded, it is dangerous, oppressive, unhealthy."[3]

No wonder marriage has become the blind leading the blind toward an unknown destination—without a map! No wonder couples haven't the slightest idea what intimacy is all about! In fact, tragically, most of us haven't the slightest idea what falling in love was meant to be!

But we human beings are a sturdy, plucky lot. Even though we see few examples of marital bliss in the media or in the society we live in, we still enter marriage expecting to establish a warm, close, trusting relationship. Only later does it dawn on us that, while we were taught to read and write, drive a car, and earn a living, no one taught us how to develop a close personal relationship.

If we grew up in a loving, close-knit family with parents who were devoted to each other, we may sense instinctively what it takes to make a relationship work. But most of us these days have not been so fortunate.

How has the American family arrived at such a state of dysfunction and despair?

The mid to late twentieth century saw the impact of the full-blown women's rights movement, the sexual revolution, rampant divorce, two-income families, and the staggering increase of single-parent homes. Amid the aftershocks of these social temblors, the search for intimacy has intensified to the point that intimate relationships have become more important than ever. Authors J. Veroff, E. Douvan, and R. A. Kulka interviewed Americans about various aspects of their lives in 1957 and 1976. They stated, "We have many different pieces of data to support the general conclusion that interpersonal intimacy has become a vehicle for personal fulfillment much more in 1976 than it was in 1957."[4]

In sharp contrast to this heightened desire for close relationships in Western society is what appears to be a declining capacity to experience them. Recent estimates of marital breakups suggest as many as two-thirds of new marriages may end in divorce.

What a tragic commentary on American life today! Think of it. Perhaps more than any other generation we yearn to experience close, intimate relationships. Yet, more than any previous generation, we have lost the *capacity* to experience them!

## THE GOOD NEWS

The good news is that genuine intimacy is attainable in your relationship, no matter how much you may have hurt each other in the past. Even if you feel your marriage has failed, there is hope. You are not helpless. You are not alone.

This book introduces the principles of *Intimacy Therapy*™—a decidedly new approach to marriage counseling that helps heal and enrich relationships, change behaviors, and create genuine intimacy between marriage partners. Based on the premise that God created us with a need for intimacy with Him and with one another, Intimacy Therapy guides couples toward a fulfilled and abundant life. Intimacy Therapy treats the whole person—body (our "world-consciousness"), soul (our "self-consciousness"), and spirit (our "God-consciousness").

Through the following pages, we will walk you through the ten "action verbs" of Intimacy Therapy: *adopt, block, think, forgive, reject, leave, mourn, understand, practice,* and *maintain.* We will guide you to an understanding of the true nature of intimacy and show you step by step how to develop deeper empathy and closeness with your mate. No longer will intimacy be an elusive dream or a wishful fantasy. You will have clear, concrete principles to guide you, plus a workable plan to build a marriage framework with a strong foundation of mutual nurturing and love.

In writing this book, David and Teresa Ferguson joined forces with two dear friends and colleagues, Dr. Chris Thurman of the Minirth-Meier Tunnell and Wilson Clinic in Austin, Texas, and his wife, Holly. They, too, have overcome significant obstacles in their marriage as they move toward achieving the kind of intimacy God desires for them. But let's let Dr. Thurman tell you about his marriage in his own words:

"Holly and I met as students at the University of Texas at Austin. She was finishing her undergraduate degree in history; I was completing a doctorate in counseling psychology. I was instantly attracted to her but didn't ask her out for months because of my own deep insecurities. Only after Holly invited me to speak at her sorority Bible study did I conjure up enough courage to ask her for a date.

"After two years of steady dating, we decided to tie the knot. We married at the beginning of my last year in graduate school, but had we known what was to come I doubt either of us ever would have married anyone at all!

"During our early years together Holly and I were both extremely immature. More concerned with getting our own needs met than meeting the other's needs, we had our share of horrible fights, saying and doing a lot of things we regretted afterwards. Being Christians, we felt an extra measure of guilt and shame for having such an unhappy marriage.

"For seven or eight years Holly and I felt more like enemies than friends. We screamed, yelled, pouted, and punished each other in our desperate effort to get what we wanted. Everything seemed hopeless. We reached a point where we knew we would either end up divorcing or we'd have to learn to truly love each other. We thank God He brought us through the misery and alienation of those early years into a loving, deeply committed relationship. Now the *we* in our marriage is more important than the *I*.

"Like any couple, we're still 'under construction.' We both have a lot of growing up to do. We know how hard it is to 'die to ourselves' and live as one in the deepest sense of the word. Thank God we've experienced a real taste of marital oneness; we're excited about how God daily continues to mature us as a couple.

"If you'd told me twelve years ago Holly and I would be getting along today and growing in our love, I'd have said, 'Impossible! Our marriage is unsalvageable.' Without God, it would have been. He is the centerpiece of our marriage."

Let us stress one point. We present these principles not only as therapists who have counseled countless couples in these matters, but also as husbands who have discovered firsthand, through trial and error, prayer and practice, the truths and the effectiveness of these concepts in our own marriages. To coin an old phrase, we speak with the voice of experience. Our wives, Holly and Teresa, would be the first to tell you that many of the battles were hard-won and a few are still in progress, but the growth and closeness we've experienced have made it a rewarding and deeply satisfying journey. And, of course, to prevent an entirely male viewpoint, our wives will share freely from their own experiences.

## HOW INTIMACY THERAPY WORKS

Come with us as we walk one couple, Marla and Jimmy Carlton, through the ten steps of Intimacy Therapy toward marital healing and closeness. Intimacy Therapy describes the destination, provides a road map, and liberates two partners to enjoy the journey. You'll see that Intimacy Therapy is different from other marriage-counseling techniques in that it does not take a Band-Aid approach to marital conflicts or merely treat symptoms; it works from the inside out, addressing the needs, emotional hurts, and heart issues of each partner while equipping couples to meet each spouse's needs. Just as you and your partner held the power to wound each other, now you hold the power to help heal your mate's longstanding childhood hurts.

How does Intimacy Therapy work? It helps couples **eliminate hindrances to intimacy** by:

1. **Identifying unmet intimacy needs.** We'll show you—as we showed the Carltons—how the need for intimacy is a basic human motivation underlying marriage behaviors. And we'll explain why it's okay to have needs. We'll examine specific relational needs that, when met, yield intimacy and when unmet, produce lies, pain, and games.

2. **Identifying and interrupting unproductive behaviors and unhealthy thinking.** We'll help you look at common marriage lies and at the games you may be playing. The Carltons needed to learn how to identify and stop the behaviors that hinder intimacy and the major marital lies that distort reality. We'll share what they learned with you.

3. **Resolving unhealed emotions.** We'll explore both inevitable marriage hurts and the family-of-origin pain that often leads to

marital unhappiness. In other words, we'll help you understand that you can't "cleave" to your spouse in intimacy until you've left your father and mother. We'll show you how to truly leave your childhood home and mourn your childhood hurts. We'll also help you grieve the losses caused by unresolved pain and guide you in experiencing the blessing when your spouse comforts you.

After we've eliminated the hindrances to intimacy, we'll walk you through our process to deepen intimacy in your relationship by:

1. **Modeling and reinforcing productive behaviors.** We'll show you how Jimmy and Marla recaptured lost romance by replacing their unproductive behaviors with positive behaviors. We'll help you implement the four necessary ingredients of intimacy— affectionate caring, vulnerable communication, joint accomplishment, and mutual giving. Just as we helped the Carltons, we'll help you begin a new cycle of giving instead of taking.

2. **Experiencing positive emotions.** We'll help you gain emotional freedom by guiding you through the positive emotional experiences of confession, forgiveness, gratefulness, empathy, and reassurance. We'll teach you the vital principles of "emotional responding," so you'll know what to say when your spouse is hurting.

3. **Internalizing healthy thinking.** We'll help you adopt a habit of positive self-talk based on the principle of Proverbs 23:7—"As he thinks in his heart, so is he." We'll also help you overcome your tendency to hide your pain or "hurl" your hurts, and lead you through the Biblical model of sharing the truth of your needs in love.

4. **Modeling and encouraging the meeting of intimacy needs.** In our final chapters, we'll help you better understand who you are. We'll guide you—as we guided the Carltons—in the disciplines of receiving intimately from your Creator then giving to your partner. We'll present tested principles that need to be embraced as a lifestyle to help you maintain a deeper marital intimacy; and fi-

nally, we'll highlight the stages of marriage, offering a proven intimacy plan to help you navigate successfully through life's major challenges, including the arrival and rearing of children, mid-life crises, and the empty nest syndrome.

It is our goal to help you, our readers, avoid the pitfalls and pains of a fractured, failed relationship and to discover the potential for intimacy that exists in your own marriage. From both our counseling and personal experiences, we offer proven techniques to help you pursue intimacy and tap into its wellspring of life-giving waters. What it took us years of trial and error—and prayer—to learn, we share earnestly and eagerly with you, that your journey toward intimacy may be joyous and abundantly satisfying for both you and your mate.

Let us speak frankly right from the start. We—Chris and Holly and David and Teresa—haven't learned all there is to know about marital happiness. No one has.

But one thing we know. We're all in this together—living, learning, exploring, and discovering nuggets of truth that make the going easier. We've been there—where you are right this moment. And we made it through. We survived. And now we're better than ever.

CHAPTER

2

# What Happened in the Beginning?

MARLA CARLTON IS one of those women who longs for intimacy but doesn't have a clue how to get it. She knows something's missing from her twelve-year marriage and she's ready to consider divorce, but she's decided to make one last effort to save the relationship. So she's come to pour out her heart to a counselor.

A burnished redhead with the saucy good looks of a Lucy or a Goldie Hawn, she speaks in quick, spontaneous spurts, her voice rising and falling with the lilting cadences of a vocalist. She gestures effusively, her hands slicing the air for dramatic emphasis. "I told myself I'd never see a shrink, and here I am! Can you believe it?"

She pauses long enough to survey her surroundings, then blurts out, "You gotta know: I wouldn't be here if I didn't still love Jimmy, but it's just no good anymore." She pauses again as her voice cracks with emotion. She shifts a little, unbuttoning the jacket of her stylish forest-green pantsuit. "Maybe I should start at the beginning. Jimmy and I met when he was doing this gig in L.A. He's a singer—we're both singers, sort of—I mean, I messed around with it a little, but not seriously like Jimmy. He was the lead singer in this little band, sort of a cross between country and rhythm and blues. It was a good little band—they traveled from Nashville to Texas to L.A. and back again—they were on the road together six years, but I don't think you would've heard of them—they never got the big breaks, you know?

"Anyway, I sang with the band a couple of times—that's how Jimmy and I met. We fell for each other right away. I mean, talk about romance and roses! We got married, and when he went on the road again I went with him. It was the most exciting time of my life. I mean, Jimmy was a real hunk. He looks like Garth Brooks, only maybe not as tall. But the same great looks, you know? And he sounds like Randy Travis. They could be brothers. I tell you, all the girls envied me. I mean, everyone loved Jimmy.

"Well, then the kids came along—two in three years, a boy and a girl. It was just too hard traveling with the band anymore, so I got an apartment and settled down with the kids while Jimmy stayed on the road. It was misery. I hated being alone with the kids, seeing Jimmy only when he was in town. Finally I gave him an ultimatum. I said, 'It's me or the band. You can't have both.' So he came home.

"I tell you, he wasn't a happy camper, but he went out and got a regular job—well, actually several jobs—first selling vacuum cleaners, then real estate—until the market collapsed—and now he's pushing insurance. Has his own office with his name on the door and a big desk and everything. Even making enough finally that I can stay home with the kids.

"But I think he hates it—being stuck in an office instead of out on the road, being a businessman instead of a musician. I don't think he's happy being married to me. Not that he'd ever tell me, of course. And that's the problem, you see? He never talks. Never lets me know how he feels. I talk at him constantly, trying to pry open his feelings, but he's like a tight little clam. Answers me in monosyllables. Little grunts or looks. The looks are the worst. He says volumes with those looks—all negative.

"I suppose we really didn't talk much during our early years of marriage—you know, about deep emotional feelings and stuff—but we had other things to keep us going. Now there's nothing except the kids. And we can't even agree on how to raise them."

Marla blinks her mascaraed lashes and swallows a sob. "The truth is, I'm always lonely, even when Jimmy's around. And I have a feeling he's lonely too—like there's something that should be there between us, like somehow we should be able to help each other or comfort each other, even if our life isn't all we wanted it to be. But we're like strangers occupying the same house. Worse than strangers. At least strangers don't have any expectations.

"Here's what it boils down to: We have twelve years of history behind us. Shouldn't that count for something? Shouldn't we feel close to each other once in a while? Sometimes I feel invisible, like I don't even exist. Am I asking too much to want my husband to be my friend? Doesn't he need me for a friend too? Why is he such a loner? It's like we each have all these needs buried down deep, but we can't reach out and help each other. Maybe Jimmy would be happier with someone else. Maybe I would too. Maybe divorce is the only answer."

No, divorce isn't the answer—although that's exactly the decision countless couples make when they've reached the same sort of stalemate Jimmy and Marla are facing. The problem isn't that they have a bad marriage or that they have opposite personality types or even that Jimmy had to give up a promising music career for the sake of his marriage. No. The major problem Marla and Jimmy are facing is a lack of intimacy in their relationship. The solution is for Marla and Jimmy to learn proven techniques for developing genuine intimacy in their marriage.

Perhaps you are facing a similar problem in your own marriage. Naturally, your circumstances are different from Marla and Jimmy's. But, like Marla and Jimmy, you recognize that something is missing in your marriage. A closeness should be there—but isn't. You often feel needy or lonely even with your mate, and you wish there were some way to communicate this sense of neediness so that you could receive comfort and understanding. Moreover, you wish you could extend such comfort to meet your partner's unspoken needs. You sense that the two of you could be so much more to each other if you could get beneath the surface of your emotions, if you could learn to be truly vulnerable and open with each other, if you could somehow nurture an environment of mutual sharing and caring.

Maybe you've taken a fatalistic attitude and decided that this is just how marriage is. The first bright burst of romance fades and winter sets in, relentlessly bleak, stark, and bone-chilling. So you decide to keep a stiff upper lip and steel yourself for the long haul.

That's how the Carltons felt about their marriage. Actually,

Jimmy was the one keeping a stiff upper lip. Marla was a lot more vocal. The fact that they were opposites in every way became evident when she persuaded him to accompany her to a counseling session with David Ferguson. After enumerating a long list of disappointments, she blurted in exasperation, "Is this what God intended marriage to be?"

"Hardly," snorted Jimmy, his arms folded across his chest.

"Marriage is part of God's answer to man's aloneness—and his loneliness," David offered. "At least that's how it all began."

"What do you mean, that's how it began?" quizzed Marla suspiciously.

"With the first single man."

"You don't mean—"

"Adam."

"Boy, you really are going back to the beginning!"

"Right. New flesh, solid sinew, strong lungs still bursting with God's breath, limitless potential swathed in love."

"I don't get it," said Marla. "This is the twentieth century. What can we learn from—of all people—Adam?"

"It's like this," David replied. "Adam awoke to sweet green grass and rose petals and blue sky and air that was fragrant with the aromas of lush ripe fruit, and best of all, he heard the whisper of God's voice in his ear and felt God brush against his arm as they walked together in the Garden. Adam had it all: God's image. God as his friend. God's work. God's place."

"Terrific," said Marla. "I still don't see—"

"But wait."

"There's more?"

"God said, 'It is not good for man to be alone . . .'"

Marla nodded. "Not so good for women either."

"Think about it, Marla," David urged. "This is one of the most incredible statements in Scripture. Over and over again God had looked upon His creation and said, "It is good. . . ." Now, for the first time, He said, "It is *not* good."

She shrugged. "Okay, I give up. What was God talking about?"

"Picture this: God created a perfect man in a perfect environment with the perfect Companion—God Himself. And yet God wanted something more for man."

"What more could there be?" muttered Jimmy.

Marla tossed him a triumphant smile. "Eve."

"Exactly," David agreed. "In spite of all the abundance God had heaped upon man, He knew Adam could never fully realize his humanity without an intimate partner: another person—like himself and yet different."

"Different? That's for sure!" said Jimmy.

"She has a right to be different," said Marla. "She's a woman!"

David smiled. "Yes, a woman: bone of his bones and flesh of his flesh. Helpmate. Lover. Companion. Friend."

"It sounds nice," said Marla, "but what do Adam and Eve have to do with Jimmy and me?"

"Plenty," David assured her. "Adam and his Eve—two separate persons who became one flesh—shared undefiled intimacy. They were naked and felt no shame. Morally innocent, they delighted in each other, reveled in the sweetness and euphoria of giving each other pleasure. They were transparent, sharing themselves fully in a joyous union of body, soul, and spirit—two people with absolutely nothing to hide."

Marla looked wistfully at Jimmy. "That's not us, but I wish it could be."

Jimmy grunted. "Save it for the movies. Or your dime-store novels," he said.

"This isn't fiction," David replied with a smile. "Intimacy is a divine idea. Literally. Intimacy in all its hues and complexities and variations. Intimacy at its fullest and most satisfying is what God wanted for the first man and woman He created. And it's what God intended for us."

"So what went wrong?" Jimmy challenged. "I don't see any couples going around acting all lovey-dovey, unless they're moonstruck kids who don't know any better. So what happened to this so-called divine plan?"

David could tell that Jimmy figured he had him now. "It's like this," David explained. "Adam and Eve wanted more."

"More of what?" asked Marla. "They had it all."

"Right. But they wanted to do their own thing. Find themselves. Develop their human potential. Become masters of their own fate. They believed a lie—that God was holding back something that was good for them. He had given them heaven on earth, and it wasn't enough. They wanted the one thing He had forbidden."

Marla sat forward attentively. "What was that?"

"It began with a tree in the center of the Garden—a green tree shimmering with lush promises as sinister breezes whispered through its branches. The serpent, coiled around the tree, told Eve, 'Eat of this fruit. You will know good and evil. You will be like God.'"

Jimmy shifted uncomfortably in his chair. "You really believe our troubles go back to this whole Adam and Eve thing? I mean, isn't it getting a little farfetched to blame our problems on them?"

"Stay with me," David urged, "and I think you'll get my point. You see, Eve believed the lie and ate. Adam ate, too, aware of the lie but choosing to disobey rather than relinquish his Eve."

Jimmy whistled under his breath. "Foolish man!"

Marla delivered a chiding kick to his ankle.

David could see he had a long way to go with this couple, but he pressed on.

"Adam and Eve were in for quite a shock. As swiftly as lightning strikes, their eyes were opened to the reality of evil. Marital bliss and intimacy went screaming off into oblivion.

"The man and woman stared at their nakedness and, for the first time, felt ashamed. Their innocence was gone. Instinctively, they hid themselves from each other, covering their bodies with hastily sewn fig leaves in a futile gesture of self-protection.

"Channels of transparent sharing and genuine communication gave way to sky-high defensive barriers. Pure love and trust were swallowed up in shame. And fear. Eve and her Adam were suddenly afraid to reveal themselves to each other on any level—body, soul, or spirit.

"Think of it. They who once had no secrets suddenly hid from each other."

Marla and Jimmy looked at each other, but neither of them spoke.

"Worse," David continued. "They hid from God, the One who had made them and walked and talked with them as their most intimate Friend, the very God who loved them beyond imagination."

Marla shook her head.

"They hid," David repeated. "And we have all been hiding from God and from one another ever since. We cover our real selves. We wear masks. We erect protective barriers, and we act out of shame and guilt rather than love and joy."

"I never thought of it like that," said Marla softly.

"Most of us don't," David agreed. "Through generation after generation we repeat the behaviors that doomed the marriage of that first couple. When God confronted them with their sin, they did what most married couples do today. They blamed someone else. Eve blamed Satan. Adam blamed Eve and then had the audacity to blame God for giving him the woman in the first place."

"We do a lot of that," Marla murmured, casting a glance at Jimmy. "We blame each other. Don't we, Honey?"

"Do you really believe it's all tied back to this Adam and Eve thing?" Jimmy questioned, his interest perking up for the first time.

"We do. Even in their lovemaking, guilt and shame tainted Adam and Eve's once pure, unsullied emotions. Before their sin, Adam and Eve exulted in their nakedness. Every act of love reflected God's perfect design for their physical, spiritual, and emotional union. But after their sin, they could not come together without feeling self-conscious and ashamed of their nakedness."

Jimmy sat forward now. "So you're saying sexual sin wasn't Adam's downfall? I was never quite clear on that."

"Not at all. Adam's sin was acting independently of God. Rejecting contentment and gratefulness for God's abundant provision, he chose disobedience. He wanted to be like God. But, of course, sin changed Adam's sexual life forever. It brought in the element of shame.

"And sin changed his marital relationship as well. Adam could no longer face his God or his wife without fear that he might not be accepted for who he was, both inside and outside. He had to find ways to hide the nakedness of his body and the nakedness of his soul. So, tragically, man's intimacy with God and with his mate was shattered by sin."

"A real downer," murmured Marla, twisting a strand of her Lucy-red hair.

David agreed. "A real downer. As a consequence of their sin, Adam and Eve were banished from the Garden and thrust into a flawed, harsh world where they had to toil for their very existence, where the joys of creativity and productivity were realized only through sweat and drudgery, and where the thrill of childbirth was lost in the pain and travail of hard labor. In other words, the stress of living in the real world made their marriage vastly more difficult."

"Tell us about it," growled Jimmy.

"Yeah, that sounds real familiar," said Marla, "too familiar."

"We're still suffering the consequences of that original sin, aren't we? So many of our marriages are troubled. So many fail."

"Why?" Marla asked with a sudden urgency. "Can you explain why?"

"Because we're still doggedly doing our own thing," David said. "We're trying to go it alone, to be independent of God. It doesn't work."

"We know what doesn't work," said Jimmy. "What we need to know is what *does* work."

"That's why we're here," David assured him. "In a nutshell here are the facts: God made us with needs, and He wants us to depend on Him to meet them. It's as if God said, 'Adam, you have a need. I will make you a helpmate.' Thus, Adam's expectations were turned to God. God didn't tell him to go out and find his own helpmate. So we, too, must trust God for our needs. But, like Adam and Eve, when we try to meet our needs independently, we become shame-based, self-protective, God-avoiding blamers, and true intimacy with God and our mate remains an elusive dream."

"It sounds hopeless," said Marla with a sigh.

"But it doesn't have to be that way. That's the terrific news we're here to share. Any couple—and that includes you and Jimmy—can develop the kind of intimacy in marriage that will satisfy your deepest yearnings."

"You really believe that?" she asked, her green eyes glinting with hope.

"Absolutely."

"Then how do we begin?"

"We begin by taking a look at the deepest needs husbands and wives bring to marriage."

CHAPTER

# 3

# Intimacy Needs—Is It Okay to Have Them?

JIMMY CARLTON SAT back in his chair, spreading his elbows over the cushioned arms, his legs crossed, one cowboy boot tracing an invisible figure eight in the air. What he lacked in verbal spontaneity, he more than made up for in body language.

Like a restless, bored little boy, he was constantly moving— tapping his foot, cracking his knuckles, tugging his earlobe. And Marla was right. He did look like Garth Brooks.

"You'd rather be somewhere else, wouldn't you?" David observed.

"Anywhere else!" he admitted with an abashed little grin.

"Do you find it hard talking about your needs?"

"I don't have any needs." He shifted, crossing the other leg and starting a new figure eight.

"No needs?"

"Nope. Marla's the needy one around here."

"We'll get to Marla, but this is your turn. Rather than saying you have no needs, would it be more accurate to say all your needs have already been met?"

"Yep. You could say that."

"What needs are those?"

Jimmy stopped drawing his figure eight and looked around blankly. "Well," he drawled, "I've got as much as the next guy, no more, no less."

"Can you be more specific?"

He tugged at his earlobe. "I've got a job, a house, and a family. I can't complain."

"But Marla seems to feel you could have more closeness in your marriage."

He shrugged. "Like I said, Marla's the needy one. Not me."

"Do you feel it's wrong to have needs?"

He thought a minute. "I suppose it makes a guy look weak. Like he can't make it on his own, be his own man."

"What about your parents, Jimmy? Did they ever express any needs to you?"

He uncrossed his legs and began a rat-a-tat with the toe and heel on his cowboy boot. "My folks? No way. They were good, sturdy stock. Never asked for a handout. If they had a problem, they kept it to themselves. I never heard my mom or dad ask anybody for anything. Whatever they got in life, they got the hard way."

"And you admire them for that?"

"Absolutely. None of this sniveling around, expecting everyone to pat you on the back and give you a free ride."

"Is that how you see Marla?"

Jimmy frowned. "She can be pretty vocal about things. You never would have heard my mother complaining the way she does."

"But did you ever stop to think maybe your mother had needs that should have been met, and weren't, because she didn't know how to express them, or she was afraid to? Maybe your mother's life would have been happier or richer or more meaningful if she had been able to share some of her needs with those she loved."

Jimmy stretched out in his chair and cracked his knuckles. "Never thought of it that way," he admitted.

Jimmy isn't the only one. Many of us are unsure about how to deal with the needs in our lives. Do we make them known? Cover them up? Feel ashamed? Blame others? Blame ourselves? Often when we feel needy we ask the question, "What's wrong with me?"

Amy asked that question. A petite brunette in her early thirties, Amy always makes sure her makeup and attire are as impeccable as her immaculately coiffed hairstyle. Her finely drawn china-doll features would be more than pretty if her face weren't so pinched with worry. By outward appearances, she looks like a woman who has it together, who knows where she's going and how to get there.

But listen to the story she shared with Chris Thurman.

"I've been married for nearly ten years, and I keep thinking it's going to get better. After all, Tom and I have a lot going for us. We're well educated. We come from good homes. We go to church. We love God and try to serve Him. Shouldn't that give us a head start on everyone else?

"To tell the truth, I feel guilty about being so dissatisfied. Like a lot of girls, I was brought up to believe Cinderella meets her Prince Charming and they live happily ever after. But I'm beginning to believe there's no such thing as living happily ever after. Marriage is a lot of hard work and responsibility, and if you can just keep the lid on things, maybe that's all a wife should expect.

"I mean, things could be a lot worse in my marriage. Tom is a wonderful guy and a good father to our three girls. He works hard to support us. He doesn't drink or run around with other women. He's home every night. I know I could trust him with my life.

"So I must sound like a real witch for complaining, right? And that's the last thing I want to do. My own mother was one of those controlling types who always got her own way by nagging or whining or complaining that she was ill. She ran all our lives that way, and my dad never spoke up, never said a word. I vowed I'd never be like that, and I haven't been with Tom. All these years I've bent over backward to be understanding and agreeable. I've never forced my own needs or wishes on him.

"But I can't help feeling like something's missing. And as the girls get older, this emptiness inside me grows. Tom and I never talk, except about things like who's picking up his shirts at the dry cleaner or when do the girls see the pediatrician or what's for dinner? It's always business as usual. We could be business associates or nodding acquaintances, for all the personal stuff we get into.

"What bugs me most is that I never know what Tom's really thinking or how he feels. And he doesn't seem to be the least bit interested in what I'm thinking or feeling either. It's like we live out our lives side by side, day by day, and yet we're strangers. Frankly, we shared more of ourselves with each other when we were dating.

"I've never had the courage to tell Tom I'm unhappy. I know it would blow his mind. He'd say, 'I break my back ten hours a day for this family, and it's still not enough. What more do you want?'

"And I'd have to say, 'I don't know.'

"Isn't it absurd? I don't even know what I'm asking for. All I know is, I feel needy—deep down inside where I really live. I want Tom and me to share the intimate parts of our lives like lovers and friends. Is that so wrong?"

## NEEDY FEELINGS ARE NORMAL

"It's certainly not wrong, Amy," Chris assured her. "In fact your feelings are very normal; but unfortunately, many of us who experience the same needs prefer to deny they even exist."

"Why?"

"Because, like you, we feel guilty. We're ashamed to admit we have unmet needs, especially considering all that God has already given us. After all, most of us have a basically good life—our faith, our health, our job, even a respectable marriage to a faithful mate who works hard. Shouldn't that be enough? Is there something we're overlooking?"

Maybe so.

Do you remember Adam's dilemma in Chapter 2? In the Garden he possessed everything there was to possess, and it was all good. He walked with God in perfect companionship. And as appointed ruler over all God had created, Adam was at the top of life's performance ladder. He had it all. Almost.

God said, *It is not good for man to be alone.*

Think about this: God Himself declared that man needed more than his companionship with the Father. Man needed more than all this world has to offer. Man needed more than the ability to perform a given job. Yes, Adam's needs went deeper than possessing or performing!

Could it be that possessing and performing don't satisfy, and it is appreciation, respect, and acceptance we need? Or it's attention, approval, and security we need?

This opens a floodgate of questions, doesn't it? Wouldn't it be selfish to need attention? Or appreciation? Or approval?

Wouldn't it be "weak" to admit we have such needs? Shouldn't God meet all our needs?

Do we dare need these things from other people?

No one teaches newborn babies to need attention; they just start crying for it. No one teaches toddlers to reach for affectionate hugs—they just hold out their arms. Notice a child's response after he or she has finished coloring a picture or building a wobbly tower with blocks. The child instinctively seeks someone's approval of his or her work.[1]

So it is with emotional-relational needs . . . often called "intimacy needs."

*Needs.* Yes, all of us have them. We are needy and God knows it because He made us that way. In Philippians 4:19 we read, "And my God shall supply all your need according to His riches in glory by Christ Jesus." The obvious premise of this verse is that we have needs. Otherwise the verse makes no sense.

From a secular point of view, Maslow and others have defined a hierarchy of needs, pointing out that our needs begin with the most fundamental, or physiological, needs (air, water, and food) and proceed up the hierarchy to the more complex needs such as love and closeness.[2] In other words, it's hard to worry about love needs when physical necessities are pressing. A soldier in combat, fighting to stay alive, won't give much thought to self-esteem problems. And a beggar on a street corner will be more concerned with finding food than in finding himself. Still, to become healthy people we need more than the basics.

## IMPLICATIONS FOR CHILDHOOD

In our counseling sessions with Amy and Tom and Marla and Jimmy we asked them to recall their childhood experiences—for good reason. Not only is much of a child's personality formed by age six, but many of his or her earliest felt needs will have a profound lifelong impact. A child's relationship with parents, siblings, and other caregivers will influence his or her future relationship with a mate.[3]

When David introduced this concept to the Carltons, Jimmy was quick to respond. "Are you saying there was something wrong with my family? No way! Maybe my parents weren't Ozzie and Harriet, but we weren't one of those—what do you call it?—dysfunctional families you hear so much about these days. My dad wasn't a drinker; my mom didn't run around. They were good, solid people."

"I don't deny that, Jimmy. But the truth is, all of us grew up with some unmet needs. It's inevitable. We grew up in an imperfect world as imperfect children in imperfect families. The major difference between healthy, functional families and dysfunctional families is that healthy families deal with the hurt of unmet needs as they go along; dysfunctional families deny the hurts, ignore the needs, or blame the children for even having needs. So no matter what kind of family we had, we're all 'undernourished' in some areas of need."

"Not me," said Jimmy. "My parents gave me everything I needed."

"Did they tell you they loved you?"

"Didn't need to. My dad showed it by going to work every day without complaining. My mom mended my clothes, fixed my meals—"

"Did they kiss you and hug you?"

Jimmy fidgeted in his chair. "They weren't mushy, if that's what you mean. It wasn't all kissy-face. Who needs that?"

"Are you willing to agree that your ideas about how people should respond to one another were influenced by how your parents treated you?"

He thought a moment, as if trying to decide whether this was a trick question. "I suppose that's an accurate statement," he said at last.

David turned his attention to Marla. "What about your childhood? What were your parents like?"

Marla was eager to talk. "Oh, they were great. Fun and free and unpredictable. Funny as all get-out. They could have come straight out of vaudeville. In fact, my great-grandfather played vaudeville back in the twenties. We've got pictures and everything. Once he even opened with George Burns and Gracie Allen."

David gently guided Marla back to the subject of her parents. "Are there particular needs you could have wished for more of while growing up?"

She examined one long, red fingernail. "My folks did as much as they could. With five kids in the family, they didn't have a lot of time for each kid. The one who got the attention was the one who talked the loudest and the fastest. Usually that was me. Or when it came to food, it was the one who grabbed first. Sometimes we were like a pack of wolves around the table, pushing and shoving and pigging out. My brothers were bigger than I, so I had to be smarter and cuter. It worked until I got older and got a reputation for being a smarty-pants."

"Were your parents affectionate with you?"

"Absolutely. We were just the opposite of Jimmy's family. We were always kissing and hugging. That's why it bothers me when Jimmy acts so cold. The only time he gives me a kiss or hug is when he wants sex."

"Hold on!" Jimmy rose to his own defense, nearly toppling his chair. "If Marla wants me to be like her family, she's got a long wait. Those people are straight out of *Alice in Wonderland!* Talk about Mad Hatters! They're all Loony Tunes!"

"That's better than being cold fish like your folks. At least my parents are warm and friendly and loving!"

David interrupted to offer an observation: "Is it possible that neither of you is aware of what your childhood needs were? The truth is, children often don't comprehend their own needs."

Both agreed this was possible. But Jimmy still wasn't quite ready to admit he had needs.

## IMPLICATIONS FOR MARRIAGE

What many couples fail to realize is that *unmet childhood needs follow us into marriage.* We unconsciously enter marriage full of hope that now we'll receive the *acceptance* we missed or the *affection* we've longed for or the *attention* we so desire.

It would be nice to think we entered marriage with a clean slate, but the truth is each partner often carries in a great deal of emotional baggage from the past. And what we must realize is that we will experience *great hurt* when these same unmet childhood needs go unmet in our marriage. Or worse yet, we may receive the painful opposite—*rejection* when we longed for acceptance, *coldness* when we needed affection, or *neglect* when we needed attention.

We counseled a woman recently who was an obsessive-compulsive housekeeper. Ida vacuumed her floors ten times a day and spent four hours cleaning the bathtub. Everything had to be spotless, and she couldn't bear to have anything out of place. If her husband dropped a sock on the floor, it was World War III. "This isn't a marriage," he lamented. "I feel like I'm living with the entire cleaning staff of a Hilton Hotel. Ida's so compulsive she follows me around with the vacuum cleaner so the rug won't show my footprints!"

As counseling progressed, we came to understand the motivation behind Ida's compulsive cleaning. Underneath her behavior was a reservoir of hurt from a raging alcoholic father who, in his drunken stupors, would yell, "I wouldn't drink if this house wasn't so messy!" Seven-year-old Ida internalized all that hurt and tried to keep her father from drinking by keeping the house immaculately clean.

It doesn't matter that Ida's husband doesn't drink and doesn't even want a spotless house. Ida is still responding to those deeply embedded childhood needs and the pain and fear she experienced with her father. It's the only way she knows how to respond to the stresses and needs in her life today. The irony is that she is destroying her marriage by responding with old, preprogrammed behaviors to those unmet childhood needs.

But just as we experience great hurt when our unmet childhood needs go unfulfilled in marriage, so the opposite is true: We experience *great love* in marriage when these same, unmet childhood needs are met by a giving, caring spouse.

As we will discover later, this dynamic of selfless giving is possible only through an intimate relationship with our Creator, receiving abundantly from Him and then giving to others.

## WARNING!

As important as it is for you to be aware of your needs, it's equally important to realize that personal needs can be hazardous to your health. Either of two extremes—exalting your personal needs or denying them—can be hurtful.

**Exalting** your personal needs can lead to *selfishness* because you focus on meeting your own needs above all else. You may find yourself developing a self-serving view of religion, a "gimme" approach to God. *What's in it for me? If God doesn't make me rich, happy, and healthy, why should I serve Him?* A whole new breed of radio and TV preachers is offering a God who looks more like Santa Claus than the Savior. People whose main priority is getting their needs met are buying into this "wealth-health" religion. But giving in to self-centeredness can damage more than your religious faith. It can destroy relationships as well. If you have an egocentric attitude, you will slip into the habit of using other people for your own ends. Rather than focusing on the needs of others, you weigh every relationship on the basis of whether it meets your own needs. You care for others, not for who they are, but for what they can do for you. As others sense this lack of genuine caring, they move on, leaving you to mope and mourn alone over your lack of supportive friends. It may never occur to you that we all have a personal responsibility to the significant people in our lives and that deep satisfaction is derived from meeting the needs of those we love.

**Denying** your personal needs can cause you to become overly *self-reliant*. If you convince yourself you have no needs or that you can meet your needs without anyone else's help, you may become a loner, isolated and insulated, impervious to love and caring. You may turn to a religion that stresses duty and orthodoxy over a genuine, loving relationship with God. You may focus on rituals and rules in your relationships with others as well. Control will be more important to you than caring. Your attitude toward life will likely reflect the sentiment expressed in Revelation 3:17: "I am rich, have become wealthy, and have need of nothing." Outward appearances may be more important to you than Christ-like attitudes within, as you wear your self-sufficiency like a medal, never realizing your profound lack of intimate ties with the significant persons in your life.

This was a large part of Jimmy Carlton's problem. He had spent his life denying that he had any needs. As we counseled him, he finally admitted that, yes, maybe he had a few unmet needs, but he was just as quick to insist that he had no idea what those needs might be. Moreover, even if he did miss something in life, it really didn't matter.

What about you? What are some of the things you believe you've missed in life? And what are your feelings about missing those things?

In counseling, we constantly encounter people who say they missed something in life, but it didn't matter all that much. They say things like, "No, no one ever told me they loved me, but I never missed it," or "No, I never felt approval from my parents, but I don't think it really makes any difference," or "Yeah, I got hit quite a bit, but not as much as my brother," or "Yes, I was abused, but it was so long ago."

Underneath their words may lie a great deal of pain they aren't even aware of. Before they can deal with that pain, they must recognize they have a need and that it *does* matter. And that brings us back to the question, *What if you don't even know what you need?* The very fact you don't know suggests you missed a great deal while growing up; healthy parenting involves statements such as these that let a child know what he or she needs:

- "Looks like you need me to hold you right now."
- "Looks like you need me to encourage you a little."
- "Looks like you need me to tell you I'm hurting for you right now."

One of our most important goals should be to understand the needs of our loved ones. Proverbs 2:2 tells us to "apply your heart to understanding." We understand with our hearts; we gain knowledge with our heads.

What happens in marriage when you don't know what you need? Then you focus on *the other person's behavior*. This is a common problem in relationships. You desperately want to be loved and to feel loved, but when you don't understand what you need, you focus on your mate's behavior. David and Teresa Ferguson noted this problem in a recent counseling session.

We asked a couple, "What do you hope to get out of counseling? What would you like to see changed or different in your lives?"

Sylvia spoke right up. "All I want is for Al to quit drinking and be home on time. Then our marriage would be great." (Notice that's what she thought *her* need was; she was focusing on *his* behavior.)

So we asked Al, "What would you like to see different as a result of our counseling?"

And he said, "I'd just like for her to quit nagging me about drinking and being home on time."

We turned back to Sylvia. "Okay, what happens tomorrow if Al shows up on time and he's sitting there in his easy chair, sober. Are you telling us you will now feel abundantly loved?"

She thought about that. "Well, no, that's not all I want."

"Well, what else?"

"I'm not sure. I never thought I'd get *that!*"

"Let's suppose you do. Al is sitting there sober, on time, in that easy chair. Would you like him to talk to you?"

"That'd be nice."

"You could sit and visit; he'd listen to you about your day and be interested in your life."

"Yeah, I'd like that. I'd like someone to talk to me, show some interest, listen to me."

We looked back at Al. "Looks like she'd enjoy spending some time with you. How does that feel to you?"

Al flashed a crooked smile. "That feels good. In fact, that feels better than being nagged about not being home. In fact, it kind of makes me want to be home."

Maybe you're beginning to realize you've been focusing more on your mate's behavior than on understanding your own needs and expressing them by faith in a loving way. Maybe you're not even sure what your needs are. Take a few moments and think about your own childhood. Then jot down answers to the following questions. You may wish to invite your spouse to participate in this little exercise as well.

Which of the needs listed below do you remember having as a child? (Check the ones that apply to you.)

| ___ Attention (care) | ___ Acceptance | ___ Appreciation |
| ___ Encouragement | ___ Support | ___ Affection |
| ___ Respect | ___ Security | ___ Approval |
| ___ Comfort (empathy) | | |

Were you aware of these needs at the time? ___ Yes ___ No

How did you demonstrate these needs to your parents? *(For instance, I tried to behave like the perfect child. I misbehaved to get my parents' attention. I became an extrovert so my parents would notice me.)*

1. _____

2. _____

3. _____

To your siblings? *(For instance, I tattled on my brothers so my parents would like me more than they liked him. I tried to copy everything my older sister did so people would like me as much as they liked her. I picked fights with my brothers because I was jealous of their abilities.)*

1. _____

2. _____

3. _____

To those outside your family—your school, church, and community? *(For instance, I tried to be the teacher's pet so she would like me best. I joined the church choir so I'd get the attention I needed. I joined every school civic organization I could so I'd feel like I belonged.)*

1. _____

2. _____

3. _____

Did you try to hide or deny your needs? _____ Yes _____ No

Explain. *(For instance, I kept my hurt feelings to myself so my dad wouldn't yell at me. I pretended everything was always okay so my mother wouldn't drink so much. I said sarcastic things so people wouldn't know how lonely I felt inside.)*

1. _____

2. _____

3. _____

How has your parents' response to your childhood needs affected the way you respond to your own mate and children? *(For instance, I have a hard time being vulnerable with my husband because I'm afraid he'll react the same way my dad did. I can't admit my mistakes to my children because I feel they expect me to be perfect just as my parents expected of me. I get angry with my wife when she tunes me out the way my mother did.)*

1. _____

2. _____

3. _____

In the next chapter, we'll take a closer look at specific needs and how you can meet them.

# 4

# Intimacy Needs—What Are They?

DAVID FINALLY GOT the usually reticent Jimmy Carlton to talk. Marla mentioned his music, and that's all it took. He was off, talking enthusiastically about his favorite rhythm and blues singers and the country-western stars he admired. He sat forward in his chair, elbows on his knees, his long fingers loosely intertwined. "Hank Williams was my favorite when I was a kid, but later it was Johnny Cash. I spent half my teenage years singing, 'I Walk the Line.' I even dressed in black for a couple of years until my mother hit the roof and said 'enough is enough.'"

"Did your parents ever see you perform?"

"A few times. They weren't much into country music—or any kind of music, for that matter. Fact is, I take after my grandfather. Now he had a voice! But he rarely sang. It wasn't the sort of thing men did in his day."

"But you didn't feel that way. You made a living at singing, right?"

Jimmy cracked his knuckles. "Yeah, for a few years, but it's not the sort of lifestyle for a family man."

"Do you regret giving up your career?"

He shrugged. "I don't think about it. It was just something I had to do."

"But if you did stop to think about it, how would you feel?"

Jimmy sat back and cupped his hands behind his head. "Maybe I wouldn't feel so good, but there's nothing I can do about it now. What's done is done."

"How did you feel when you were on stage singing?"

He smiled wistfully. "I felt good, special—like I had the world by the tail and I could do anything. Especially when everything was going right. The people would let you know when you made them happy. They'd whistle and applaud and shout for more."

"Sounds like you miss the applause."

"Sure. Who wouldn't?"

"So then maybe that's a need you still have. Maybe appreciation is still important. Would you agree?"

"Maybe so. But so what? I can't go back on the road."

"No, but you can have some of those needs met in your relationship with Marla."

He chuckled wryly. "Sure, I'm gonna do a one-man show for a one-woman audience!"

"Not exactly, Jimmy. The point we're making is that needs are often relational. In other words, your deepest yearnings can be met in the context of a relationship—with God, with another person. Let's recap a little to show you what we mean."

## RELATIONAL NEEDS

Genesis 2 reveals that God placed Adam in a perfect environment with abundant provisions. Adam's mind was pure (that means he had no faulty thinking), his feelings were undefiled (he experienced no hurt, fear, or guilt), and his behavior was innocent. Yet in the face of all this, God said, "It is not good that man should be alone" (Gen. 2:18).

But what made it "not good"? The fact that Adam had been created by God with needs—for acceptance, affection, and encouragement, among others—which could be met only in the context of relationships. Our heavenly Father desired not only that Adam be the recipient of *His* divine acceptance, affection, and encouragement, but that Adam also receive such love and acceptance from meaningful *human relationships*.

That's why God established the marriage union (Gen. 2:24), the family (Gen. 4:1, Ps. 127:3), and the church (1 Cor. 12:27). God wants us to love as we have been loved (1 John 4:11), to comfort as we have been comforted (2 Cor. 1:4), and to forgive as we have been forgiven (Eph. 4:32). God's plan is one of grateful stewardship: First *we receive from Him,* and then with grateful hearts *we share with others.* Clearly, the divine intention for marriage and family intimacy is *mutual giving.*

## MEETING NEEDS IS WHAT LOVE IS ALL ABOUT

First Corinthians 13, the Love Chapter, speaks of love in these ways:

"Love suffers long and is kind" (v. 4).

"Love . . . does not seek its own, is not provoked" (v. 5).

Demonstrating such love involves not only giving attention to your mate's external or superficial needs, but also caring for the deeper needs of the "real" person inside. Just as valid as your husband's need for food is his need to be *appreciated* by you, his helpmate. He needs sleep, but he also needs your *attention* as you "prioritize" him above all other humans. He may thirst for water, but there's an even deeper longing for your *acceptance* and *affection.*

Think a moment about Christ's love. He gave Himself for us that we might know life and love, joy and peace. His is not merely a shallow love focused only on our temporal comforts; it's a deep love focused on our eternal needs for acceptance, forgiveness, and a new nature. Deep love touches deep intimacy needs.

God wants to love like that through us.

### Two Equations at Work

Whether you realize it or not, two significant equations are at work in your relationships. These equations are either working for you or against you.

### *1. Basic Needs That Are Met Equal Fulfillment.*

This equation might read, *Basic Needs + Met = Fulfillment.* Relationships such as marriage and family tend to have identifiable basic needs that, when met, produce a sense of abundance, joy, and fulfillment. Some of these basic needs are easily identified and others are discovered by trial and error. For example, needing to feel secure regarding marital fidelity might be a rather easily identified need. The need to be appreciated for your contributions to your family or for your character strengths might be less obvious—until you explode in frustration after being taken for granted too many times.

A marriage with an abundance of met needs will experience more of God's intended abundance, retain romance, and be better protected from temptations. A family that focuses on giving to meet one another's needs will feel close, build self-worth, and serve as a powerful example to a self-centered world. It's from this secure platform of Christ-centered mutual giving that an effective ministry to others can be launched.

David pointed out to Marla that maybe part of Jimmy's problem was that he needed more attention and recognition from her. From his viewpoint he had given up his singing career for his family, and no one seemed to appreciate that fact. It had been easier for him to deny the need than to try to figure out how to meet it. Marla had inadvertently contributed to Jimmy's pain by never bringing up the subject of his lost career.

"It was a sore spot for Jimmy," she admitted, "so I never talked about his singing days. I didn't want to rub salt in old wounds."

But Jimmy grudgingly admitted that, yes, maybe he would feel a little better if once in a while someone recognized what he had given up. "My dad always says a man does what he has to do, so I didn't want to sound like a whiny little kid. But, yes, it feels good when someone says, 'You had a good career, but you did good putting your family first.'"

Marla reached over and took Jimmy's hand and looked him in the eye. "Jimmy, I know how much your career meant to you. I know because I was a singer, too, and I miss it. But it was never my life like it was yours. I know it took a lot for you to put that behind you and get a desk job with the insurance company. I really appreciate what you did for the kids and me."

David looked over at Jimmy. "How does that make you feel?"

He grinned broadly. "Like I just heard the whistles and applause!"

## 2. Basic Needs That Are Unmet Equal Frustration.

This equation might read, *Basic Needs - Unmet = Frustration.* You have a basic physical need for sleep, and when that need goes unmet you feel uptight, irritable, and easily frustrated. Remember the last time you tossed and turned until dawn and then had to get up and trudge off to work or face a houseful of bickering, screaming kids? You didn't handle it too well, did you? Bleary-eyed, your head feeling as if you'd stuck it in a bucket of cement, you stomped around and muttered a few choice words of complaint or maybe even did a little screaming of your own. Why? Because your body and mind hadn't experienced the restorative powers of sleep; you were physically weary and emotionally thin. Your nerves were frayed from all those hours of staring wide-eyed into the darkness, silently begging for just a little shut-eye before your alarm jangled.

It's a fact: To remain physically and mentally healthy, we all need sleep.

It's the same with basic relational needs.

A marriage partner who goes for long periods without attention, affection, or appreciation can easily become vulnerable to moodiness, retaliation, or rejection. A wife may turn inward and become uncommunicative, a husband may retaliate by beginning an affair, or both partners may find a hundred minuscule ways of rejecting each other every day. She fixes his least favorite meal. He doesn't remind her that her favorite TV program is on. Their cuts and digs and little betrayals are limited only by the boundaries of their own imaginations. These various creative relationships are never justified; in fact they are wrong and sinful. In order to avoid them and even stop them we must often come to better understand them.

But relational needs aren't limited to adults. A child who misses out on attention, acceptance, or affirmation may begin to "act out" in order to gain attention or strike out against those who withhold his or her basic needs.

Remember the Los Angeles riots in the spring of 1992? We all sat in stunned horror as unimaginable violence and devastation blazed across our TV screens. Later, as TV reporters talked with both victims and offenders, a common theme became evident: People—especially young people—were striking back at a system that they felt abused and deprived them of their basic rights.

As husbands and wives we aren't likely to start any riots in our households, but a spouse's discontent can become just as deadly to the marriage. Surveys consistently indicate that marital affairs are not primarily sexually motivated. Instead, infidelity usually begins with emotional bonding. An acquaintance becomes more than a friend; add a little flirtation, and temptation can't be far behind. Surprisingly, the typical "attraction" is based not so much on physical as emotional needs. In other words unmet needs lead to frustration, frustration leads to vulnerability, and vulnerability can lead to an affair.

Danny's case offers a good illustration. "I wasn't even thinking about sex when I met Diana," he explains. "I was just mad at Karen. We'd been married fifteen years and all she wanted to do was play bridge with the girls or get involved in some social affair. She never had time for me. In fact, whenever I had a day off, Karen acted like I was spoiling her fun. And when I wanted her to go somewhere with me, she'd go grudgingly, but she made sure I knew she wasn't happy about it. She made me feel like I was dirt under her feet.

"But when I met Diana, she gave me this big smile and her eyes actually lit up like I was Tom Cruise or something. Then, when we started talking, she acted like she was really interested in what I had to say. Man, I could have talked for hours! And when I asked her out, she acted real flattered. I could tell she really wanted to be with me. The truth is, she wasn't even as pretty or as sexy as Karen, but she made me feel like a million dollars. A feeling like that is hard to turn down."

Allison tells a similar story. "I never thought I'd turn to another man. But when Jason worked late night after night, I got so lonely I started working late too. My boss wanted to show his appreciation for all the overtime I was putting in, so he took me out to dinner after work. Gradually it became a regular routine. My boss listened to me and valued my ideas in a way Jason never had. Having sex with him wasn't even important to me; I thrived on those intimate conversations when he made me feel like the most wonderful person in the world."

We could all learn a lesson from Danny and Allison. But how do you put that lesson into principles you can apply in your own life? How do you "affair-proof" your own marriage? It's important to begin by understanding your spouse's emotional-relational needs.

Dr. Les Carter, in his book *Broken Vows*, shares reasons given for extramarital affairs. One of the most common arguments is, "My wife (husband) and I don't ever talk anymore. I was just looking for some companionship."[1]

This comment highlights significant unmet needs. For example, "We don't talk anymore" might really mean, *I'm needing attention, understanding, and empathy.* "Looking for companionship" might be expanded to include the unmet needs of support, appreciation, acceptance, or affection. When these emotional-relational needs are met, a mate is much less vulnerable to other "companionships."

Keep in mind that marriage is a role model of the relationship between Christ and the church. Ephesians 5 speaks of Christ loving the church as He gave Himself for it (v. 25). During your private times of prayer and fellowship, God meets your needs for intimacy with Him. As you share your innermost self with Him, you receive His love and acceptance, and your deepest emotional yearnings are satisfied. Then you share with your mate the same love, comfort, and acceptance God has given you. When both you and your mate have spent time basking in God's love, you are likely to come together with an overflow of love for each other.

Lynne confirms this fact from her own marriage. "When I've spent time in the presence of Christ and feel His love surrounding me, I'm a different person when I return to my family. I'm not bothered by things that normally would have irritated me. I can feel God's love flowing through me to my husband and children. It may sound funny, but it's almost a transcendent feeling. It's not me showing them that special love; it's Christ through me. It's a wonderful, joyous feeling. And it's contagious. My family responds to me with patience and love. It's a snowballing effect, and I find myself thinking, *Yes! This is the way it was meant to be!*

"But I have to admit it doesn't happen like that often enough. Usually I just stumble along, trying to love my family in my own strength. They can tell the difference. Boy, can they tell the difference! When it's only me, my love wears pretty thin sometimes and I'm not as patient as I want to be. I get downright grouchy and then I just wish they'd leave me alone.

"But at least I know what it takes to have the kind of love I should show my family. It means spending time in the presence of Christ and experiencing His love on a daily basis. And then letting that love spill over to my family in the ordinariness of life. With God's help, that's the goal I'm working toward."

John 13:34 sums up what Lynne is seeking to put into practice: "A new commandment I give to you, that you love one another; as I have loved you, that you also love one another."

Matthew 10:8 underscores this admonition: "Freely you have received, freely give." Since we have freely received from Christ, with gratefulness we can freely give to others.

Now that we better understand how important it is to mutually give to intimacy needs, let's look at the top ten intimacy needs in a marriage.

## UNDERSTANDING INTIMACY NEEDS

David shared the chart below with Jimmy and Marla and asked them to consider which of these intimacy needs were most important to them.

### A RECENT SURVEY OF THE TOP TEN INTIMACY NEEDS

- Attention (care)
- Acceptance
- Appreciation
- Support
- Encouragement

- Affection
- Approval
- Security
- Comfort (empathy)
- Respect

Jimmy squirmed a little. The fact that he had needs was still new to him; he wasn't ready to articulate which ones took prominence in his life.

But Marla was more than ready with an answer. "You've heard the old vaudeville routine: A man marches out on stage declaring, 'Attention! Attention!' Everybody's ears perk up. Then comes the punch line. The guy smiles sheepishly and gushes, 'I *looooovve* attention!' Well, that's me," Marla admitted. "With five kids in the family, we all had to stand on our heads—or worse—to get attention. That's why I started singing. It was the only time my family shut up and listened to me. Of course, I wasn't as good at it as Jimmy. But I did love the attention."

David suggested a closer look at the top ten intimacy needs, one by one, and he recommended that the Carltons weigh the importance of each one in their own lives. We suggest you do the same.

1. **Attention (Care).** To take thought of another and convey appropriate interest, concern, and support; to enter into another's "world." (See 1 Cor. 12:25.)

Christ set the great example. He cared so much for us He stepped down from His celestial realm into the earthy mire of a manger. He entered our world and became one of us, willingly putting on the straitjacket of our humanity. He did it because He loved us.

Undoubtedly you long to have a mate who willingly enters your world and affirms your significance, but instead of expressing your need directly you may nag or tease, thus alienating your mate. In the last chapter we described how Al and Sylvia faced that problem. Sylvia nagged Al about his drinking and tardiness, but underneath, what she wanted was for him to pay attention to her and show affection.

When you feel needy, do you find yourself saying things like:

- "Why aren't you ever home on time?"
- "Why do you pay attention to all the other girls at the party?"

- "You're never here when I need you. Don't you love me anymore?"

- "If you loved me, you'd listen when I talked to you!"

Such remarks will only alienate you from your spouse. Instead of making accusations, simply examine and state your own neediness as you see it. For example:

- "You work such long hours, I worry about you. And today I'm feeling especially lonely. Could we spend some time together?"

- "When there are other pretty girls around, I get afraid you don't think I'm pretty anymore. It helps when I'm reminded how much you care."

- "I miss you when you're away. It helps so much to be reassured of your love."

- "Sometimes I feel I'm not saying things in a way you understand. Your eye contact and feedback reassure me that we can still communicate with each other."

Notice how the second set of comments is nonthreatening, focusing on your own neediness, not on the errors and omissions of your spouse. Such statements open the way to further dialogue rather than erecting a defensive barrier. Being open and vulnerable about our neediness is an important element in developing intimacy. In fact, sharing the truth in love about our needs is one of the most faith-stretching exercises we can enter into, inspiring a confidence that our heavenly Father will be there for us even if we're rejected by our spouse.

Like Marla, Teresa Ferguson admits she needs attention, but it took her years to communicate that need to David. "I'm an outdoor person who likes to work in the yard. My fondest childhood memories are of being outside with my family; I felt closest to them then. So I'd ask David, 'Honey, would you come outside with me and pull weeds?' But he figured I was just trying to put him to work, so he'd say, 'Go hire someone to do it.' Well, what I was really trying to say was, 'I'm lonely out here and would enjoy having you with me.' It took David ten years to figure out I wanted his company, not a lawn service! If we're going to have an intimate relationship, we've got to learn to get into another person's world and understand what he or she needs."

2. **Acceptance.** Deliberate and ready reception with a favorable positive response. (See Rom. 15:7.)

God offers unconditional acceptance when He looks beyond your faults to see your need. Similarly, it's this looking beyond to see need that makes marriage work—looking beyond differences, idiosyncrasies, irritations, and disputes to see the worth of your spouse. In fact, one of the best definitions of love is, "an unconditional commitment to an imperfect person."

In what ways do you show unconditional acceptance of your imperfect partner? And how does your partner show acceptance of imperfect you?

3. **Appreciation (Praise).** To communicate with words and feeling personal gratefulness for another. (See 1 Cor. 11:2.)

Tragically, the focus in marriage is often on the negative. *Why is he so sloppy? Why is she always late? Why can't he get a better job? Why does she spend so much money? Why does he keep his nose glued to the TV? Why doesn't she fix something besides TV dinners?*

We're often so busy counting up wrongs and focusing on flaws we overlook the good qualities of our mates. We all have our faults, so it's a cinch we'll find something negative if that's what we're scouting for. Meanwhile, we'll miss out on all the positive traits that originally drew us to our partners.

Think back. What originally attracted you to your spouse? Make a mental list. Have you stopped to think that God knew you needed a person with just those qualities? How long has it been since you've praised your mate for those special traits?

Chris Thurman admits in the past he had trouble showing his appreciation for Holly. "Holly is very compassionate. I love that about her. She needs to feel appreciated for who she is, but in the past I tended to notice only what she hadn't done, not what she had done. Now I know that, even more important than appreciating what our mates *do* is being grateful for who they *are*—their personal character qualities. We should remember to express our appreciation for them, and it should be sincere, not spoken just to get something back."

4. **Support (Bear Burdens).** To come alongside and gently help carry a load (problem, struggle); to assist; to provide for. (See Gal. 6:2.)

If you're truly supportive, you notice your mate's need, take the initiative, and quietly give of yourself. A healthy relationship is characterized by two people freely giving to each other out of God's abundance, with each partner being vulnerable enough to admit his or her need, share his or her struggles, and receive support. Having freely received God's blessing, they "freely give" to each other (Matt. 10:8).

Holly Thurman shares how her husband, Chris, consoled her when she had to undergo surgery for a tubal pregnancy. "When I awoke from the anesthetic, Chris was sitting beside me, gently wiping my forehead. I was so glad to see him! For as long as I needed him, he stayed by my side, holding my hand, whispering words of reassurance and love. He sensed how much I needed him. I didn't have to say a word. He was there for me, completely focused on my needs."

Contrast this point of view with the "take-all-you-can-get" attitude so prevalent in today's society. No wonder marriages flounder when the emphasis is on "my rights" and "what's in it for me?" When both partners are bound and determined to milk a relationship for all it's worth, there's little opportunity to "catch the vision" for giving unselfishly to the other. Many marriages collapse because of this vulture mentality; couples selfishly feed off each other until there's nothing left of the relationship, then they take off in search of someone else to feed off of.

5. **Encouragement.** To urge forward and positively persuade toward a goal. (See 1 Thess. 5:11, Heb. 10:24.)

Couples sometimes have the mistaken idea they should offer encouragement only when a spouse is discouraged. Wrong! Encouragement is a gift you can give anytime, and the benefit is a sweet intimacy and marital closeness that dispels loneliness.

Try this experiment: When you're alone with your mate during an ordinary moment, offer sincere words of encouragement. Something like this: "Honey, I've sure appreciated your help lately . . ." Finish the sentence with something appropriate: "with the kids," or "at work," or "around the house," whatever. Or say, "Sweetheart, I don't tell you often enough what you mean to me. You're really sensitive to my needs, encouraging of my career, etc. . . ." (Finish the sentence, but make it good and keep it honest.)

6. **Affection (Greet with a Kiss).** To communicate care and closeness through physical touch. (See Rom. 16:16.)

Studies consistently document a newborn's need for nurturing, touch, and affection. Babies who receive no love, attention, and cuddling are more likely to die, even though their physical needs are met. Babies who are held, cradled, and touched usually thrive.

From infancy, we all need the tender, nurturing touch of another human being to assure us of our own unique worth. For bonding to occur, children need the caress of their parents; for marriages to survive, couples need to touch each other with warm affection. A husband needs his wife's intimate touch to reassure him he's sexually attractive. A wife needs her husband's nonsexual embrace to remind her she's loved for more than her body, she's also appreciated as a unique and admirable person beyond the physical attributes that give her husband pleasure. Often, touch conveys more than words. It can say, *I'm here. I'll take care of you. You're not alone. I care. I enjoy you.*

7. **Approval.** Expressed commendation; positive affirmation; to bestow favor; to think and speak well of. (See Rom. 14:18.)

Many of us go to any length to win approval. We ride hot-air balloons or go skydiving to look brave. We bake in the sun to look gorgeous. We work eighteen-hour days to look ambitious, drive fast cars and spend money to look rich, experiment with extramarital affairs to look sexy, and spend a mint on diets and plastic surgery to look eternally young.

Why?

We want people to like us.

Why?

Who knows?

But it's there inside us—this deep-seated desire for people's approval.

And when we marry, we expect the starry-eyed idealism to remain in place forever. But blindness to your mate's faults vanishes with the rose-tinted glasses. All too soon you see the flaws, like the fine network of cracks in a Renaissance masterpiece. But as you focus on the intricate road map of lines, you miss the beauty of the painting. Your spouse's faults take on gigantic proportions while his or her positive traits take a backseat.

It's all too easy to criticize and find fault. Try making a list of your spouse's traits that win your "A" seal of approval. You may be surprised to find your mate has a list of good qualities too.

**8. Security (Peace).** Confidence of harmony in a relationship; freedom from harm. (See Mark 9:50.)

Bert and Rhonda worked for twenty years to amass a small fortune in the entertainment industry. Their million-dollar home in the Hollywood hills was designed by a renowned architect. They traveled in the elite circles of the Hollywood rich and famous, throwing fabulous parties for every occasion and vacationing in the fun spots of the superstars. But when it came to the strength of their marriage, they had built their mansion—and lifestyle—of flimsy papier-maché. When they divorced, their house of cards collapsed with them; they had nothing of substance to build on.

Many couples have been deceived into thinking security comes from possessions and social status—from luxurious homes, fancy cars, and high-paying jobs. Genuine security is something internal, something of the heart.

"Security is different for everyone," says Teresa Ferguson. "I discovered that some of my security needs were tied to things my dad used to do for us. But David isn't my dad, and his way of showing me security is different. I realized I shouldn't expect David to know automatically what I need. I need to express my needs to him so God can, as He desires, work through David to help meet them."

**9. Comfort (Empathy).** To come alongside with word, feeling, and touch; to give consolation with tenderness. (See 1 Thess. 4:18.)

David Ferguson, who admits he hasn't always been the greatest at offering his wife comfort, gives this advice: "When your wife needs comfort, here are a few things you *shouldn't* do: Don't blame her ('What's wrong with you this time?'); don't give advice as you try to 'fix' it ('Next time, do it this way!'); and don't be a martyr ('This is all I need! I should have stayed at work!'). When your mate shares sincere emotion, don't answer back with logic, reason, or facts. Emotional hurt is not healed with explanations or criticism."

What *should* you do?

Answer emotion with emotion. Offer comfort by carefully listening and gently touching your mate while she talks. (Women, this works for men too!)

Holly Thurman shares how she meets Chris's need for comfort. "He likes it when he comes home from work and I ask about his day in detail, not just, 'How was your day? Excuse me, I've got to go change a diaper!' I get into his life, what he's all about, what he's feeling. I tell him about funny bumper stickers I see—he loves them. Or we talk about sports. I make it a big deal when he comes home, greeting him, kissing him, letting him know he's special."

Wives, believe it or not, your husband needs you. He's not the self-reliant, self-sufficient person he pretends to be. Under a rough, tough-guy exterior lives a fearful, insecure little boy. A *wise* woman learns to look beneath a man's external behaviors to find his deeper needs. A *sensitive* wife will so understand her husband that she "senses" his emotional state and needs as soon as he enters her presence. A *loving* wife will focus on giving to meet her husband's complex and unique "little-boy" needs.

Cindy discovered the little-boy side of her husband Jack when he lost his job. Always before, he was the tough guy, the superjock, the first father in the neighborhood to volunteer to coach the boys' baseball team, the first to look for a prowler when he heard a noise outside, the first man Cindy knew to try skydiving (against her wishes, she adds).

She had never seen Jack shed a tear or back down from a fight or give in on an argument or compromise his principles. He was a man's man through and through—until he was suddenly laid off when his company "down-sized" during the recession. The day he came home with his walking papers, Cindy saw a new side to her husband. He sat down at the kitchen table, buried his face in his hands, and cried like a baby.

Cindy didn't know what to do, but instinctively she went to her husband, wrapped her arms around him, and let him weep, allowing a few tears of her own to escape. But she never said a word or asked a question until he was ready to talk, and later she was careful not to mention his tears. It was a private moment between them, something she remembered later as a special time of bonding, when she accepted her husband as he was without question, without criticism, without condemnation. In fact, Cindy recalled the event with warm feelings because she had felt truly needed. No one else could have provided the comfort she gave Jack that day, and that made her feel special.

But suppose Cindy had responded differently, with one of the following reactions?

"Come on, Jack, there's nothing to cry about. Everything's going to be okay. You'll find another job." (With this response she would have been belittling the importance of the situation to Jack. He would have felt angry or misunderstood.)

"Really, Jack! You're a grown man. What if the children see you crying?" (Jack would have felt put down and humiliated by this response.)

"Please, Jack, don't cry. I can't stand to see you so upset!" (With this response Jack would have felt obligated to stifle his tears and put on a happy face to keep his wife from feeling upset.)

**10. Respect (Honor).** To value and regard highly; to convey great worth. (See Rom. 12:10.)

Teresa Ferguson shares a time when she failed to respect her husband's leadership. "It was a family barbecue, and I wanted everything to be perfect. Fat chance! David announced he was going to barbecue the steaks, and they were expensive steaks, the best I could find. I thought, *David, you've got to be kidding!* But, of course, he wasn't. So I decided then and there to tell David exactly how to cook them, and of course I hurt his feelings. He felt patronized and put down. When I realized what I'd done, I apologized, and you can bet the next time David offered to barbecue steaks, I handed them to him with a smile and never said a word."

Teresa adds, "If we don't respect our husbands, how do we expect our children to respect them? Our kids pick up on our feelings without our ever saying a word. Anytime a wife belittles her husband, there will be chaos in that home."

Ephesians 5:33 reminds us, "Let the wife see that she respects her husband." Wives communicate that respect when they are supportive of their husbands' leadership and decisions. Husbands show respect when they seek to meet their wives' significant needs, lovingly sacrificing themselves as Christ did for the church.

"I think I'm getting the hang of this," said Jimmy Carlton with a sly little smile after David explained this list of top ten intimacy needs. "What you're saying is, if I admit I've got these needs and I see these same needs in Marla, and I start meeting some of her needs and she does the same for me, then we're gonna start feeling close to each other, right?"

"Right, Jimmy. In fact, you'll notice a difference in both your personal life and your marriage," David told him.

"Remember what Matthew 5:3 says about the 'poor in spirit' (or needy) receiving the kingdom? When you're sensitive to someone's needy inner soul, you receive something back; you experience greater self-awareness and empathy with others. In other words, you're rewarded emotionally when you keep your spiritual antennae tuned to the deep, secret hungers of the human heart. In that way you're reminded of how God has abundantly blessed you and how He is at work through you to bless others.

"As you come to understand and meet each other's needs through mutual giving, intimacy deepens and your sense of connectedness grows. You develop an emotional bond strong enough to ward off the slings and arrows of an increasingly complex and hostile society. Your marriage becomes a refuge, a stabilizing force and source of comfort as you face the daily stress and grind of surviving in today's world."

Marla sat back and closed her eyes, a smile playing on her lips. "That's the kind of marriage I want," she sighed. "The kind I've always dreamed of—and never knew was possible." Her smile faded and her tone grew serious. "But is it more than a fairy tale? Does God really want Jimmy and me to have a relationship like you've described? Does He really care about our needs?"

## GOD SEEKS TO MEET NEEDS

"Yes, Marla," David assured her. "Our God is a good God who desires to give us good gifts. He gave His own Son to meet our need for redemption. According to James 1:17 every good and perfect gift comes from above, so we need to look to Him for our provisions. You see, if we look only to ourselves or make excessive demands on others, we'll just be disappointed. Our faith should be placed, not in ourselves, or in others, but in the One behind the promise of Philippians 4:19."

Marla and Jimmy were beginning to understand. A sovereign God is always free to do what He wishes! Therefore, in His plan to meet human need God is free to involve people as He desires.

What about you? Have you caught the full implications of this truth? Many of your needs will be met directly in the intimacy of your relationship with God while other needs may be met as God involves significant people in your life. Maybe a more sobering implication is that God wants to involve you in giving to important needs in your partner's life—your children's lives![2]

## God Can Use a Wife to Meet Needs Like No One Else!

Think again about the Genesis 2 account. Before Adam met his Eve, God paraded past him every animal He had created—alligators, elephants, monkeys and mice, gazelles and giraffes. And even though all God had made was "very good" (Gen. 1:31), it became abundantly clear there was not a suitable helpmate among the entire lot. Why then did an omniscient God bother with such a spectacular exhibition when He already knew what Adam needed wasn't among them?

He did it to prove to Adam that only Eve could meet his unique needs for love, intimacy, and companionship.

And that message is as true today as it was then.

Wives, no matter how much your husband needs appreciation and approval at work, no one's praise is more important to him than yours. He may value the encouragement of his peers, but he will treasure your support far more. And remember, the affection and comfort he receives from his children or other family members will never have the same impact as yours!

## God Can Use a Husband to Meet a Wife's Needs

First Peter 3:7 says simply, "Husbands . . . dwell with [your wives] with understanding." Some men might be quick to respond, "Understand my wife? You must be joking! Try communicating with someone from another planet!"

I'm sure you've heard husbands voice such opinions. Jackie Gleason, in his 1950s television classic "The Honeymooners," used to wave his fist in the air and sputter, "One of these days, Alice. *Pow!* Right to the moon!" He rarely understood his wife—just as his neighbor Ed rarely understood his wife, Trixie—until the last few minutes of the show. Then, while Alice nailed her husband with her patient, long-suffering gaze, Ralph (Jackie Gleason) would look painfully abashed and fumble around, wearing his discomfiture like an outgrown suit. Contrite and shamefaced, he'd mumble his apologies, closing with his famous line, "Alice, you're the greatest!" And the scene would fade to black with a kiss.

Naturally, life isn't as black and white as it was portrayed in the innocent days of black and white TV. But God's message for husbands and wives is as true now as it was then. And for you husbands, the instruction is clear—to live with your wives in an understanding way. Admittedly, developing an ongoing attitude of understanding will require a considerable investment of your time, sacrifice of your own "agenda," and most importantly, a divine work of enlightenment and power.

However, the results are numerous and abundant. An inexpressible *joy* comes in giving to meet the deepest needs of another (1 Pet. 1:8). There is an inner *security* in seeing God use you in the life of another person (your wife) like no other human being (Eph. 5:28). You experience a *gratefulness* that God is entrusting you with His divine resources and trusting you to share them as a good steward of His all-encompassing grace (1 Pet. 4:10).

## Understanding Your Wife Begins with Her Intimacy Needs

Your wife may seem overwhelmingly complex, so different from you in her emotions and intuition, so given to seeing things differently from you that you're sometimes not sure she's seeing the same "reality" you are. How can you possibly understand her?

Underneath these differences you'll come to find a set of very basic human needs—just as essential as air, food, and water. These intimacy needs are the keys to understanding your wife. Understanding what she needs will give you insight into how she *thinks*, *feels*, and *behaves*; it will motivate you to seek a deep closeness; and it will serve as the beginning of your discovering how you can truly love her (Eph. 5:33).

Now that we've taken a look at the intimacy needs of husbands and wives, in the next chapter we'll consider how you can genuinely love your spouse—body, mind, and spirit.

# 5

# Loving Your Spouse: Body, Mind, and Spirit

"DARLING?"

"Yes, Dear?"

"I was just thinking . . ."

"Yes?"

"About us."

"Us?"

"Our relationship."

"What about our relationship?"

"I don't know, uh, don't you think it's about time . . ."

"Time for what?"

"Time to get a little more . . . intimate?"

"Intimate?"

"You know. *Intimate*. Sharing our feelings, being close."

"I suppose you're right, dear. How about Tuesday morning?"

"Can't. I have a hair appointment. How about Wednesday night?"

"Sorry, I'll be late. I'm meeting that client out of town."

"Friday perhaps?"

"Meetings all day. Saturday?"

"My mother will be in town. Sunday?"

"I promised the guys I'd be in that bowling tournament."

"Well, maybe the following week . . ."

"Sure. I'll check my calendar."

"Good. And I'll check my appointment book."

"Come on, Darling. Don't look so sad. We still have time."

"Time?"

"For intimacy, of course."

"You're right, Dear. After all, we've only been married *two* years!"

Does this conversation sound absurd?

Or maybe a better question would be, Does it sound *familiar?*

As standard practice, a married couple doesn't awaken one Monday morning and decide, "Let's become intimate this week!" Intimacy usually isn't something you plan for or announce as a conscious objective of your relationship. Marital intimacy emerges and is deepened not when it is demanded or declared as a specific goal; rather, it evolves spontaneously through the enjoyment you experience during the day-to-day process of relating to each other. This process involves several "ingredients" that, when mixed into a relationship, produce the closeness, feeling, and experience of intimacy.

You probably laughed at the couple above for trying to schedule intimacy into their busy lives. You recognize that if they've been married two years and still haven't managed to develop some sense of intimacy in their relationship, they don't stand much of a chance now. But hold on. You may find yourself laughing a bit uneasily because you *do* recognize some similarities between the couple above and yourself. Sometimes it may get to the point where you're trying to carve out bits and pieces of time to spend together as husband and wife. Sometimes you may wish you *could* write on your appointment calendars, "time for intimacy with my mate." Perhaps we shouldn't be too quick to laugh after all.

## A CLOSER LOOK AT INTIMACY

Intimacy is a paradox. It develops and deepens as you and your mate share experiences that draw you together. You may already have noticed it doesn't just happen without effort, but neither can intimacy be programmed to happen. Couples grow in closeness as they encounter one another spiritually, emotionally, and physically. Think about a recent time when you felt especially close to your mate. Maybe it was an ecstatic moment of shared joy after the birth of your child or a tearful apology after a lovers' quarrel or an affectionate embrace that launched an evening of romance. Since these special moments rarely just happen and can't be programmed, you as a couple need to learn how to *maximize* your experiences to deepen your marital closeness.

## John and Mary and Rick and Annie

To better understand how intimacy works, let's step for a moment into the maternity ward of your local hospital. We see two couples. John and Mary have just gone through the exhilarating experience of birthing their first baby—a healthy, bouncing nine-pound boy. Rick and Annie have also endured the long, difficult hours of labor and delivery, but their child was stillborn.

Both couples now face experiences that are ripe with the potential for marital intimacy. The days and months ahead offer countless opportunities for growing together . . . or for growing apart. The small, moment-to-moment choices each couple makes will determine whether this event in their lives strengthens their marriage—or weakens it.

For example, John and Mary are thrilled with their new baby. John is busy snapping photographs and handing out bubble-gum cigars (he's one of these nineties men who wouldn't think of polluting his son's environment with cigarette smoke). Mary watches him and her tiny infant from the vantage point of her homey, comfortable bed in the birthing room, with its frilly curtains, bright wallpaper, and quaint bedroom furniture. She basks in her husband's warm smiles of approval; she feels special; life has never been richer or more meaningful.

If John and Mary continue to share these warm and tender moments together, their relationship will deepen and their sense of intimacy will grow. They will feel a bond with each other and with their son that will make their marriage stronger than ever. They will grow as a family, not just because they have the same last name or live under the same roof, but because they are sharing themselves fully with each other through the treasured milestones of a marriage.

So, you say, what's wrong with this picture? What could possibly go awry in such a perfect setting?

Plenty.

As John and Mary bring the baby home and try to establish a regular routine, John might discover, to his dismay, that he can't get any sleep with the baby crying all night, that the bathroom reeks of dirty diapers, that his wife is too busy nursing the baby to have sex with him and too tired to fix the delectable dinners she used to serve every evening. What's worse, he's no longer the center of attention in his home. Whereas Mary used to have eyes only for him, now she has eyes only for Junior; it's as if she's fallen in love with the little tyke and they're having their own little romance that leaves John out. So he might as well spend more time at the office since he's obviously a fifth wheel around the house these days.

Meanwhile, Mary seethes inside as she watches John become more and more distant. Wasn't the baby supposed to draw them closer together? Why isn't John as attentive as he was when the baby was born? Why doesn't he offer to help with his son once in a while? It's his baby too. Doesn't he know how tired she is? Why doesn't he understand that things are different? She doesn't have the energy she once had for sex and housekeeping and fancy dinners. In fact, she feels exhausted and emotionally drained all the time. When the baby was born she felt so special; now she's just a workhorse, a drudge, and a milk machine. While she's stuck at home with the baby, John dresses up and goes off to work as if nothing has even changed. If this is what being a family is all about, Mary wants out.

You can see how quickly the intimacy deteriorates into irritation and alienation when a couple stops sharing their feelings and needs during seemingly overwhelming circumstances. Imagine what would have happened if just once John and Mary had shared their true feelings and needs with each other. Mary might have said, "John, I love you as much as ever and I miss our times together, but I'm so tired these days. I know it'll get better, but right now I feel alone and overwhelmed. I need to know you're with me in this. I need your support and encouragement. And the baby needs you too. We both need you. We can't make it without you."

Or John could have said, "Mary, you and the baby share such a special closeness, I sometimes feel left out. I feel as if our whole world has changed, and I don't know where I belong or what I'm supposed to do. I'm all thumbs around the baby and I don't know how to help, so I end up spending more time at the office. I think I need to be reassured of your love and reminded that you want to prioritize us as a couple."

You can imagine the exclamations of discovery and surprise that would follow such revelations. What wonderful conversations John and Mary could have as they explored their feelings and admitted their needs. They would be well on their way to putting down deep roots of intimacy in their relationship.

But let's take a look now at Rick and Annie. They were in the maternity ward that evening too. But unlike John and Mary, they went home empty-handed. Sure, they spent some time with their stillborn son, holding him, weeping over him, murmuring expressions of love. In the old days, the nurse would have whisked the child away before they even had a chance to see their son, supposedly to minimize their pain; but in these enlightened days, nurses realize the importance of a proper good-bye, so they encouraged Rick and Annie to take as long as they like to take pictures, get a footprint; save his little blanket . . .

Rick and Annie have never faced anything more traumatic in their marriage than a few burned dinners and a handful of misunderstandings. Now they must accept death—not just the lofty concept of death, but the personal reality of profound loss. They will internalize this loss and struggle to cope with it in a thousand different ways in the days and months to come. At the moment, as they cling to each other and weep together, they share a closeness they've never experienced before. They are one in their grieving.

But in the days ahead, unless they are careful, their loss will drive them apart. Just when each one needs the greatest amount of comfort and support, the other one is in too much pain to offer it. Death rarely draws a family together; in fact, a high percentage of couples separate within the first year after losing a child. If Rick and Annie don't want to be another statistic, they need to open up and share themselves more than ever before.

Annie quickly discovers how divergent the paths of grief can be. She finds comfort in weeping, talking about her baby, and looking at mementos. She wants people to know her son existed and his life had meaning. After all, she carried him and he was *alive*; he was real and she will never forget him. She feels wounded when people act as if her grief should be put on a timetable so she can get on with her life.

Rick, on the other hand, feels it's best if they put the whole thing behind them as quickly as possible. He refuses to talk about his son, and Annie has never seen him shed tears of grief since leaving the hospital. Instead, Rick throws himself into his work and seems to shut Annie out, as if seeing her reminds him of their stillborn baby. When he does turn to her for a little sex and affection, she turns a cold shoulder on him, making him wonder if there's anything left of their marriage.

Do Rick and Annie stand a chance with their marriage? Yes!

If they can open up their wounded hearts and truly share their pain, they can begin to build a real foundation of marital intimacy.

Consider what would happen if Rick told Annie, "I loved our baby as much as you do, but it hurts too much to talk about it. I'm afraid I'll break down and you'll see how vulnerable and weak I really am. I work long hours because I don't know how else to deal with the terrible ache I feel. I avoid you because the pain I see in your eyes reflects the pain in me. Even though it is painful for me, I need you to be close to me and lovingly encourage me to talk about my sadness while you comfort me."

Or imagine the scene if Annie told Rick, "I love you as much as ever, but I have a hard time showing it physically. I want your closeness and comfort, but having sex is a painful reminder of how our baby was conceived. Besides, I feel selfish and guilty enjoying sex when our baby's dead. I feel like I failed as a mother because I should have been able to keep our baby alive. I'm scared, too, because I feel I'm losing you. I think you're disappointed in me for not giving you a healthy son. Even though he's gone, I need to hold on to him for a while longer, but everyone makes me feel guilty because I'm not ready to forget. Please just hold me so I'll know I'm not alone."

Can you imagine the closeness Rick and Annie could feel if they could only articulate their needs and feelings with such openness and honesty? Think of the ways they could comfort and reassure each other. What a healing balm their words and actions could be if they allowed this tragic experience to build a deeper level of intimacy in their marriage!

## WHAT GOD ORIGINALLY INTENDED: FRIENDS, LOVERS, AND SAINTS

Imagine it! God wants the works for us. He didn't create us just to be friends with our mates or just to be lovers or spiritual soul mates. He wants us to be all of these—and more! Much more! But if our relationships are to be knit together intimately in marriage, *sharing* is vital. Sadly, all too often these days we find families that are nothing more than a house of strangers. Family members move about in a vacuum, each going about his or her business rarely connected to other members by habits, rituals, or routines. Each one grabs breakfast on the run, eats lunch at a fast-food restaurant, then sticks a frozen dinner in the microwave and plops in front of the TV. Talk about one-sided communication! We used to lament that families gathered in front of the "boob tube" to watch their favorite show rather than carry on a conversation. But today's family members scatter to different rooms to watch their personal TVs alone. They don't even share the "togetherness" of watching the same show! Talk about being a long way from intimacy!

In our practice of Intimacy Therapy, we often find we must take a couple back to the basics to begin establishing intimacy. We point out that "becoming one" in marriage involves the freedom to share *all* of yourself with your spouse—spirit (your God-consciousness), soul (your self-consciousness), and body (your world-consciousness).

Take a look at the chart *Dimensions of Marital Intimacy*, which shows the dimensions of marital intimacy. Most couples don't stop to realize that marriages need nourishment and attention in each of these dimensions. Just as certainly as you need air, food, and water to live, so also your marriage has essential nourishment needs. A growing, healthy, balanced marital relationship is one in which each partner is enjoying an abundance of intimacy—in spirit, soul, and body.[1]

What often happens is that one or more of these areas is lagging or even short-circuited. Couples may enjoy a certain level of spiritual compatibility, a tolerable friendship with one another, and a good-to-great sex life. Other couples might enjoy a growing friendship, a problematic sex life, and no real spiritual closeness. Countless other

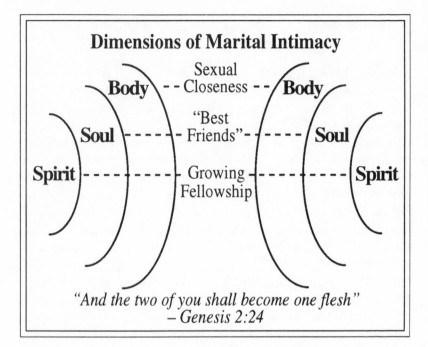

**Dimensions of Marital Intimacy**

Body --- Sexual Closeness --- Body

Soul ----- "Best Friends" ----- Soul

Spirit ----- Growing Fellowship ----- Spirit

*"And the two of you shall become one flesh"*
*– Genesis 2:24*

patterns exist, but our goal is to help you establish a balanced and growing intimacy in all three areas. In other words, the best of all three worlds would be a married couple who consider themselves best friends, have a terrific sex life, and share a growing spiritual fellowship. How would you assess your own marriage in these three areas?[2]

Remember our definition: *Marriage intimacy is the freedom to share all of yourself . . . spirit, soul, and body with your spouse.* As God's special creation, you have the potential to experience and enjoy intimacy in all three areas. Genesis 2:7 says, "God formed man's *body* out of the dust of the ground, and breathed into him the *spirit* of life, and man became a living *soul*" (our paraphrase and emphasis). It shouldn't surprise us then that the triune God who manifests Himself as Father, Son, and Holy Spirit would create us as similarly complex! The complexity is compounded, of course, as two become one in the marriage relationship. So let's take a closer look at this multidimensional aspect of intimacy.

## Loving Your Spouse—Spirit, Soul, and Body

To better understand God's view of intimacy, let's look at three uniquely different Greek words for love that shed light on the different dimensions of intimacy.

### Agape.

This word is used in the New Testament to describe the attitude of God toward His Son (John 17:26), toward humanity (John 3:16), and toward those who believe on His Son (John 14:21). *Agape* conveys God's desire that believers share this love with others, including their spouses and children (John 13:34). *Agape* is demonstrated through *action, commitment, and giving,* not through *feeling.* Because *agape* love is an expression of God's Spirit, it is impossible for us to produce such love through our own self-will.

### Phileo.

This kind of love is distinguished from *agape* in that it speaks of tender affection and represents the emotional aspect of a relationship. *Phileo* characterizes two hearts knit together in the tenderness of a mutual companionship. It's the emotion we feel when we affectionately *cherish* that special person.

### Eros.

This is the word from which **erotic** is derived; it speaks of sensual fulfillment and the physical pleasures of sexual expression. Scriptures stress a God-given boundary to confine these pleasures to the marriage relationship (Heb. 13:4).

## MAPPING MARITAL INTIMACY

Take a look at the chart *Theoretically "Ideal" Intimacy,* which shows a model of theoretically ideal intimacy. On the ideal model you'll notice that each of the three types of love—*agape, phileo,* and *eros*—is paired with one of the three dimensions of marital intimacy—body, soul, and spirit. As each partner receives God's *agape* love, the Holy Spirit within urges you to share it with your spouse, which produces fellowship. Your soul encompasses *phileo* love and leads you to deeper friendship. Your body focuses on *eros* love, which stimulates passion.

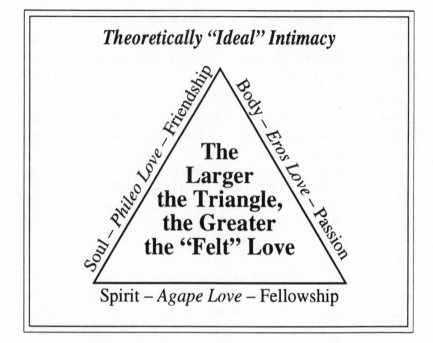

*Theoretically "Ideal" Intimacy*

Soul – *Phileo Love* – Friendship

Body – *Eros Love* – Passion

**The Larger the Triangle, the Greater the "Felt" Love**

Spirit – *Agape Love* – Fellowship

Using the dimensions of body, soul, and spirit as a framework, it's possible for you to graphically portray an intimacy history for your own marriage, as demonstrated in the examples shown in *Example Intimacy "History."* With the dimensions of body, soul, and spirit forming the sides of a triangle, the ingredient you perceive as most important forms the base, while the length of the sides represents your perception of the other dimensions' magnitude in your relationship.

A theoretical ideal would include spiritual oneness as the foundation upon which growing friendship and passion expand proportionately as the relationship matures. Using the examples in *Intimacy "History"* you can develop an intimacy history illustrated by a series of triangles drawn at different stages to reflect your marriage journey.

For example, Cal and Debbie are in Stage 1—a less than ideal but common stage, in which their premarital relationship emphasizes the physical dimension; the friendship dimension is adequate, but there is little spiritual fellowship. Whenever they're together, they are pre-occupied with kissing, touching, and caressing. Even when they are studying together or seeing a movie or visiting with friends, they're aware of an undercurrent of physical excitement between them. Their family and friends tease them about being so in love they can't see straight, and there's a certain amount of truth in that observation.

While Cal and Debbie certainly consider themselves good friends and while they even attend church together and pray occasionally at the end of a date, the foundation of their relationship at this time is physical. The passion they feel for each other is uppermost in their minds no matter what else they may be doing. They expect to feel this way forever, but the truth is that no relationship could retain this degree of intensity for long without burning itself out. Eventually their relationship will settle into the less emotionally and physically charged Stage 2.

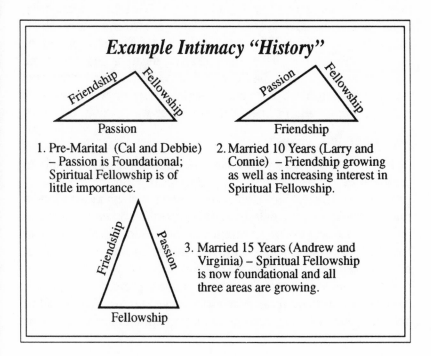

### Example Intimacy "History"

1. Pre-Marital (Cal and Debbie) – Passion is Foundational; Spiritual Fellowship is of little importance.

2. Married 10 Years (Larry and Connie) – Friendship growing as well as increasing interest in Spiritual Fellowship.

3. Married 15 Years (Andrew and Virginia) – Spiritual Fellowship is now foundational and all three areas are growing.

Married nearly ten years, Larry and Connie are in Stage 2. Friendship is their dominant theme, and there's an adequate amount of passion in their relationship, with their spiritual fellowship steadily increasing. Larry loves camping, hunting, and fishing while Connie has a penchant for photography. In the early years of their marriage they pursued their hobbies separately. Then they discovered they could have more fun by combining their interests. Now Larry and Connie go camping together and she takes her camera. Larry enjoys helping her find perfect photographic compositions, especially when they involve his latest trophy or catch. These days it's hard to tell where his interest in the outdoors leaves off and her interest in photography begins because their interests have become wonderfully intertwined into a close and enjoyable marital lifestyle.

Andrew and Virginia have been married more than fifteen years and are comfortably ensconced in Stage 3 of their relationship. Spiritual fellowship plays a major role in their lives, enhancing their growing marital passion and friendship. Their conversation is peppered with "we" rather than "you" or "I": "We should take a drive to the mountains this weekend," or "What are we going to do about Johnny's grades?" or "Why don't we invite the Smiths over tonight for our Bible study?" They enjoy praying together and discussing spiritual truths; in fact, the closer they grow to the Lord, the closer they feel to each other. It's a comfortable, satisfying three-way partnership. They couldn't imagine it any other way.

## Your Courtship Triangle

We suggest you and your mate each draw your own triangle to demonstrate your courtship. What do you recall to be the base of your dating relationship—fellowship, friendship, or passion? Map this element as the triangle base, then draw the other two sides in proportionate lengths. For example, if friendship was the base and therefore the longest side, decide whether fellowship was more important than passion. Or was it vice versa?

Keep in mind that this courtship triangle represents your *perception* of how important these three elements were in your relationship. You and your mate may come up with very different triangles. This difference may graphically document some of the adjustment struggles the two of you have been through. After each of you has drawn your triangle, share and discuss your drawings with each other.

## Your Journey Triangles

Using your courtship triangle as a starting point, draw three or four other triangles representing your marriage journey. The second triangle might represent the early years of your marriage and a third triangle might illustrate your relationship after children were born. Maybe another triangle could show when your children became teenagers or were grown.

In each triangle, does the base change over time? Does the relative length of each side change? Does the area of love increase? Complete your journey triangles and share them, considering your marriage relationship from your spouse's perspective.

## The Perceived Triangle

Now draw a triangle to represent what you think your spouse *currently* feels about your relationship. Consider the following questions as you draw this triangle:

*Friendship.*
Does your spouse believe you have fun together as a couple? Share common interests? Does he or she feel you are emotionally supportive?

*Fellowship.*
Does your spouse feel secure in the permanence and fidelity of your marriage commitment? In your spiritual closeness? In your common eternal goals?

*Passion.*
Describe your spouse's perception of your sex life. Is he or she comfortable with your touching? Kissing? Performance and frequency? Is this area more a priority to you or your spouse?

Complete this triangle and then share your triangles with each other.

Now that you've defined the dimensions of intimacy (spirit, soul, and body) and identified various intimacy needs, you're ready to take the plunge into Intimacy Therapy. In Part 2, we'll show you how each of the ten steps of Intimacy Therapy—adopt, block, think, forgive, reject, leave, mourn, understand, practice, and maintain—can nurture greater intimacy between you and your spouse.

# THE TEN STEPS OF INTIMACY THERAPY

CHAPTER

# 6

# Adopt the Four Necessary Ingredients of Intimacy

Marla and Jimmy Carlton were making progress. Jimmy no longer came to Intimacy Therapy sessions scowling and dragging his feet. He no longer sat with his arms crossed and his lower lip stuck out, daring anyone to make him speak. In fact, this time he wore the hint of a smile.

Marla was beaming. "Would you believe, we stayed up half the night talking? We haven't done that since before Jeffy and Anna were born. It was terrific."

"What did you talk about?"

"Everything. And nothing. Of course, I did most of the talking. You know me and my big mouth—er, maybe I should say my gift of gab. But the beauty of it is Jimmy talked too. He shared some things he's never told me before."

"How about it, Jimmy? Would you like to tell me?" David Ferguson asked.

He shrugged. "Marla's doing okay. Let her tell you."

Marla's words nearly toppled over one another. "Jimmy and I talked about the good old days, singing with the band. We reminisced about the great times we had with everyone. We were all real close, you know? Traveling from city to city, Scranton to Indianapolis to Detroit—wherever, one gig after another. It was hard work, but it was exciting too. We were footloose and fancy-free. When you're on the road like that, you have this feeling you can go anywhere and do anything, and you thrive on the applause. It's almost like a narcotic."

75

Marla paused, perhaps realizing she was "stealing the show." She wanted to give Jimmy a chance to verbalize his feelings.

"Anything you'd like to add, Jimmy?" David asked.

He crossed one lanky leg and started drawing the familiar figure eight with his cowboy boot. "Can't think of much. Except I told her I miss singing with the band like all get-out. But if I had to choose between her and the band, I'd still choose her."

"It really helped me to hear that," said Marla. "You wouldn't believe how many years I've lived with the fear that Jimmy regretted leaving the band to stay home with me and the kids."

Jimmy reached over and patted her hand. "I still love you, girl."

"I love you, too, Jimmy."

Their progress was so obvious, David decided it was time to introduce Jimmy and Marla to the four intimacy ingredients—affectionate caregiving, vulnerable communication, joint accomplishment, and mutual giving—that would help them determine exactly where they were in their relationship.

## 1. AFFECTIONATE CAREGIVING: "I CARE ABOUT YOU"

"Marla, what did you do last night when Jimmy told you how much he missed singing?" asked David Ferguson.

"Well, let's see. I put my arms around him and told him I understood. I kinda nuzzled up to his neck and let him know I care."

"Good. That's the intimacy ingredient we call 'affectionate caregiving.' It's the emotional element in your relationship that offers empathy and reassurance when your spouse is hurting. It can include words of encouragement or even physical affection. The important message is, 'I care about you.' Can the two of you think of any other ways you communicated that message?"

"I gave her my undivided attention while she talked," said Jimmy. "I admit, that was a rarity for me."

Marla nodded. "He also took the time to be with me. Usually our conversations run only a few minutes and then he's off doing something else. But last night he actually sat and talked with me for several hours. That meant more to me than anything else."

"We even said a little prayer for each other before we fell asleep," said Jimmy. "Does that count?"

"Absolutely! What better way to show you care than to pray for each other?"

"Well," Jimmy drawled sheepishly, "Marla found a way. She was pretty affectionate after our long talk. I figure we gotta have more of those long talks."

Marla nudged him playfully. "You don't fool me, Jimmy Carlton! It's what happens *after* the talks that's on your mind."

## 2. VULNERABLE COMMUNICATION: "I TRUST YOU"

"Jimmy and Marla, I think the two of you experienced some 'vulnerable communication' during your talk last evening. That means you risked being open about your feelings, needs, and hurts. Is that right?" David asked.

Marla nodded. "For most of our marriage I've never known how Jimmy felt about anything. He just doesn't talk about how he feels or what his needs are. But last night he opened up and talked about his career. He admitted what he's doing now in the insurance business isn't meeting his needs like singing did. We know now we've got some things to work out. We have to find new answers, but at least now we've got something to work with."

"How did you feel about sharing your needs, Jimmy?"

He tugged at an earlobe. "To tell you the truth, I didn't plan on spilling my guts. It just sort of happened. Until we started this Intimacy Therapy thing, I didn't know I had any needs. I guess I buried 'em real deep. But once Marla and I started talking, it just felt right to say what was on my mind. I don't even know where the feelings came from. They were just suddenly there, and they hurt bad. I had to get 'em off my chest."

"Were you worried about how Marla would react?"

"Maybe a little at first, but I had a feeling she'd been waiting to hear that stuff for a long time."

"Then you felt secure that you wouldn't be ignored, rejected, or hurt even more?"

"Right. For the first time I felt like I could let my defenses down."

"Jimmy, you've captured the essence of vulnerable communication. As your fears eased, you let down your walls of self-protection and became transparent, letting Marla see how you really felt. The more the two of you share like that, the closer you'll feel."

"I like it," said Marla. "I'm wanting more."

David smiled. "Keep it up. You deepen your trust in each other as you openly share your lifelong fears and dreams—all without fear of being rejected. You also communicate your vulnerability as you confess your wrongs to each other—read it in James 5:16—or as you honestly share your hurts or needs with each other—take a look at Ephesians 4:15. Each of you needs to ask the other, 'Can I let you know how I feel, what I need, and what I enjoy, without fearing your criticism or rejection?' "

Marla and Jimmy looked at each other. "We're going to work at it," said Marla. "In fact, we're already on our way!"

## 3. JOINT ACCOMPLISHMENT: "I NEED YOU"

"Well and good," David agreed. "But there's more. Joint accomplishment is an ingredient in closeness that comes from feeling, 'We did it! Together! You and I! We're a team!' Maybe you share common interests, hobbies, sports, or civic activities. Maybe it's a project you've worked on together—anything from finishing a household project like painting or remodeling the basement to looking forward to the arrival of a new baby. Maybe it's just managing to make a living and have a comfortable home. You get this sense of closeness by setting goals and working together to accomplish them. Remember the question in Amos 3:3, "Can two walk together, unless they are agreed?"

Jimmy and Marla were silent a moment. Then, surprisingly, Jimmy spoke up. "We have our music. We both love to sing. We should try it again. Maybe look up some of the old band members— just for fun, of course."

Marla was so pleased she bounced in her chair. "I can't believe he's actually suggesting that! I didn't think he'd ever want to sing with me again!"

David smiled knowingly. "Looks like finding a common interest shouldn't be hard for the two of you." He paused. "But beware. Joint accomplishment can be hindered by your natural tendency to be self-sufficient."

"I guess I'm guilty of that one," murmured Jimmy, almost under his breath. "I still have a hard time admitting I have needs. I suppose I always will."

"But you're doing better," said Marla. "That's what counts."

"Having needs is part of what builds intimacy," David explained. "Jimmy, it's difficult for you to feel close to Marla if you don't have needs she can meet. And vice versa."

"That's for sure. I like feeling needed," said Marla.

"Remember how the apostle Peter resisted Jesus' desire to wash his feet? He figured he just didn't need it, but his self-sufficient attitude almost robbed him of a very special time with his Lord."

"How do people get that way, feeling like they don't need anyone?" asked Marla.

"There are lots of causes. A child may grow up seeing self-sufficiency modeled by his parent or another family member. Sometimes it's a cultural thing—you know, the stoic superhero who needs no one. Sometimes people become overly self-sufficient when they go for a prolonged time without having their needs met. They feel hurt, and that drives them to deny their needs. Or they may turn to self-indulging ways to meet their needs."

"Self-indulging? What in the world is that?" asked Marla.

"It means overeating, fantasizing, overachievement, perfectionism, or other escapes—anything to dull the pain."

Marla nodded. "That describes a lot of people I know, including Jimmy and me. I do everything in a big way—talking, eating, fantasizing, achieving. Jimmy tries to be silent and perfect and never need anything. My family's like me; his family's like him. You should go to dinner with his family sometime. Everyone sits and eats in silence. No one talks. They don't even ask anyone to pass anything. I guess they don't want people to know they need anything, even if it's just the butter or the salt and pepper."

"You're gaining some good insights, Marla. Recognizing some of the problems means you're on your way to solving them," David noted. "Maybe it's time we talked about how you can block the robbers of intimacy."

## 4. MUTUAL GIVING: "I LOVE YOU"

The final ingredient of intimacy is mutual giving. It involves two people thinking more highly of each other than of themselves. It's covered in Philippians 2:3: "Let nothing be done through selfish ambition or conceit, but in lowliness of mind let each esteem others better than himself." The focus is on giving rather than taking—giving to meet the needs of your partner; this is the basis of a healthy relationship. God honors a motive of giving; it's the secret to deepening marital intimacy and the crucial ingredient for producing joy and grateful appreciation in a relationship. As spouses receive of God's abundance, so they "freely give" (Matt. 10:8).

In sharp contrast is a relationship in which "taking" is the paramount objective. We've all known people whose motives are dubious, to say the least. The salesperson who offers an exaggerated compliment, then jams a hard sales pitch down your throat. The child who tells Mommy she's beautiful, then begs for a cookie. The date who showers you with flowers, then tries to compromise your virtue.

Naturally, selfish manipulation and wrong motives are infinitely harder to contend with in a marriage, and God has His own opinion of such a person: "All the ways of a man are pure in his own eyes, / But the LORD weighs the spirits" (Prov. 16:2).

Mutual giving is the key to healthy relationships.

### Healthy versus Unhealthy Relationships

To understand the difference between healthy and unhealthy relationships we focus on the issue of expectations: Who do you expect to meet your need? Partners in a healthy relationship look to God for satisfaction and blessing. Those in unhealthy relationships expect another person to be their source of happiness, as shown in the following chart. Let's carry this another step. If you are in a healthy relationship in which God is meeting your needs, you can feel free to trust other people to the Lord. In other words, you may desire that your wife be more supportive as a helpmate, but your faith is that

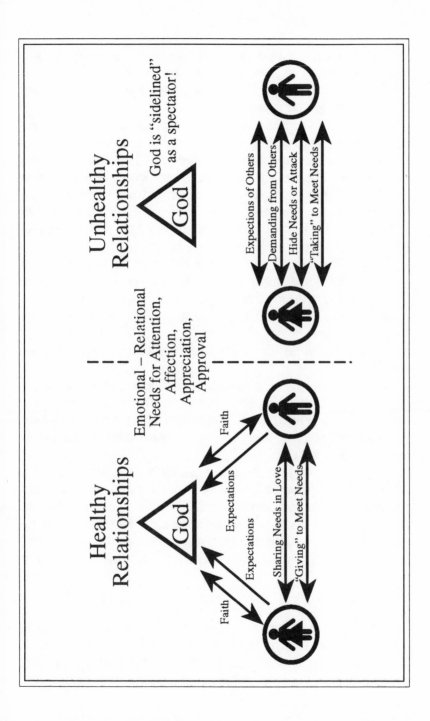

God can be trusted with both your need and your wife! In contrast, those in unhealthy relationships will expect other people to please them, and when their needs aren't met, they will likely become angry, demanding, and manipulative.

George and Gloria presented a classic example of an unhealthy relationship. While struggling with some of the same problems Jimmy and Marla Carlton experienced, George and Gloria faced an added complication. The son of an alcoholic father, George began drinking in college. At first he tried to hide his dependence on alcohol from his wife, but soon everyone was aware of the problem. George had several minor traffic accidents and even spent a night in jail, but he still refused to admit his problem with booze.

Gloria tried again and again to break through her husband's wall of silence. She desperately wanted to help George, but the more she tried to reach him the more he turned away. She was convinced if she could just get him to open up and talk to her, he might begin to heal some of the hurts he had buried so deep. But whenever she urged him to talk, he cut her off with "Everything's fine. Leave me alone. I'm okay."

"But *I'm* not okay!" she shot back once, her anger spilling out in spite of her resolve. "You won't talk to me. You won't ever tell me how you feel. You hide all your emotions. Do you feel anything? Do you need anything from me? Do you ever want to know what I need from you? Do you even care?"

Sadly, Gloria was learning a very painful lesson: The person who refuses to admit he or she has any needs usually refuses to recognize the needs of his or her partner as well. Just as George denied his own needs, so he also blocked out Gloria's needs. There seemed to be no way to begin establishing a healthy relationship until George admitted he needed help and allowed a chink in his armor for Gloria to reach through.

## Sharing Needs in Love versus Hiding Needs or Attacking

In healthy relationships needs are expressed openly and in a loving way: "I've been missing our being together. Can we plan a special date, just the two of us?" "I need a hug." "I feel good when you tell me you love me."

Unhealthy relationships usually follow one of two extremes:

1. Not sharing the truth about needs. In other words, one or both mates hide their needs (as George did) and are overly self-reliant, expressing such attitudes as, "I'm fine. Nothing's the matter. Leave me alone!"
2. Sharing needs but not in love. This happens when one mate says, for example, "You don't care what I want. The kids are more important to you than I am! You never pay attention to me anymore!"

When Gloria finally persuaded her reluctant husband to see a therapist, Chris Thurman encouraged them both to share their needs with each other openly and lovingly. Gloria admitted she had become a bit strident lately, prompting George to clam up even more. He admitted he probably should express his feelings more candidly, but it was his nature to be reclusive. Chris urged both of them to give a little. He suggested Gloria share her needs *only* in a loving manner and that George make a real effort to verbalize his feelings occasionally rather than withdrawing. It was slow going at first, but gradually they learned to share their needs more often than they hid them or attacked each other for ignoring them. In fact, George was on the verge of admitting he needed help with his alcoholism.

### Giving versus Taking to Meet Needs

Mutual giving is the key to healthy relationships . . . two people giving to meet their mate's important emotional needs, with neither person taking from the other. This follows the admonition of Acts 20:35: "It is more blessed to give than to receive."

In contrast, nothing destroys intimacy faster than feeling someone has taken something from you that you didn't choose to give. Unhealthy relationships typically end up with two emotionally bankrupt people trying desperately to take from each other—the mark of a codependent relationship! Notice that taking is characterized by a very conditional love:

I'll love you if . . .

I'll love you when . . .

Tragically this performance cycle is never ending, and it never satisfies!

George and Gloria had started out as two bankrupt people, one wanting to take, the other refusing to give. But with work and determination they began to restore their relationship. It took several months of counseling before George and Gloria felt comfortable with their new pattern of behavior. At first George frequently slipped back into his old habit of turning to booze and concealing his emotions, insisting nothing was wrong.

Gloria's first impulse was to pressure George to stop drinking and talk about his feelings, but she resisted the impulse and practiced expressing her needs in a loving, gentle way. The less pressured George felt the less he drank and the more willing he was to be open and vulnerable—at least often enough that Gloria felt they were making progress. As George acknowledged his needs, he began seeking help in overcoming his addiction. Now, with a smile, Gloria shares that she's beginning to remember why they fell in love in the first place.

## Trust Issues in a Healthy Relationship

Think about your own marriage in terms of the three dimensions of body, soul, and spirit. Then read each statement below, asking yourself how accurately it portrays your personal goals in your marital relationship. Imagine that you are speaking directly with your mate.

I will walk intimately with God, receiving abundantly from Him.

I will trust God to direct and change me as He chooses.

I will trust God to direct and change you as He chooses.

I will give priority to meeting your needs.

I will empathize with you and help heal your hurts.

I will share the truth of my needs with you in love.

I will share the truth of my hurts with you in love.

I will treat the truth you share with me confidentially as *our* truth.

# 7

# Block the Robbers of Intimacy

"BLOCK THE ROBBERS of intimacy? Sounds like a football game or a crime drama," mused Jimmy Carlton. "What are we supposed to do—come up with some new strategy for blocking and tackling?"

"That's a good way of putting it," agreed David Ferguson. "It's just what you might need to do if you're serious about journeying through the ten steps of Intimacy Therapy."

"Oh, we're serious," said Marla, "but when I tell people Jimmy and I are learning how to put each other first and give instead of take, and all that good stuff, they look at me like I'm daft. I mean, everywhere we go we hear people talking about how you should get what's good for yourself. Take care of Number One. If you're not getting what you need out of a relationship, get out. It's hard to think of turning that concept around, turning it inside out and making it work. But I'm willing to try if Jimmy is."

Jimmy drew a figure eight with his boot. "Why not? We've come this far."

"Good," said David. "Now let's look at some of the hindrances you're going to encounter as you try to put these four intimacy ingredients to work in your marriage."

Marla sighed. "I suppose it was too much to expect we could sail blissfully along now that we know these intimacy techniques. Go ahead. Tell us the worst."

"You're right, Marla. As sure as we are that God wants us to experience intimacy with Him, with our mates and children, and with the body of Christ, we can be just as sure that hindrances will follow. After all, on the heels of the Genesis declaration that Adam and Eve's relationship was 'very good,' the thief was there to 'steal, and to kill, and to destroy.' Check it out in Genesis 3:1 and John 10:10. But forewarned is forearmed, right?"

## EMOTIONAL HINDRANCES: DESTROYERS OF INTIMACY

For many of the couples we see in counseling, the hope of intimacy has long since vanished. They may never even have seen an intimate marriage, let alone possess one. All too often, as God is sidelined in a relationship, a couple's needs go unmet and each begins taking from the other. Their unmet needs affect their thinking, then their feelings, and finally their behavior. For example, as their needs for attention, affection, or support go unmet, they develop thinking patterns like this:

*You don't care about me anymore.*

*I'm not important to you.*

*Maybe there's someone else.*

This type of thinking produces emotional pain that may be experienced as *hurt, anger,* or *fear:*

Deep hurt springs from feelings of rejection, loneliness, disappointment, embarrassment, or sadness.

Anger can motivate a person to strike out in retaliation, seethe in sarcasm, or repress his or her feelings, causing depression.

Fear of being hurt again may prompt a person to withdraw, to escape into work or other relationships, or to build impermeable walls of self-reliant protection.

And what began as a thought (*He doesn't love me anymore*) soon becomes an emotion (*I feel hurt and I want to make him hurt too*) that quickly evolves into a behavior (*I'll attack him with criticism and cruel words to spite him for hurting me*).

As this destructive spiral continues, a couple will settle into these unproductive patterns, or games, that destroy intimacy:

**Performance pressures:** Partners manipulate or leverage their mates into meeting their needs.

**Poor communication patterns:** Partners hide their needs from each other or hurl verbal attacks rather than vulnerably sharing.

**Sexual struggles:** Instead of viewing sexual expression as a means of giving to each other, partners become obsessed with the frequency of sex and in trading sex for chores.

Consider how the following common marital complaints (compiled by Bernard Greene in a study of 750 couples complaining of marital problems) could be sorted into the three common patterns:

| | |
|---|---|
| Lack of communication | Infidelity |
| Constant arguments | Conflicts about children |
| Unfulfilled emotional needs | Domineering spouse |
| Financial disagreements | Suspicious spouse |
| In-law trouble | Physical attack[1] |

In counseling, we have encountered every type of marital problem imaginable. We've seen narcissistic spouses who were so self-centered they could perceive no one's needs but their own; couples who had never experienced a positive, meaningful relationship, who were totally indifferent to the partner's feelings or were incapable of "stroking" (reinforcing) each other; wives who were so inflexible they couldn't deviate from a fixed pattern of behavior; and husbands who lacked both verbal and nonverbal communication skills. Some couples were in crisis because one partner avoided communication by withdrawing, leaving the spouse to feel rejected; other couples had become experts at miscommunication by distorting the messages they received from their mates.

Then there's the matter of affairs. Various surveys present shocking numbers. The *Hite Report on Male Sexuality*, published in 1981, reported an almost unbelievable 70 percent of married men had cheated on their wives.[2] According to an 1988 survey conducted by *Christianity Today* of both men and women readers, fully 28 percent indicated they had been involved in sexual contact outside the marriage.[3] While the validity of anonymous self reports is sometimes questionable, the concern over extramarital affairs cannot be mini-mized. Jerry Jenkins, in his work entitled *Loving Your Marriage Enough to Protect It*, bluntly states "Sexual immorality hits frighten-ingly close to home. Without being aware of the need to protect our-selves against it, we are vulnerable."[4]

There are two significant aspects to every affair: the deprivations at home and the attractions away from home. But we should point out that many people have nonsexual, nonpersonal affairs—with their jobs, their hobbies, their drive for further schooling, their churches. In essence, something else is receiving the care and atten-tion that rightfully belongs to the marriage.

Some people are reared in an atmosphere of neglect. Deprived of much-needed attention, they may lack the capacity to feel important or be concerned with others' feelings. They may run from one per-son to another, hoping each one will supply that missing ingredient in their lives. With a seemingly insatiable need for love, warmth, and attention, they are perpetually dissatisfied with their relationships with others, including their spouses.

Typically, this person longs for a deep, intimate relationship, but his needs are so pervasive he constantly wants to be parented. (Obvi-ously, the person could be either male or female.) And even if his spouse were able to get that close, he would be unable to accept the attention he needs because he would fear his spouse wouldn't like him if she really knew him intimately.

In many ways James Barrie's classic character Peter Pan presents just such a person—the little boy who never wants to grow up and accept adult and family responsibilities, but who desperately needs his Wendy to nurture and mother him. To their consternation and regret, many wives have stepped into Wendy roles and find them-selves forever mothering and rescuing their "little-boy" husbands. Yet these wives may be reacting out of a deep unmet need to nurture, and thus we come full circle to the importance of understanding inti-macy needs.

The chart *Understanding Intimacy Needs* presents both the poten-tial and the pain of personal needs and gives an overview of the con-nection between your needs, thoughts, feelings, behavior, and the quality of your adult relationships. Depending in large part on whether your needs are met or unmet, you will take the "high road" to healthy relationships or the "low road" to unhealthy ones. If your parents and other caregivers generously gave you affection, attention, praise, and positive instruction, then you probably developed healthy thinking: *I must be important . . . I'm really loved . . . I can do it!* You probably felt worthy, confident, secure, and grateful, and such positive emotions likely produced productive behaviors such as kindness, consideration, generosity, and a desire for excellence. As a child experiencing such early positive feedback, you were likely to develop a trusting heart open to a personal relationship with Christ. As this relationship was established and nurtured, you probably developed a good self-image and a mature personality, and you were able to establish intimate relationships in the context of a functional family.

On the other hand, if your childhood needs remained largely unmet—if you experienced neglect, abuse, excessive criticism, or rejection—then you probably developed unhealthy thinking: *What's wrong with me? I don't matter . . . Maybe if I try harder, they'll love me.* Such negative thinking could have spiraled into negative feelings. You probably felt unworthy, hurt, anxious, and bitter. In turn, these unhealed emotions could have provoked unproductive behaviors, including manipulative games, addictions/compulsions, and self-abuse. Struggling against a poor self-image and possible personality disturbances, you likely experienced problems in living and established a dysfunctional family similar to the one you came from. Such an environment would make trusting difficult and actually hinder you from coming to know Christ.

To illustrate this process, imagine a four-year-old drawing a picture with his crayons. Little Johnny calls out, "Mommy, Daddy, come look!" If they don't respond immediately, he runs and clutches his father's leg or waves his drawing in his mother's face. Suppose his mother replies, "Not now, Johnny, I'm busy." And his father shoos him away, declaring, "I have to go to work. Go play by yourself."

Johnny slumps away, his need for attention and approval unmet.

# Understanding Intimacy Needs

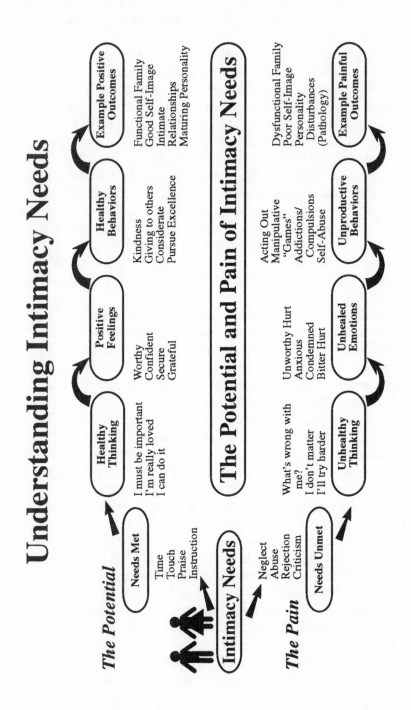

## The Potential

**Needs Met**
Time
Touch
Praise
Instruction

**Healthy Thinking**
I must be important
I'm really loved
I can do it

**Positive Feelings**
Worthy
Confident
Secure
Grateful

**Healthy Behaviors**
Kindness
Giving to others
Considerate
Pursue Excellence

**Example Positive Outcomes**
Functional Family
Good Self-Image
Intimate Relationships
Maturing Personality

## Intimacy Needs

Neglect
Abuse
Rejection
Criticism

# The Potential and Pain of Intimacy Needs

## The Pain

**Needs Unmet**

**Unhealthy Thinking**
What's wrong with me?
I don't matter
I'll try harder

**Unhealed Emotions**
Unworthy Hurt
Anxious
Condemned
Bitter Hurt

**Unproductive Behaviors**
Acting Out
Manipulative "Games"
Addictions/Compulsions
Self-Abuse

**Example Painful Outcomes**
Dysfunctional Family
Poor Self-Image
Personality Disturbances (Pathology)

He might be thinking, *Mommy and Daddy aren't interested in what I do. I'm not important to them. What's wrong with me?* He might feel rejected, unloved, insecure, perhaps even afraid to try to win his parents' approval again.

How might he act? He might tear up his picture, hide in the closet and cry, or begin coloring on the wall (surely that would elicit his parents' attention!), or he might hit his baby sister. After all, why should she sit there smiling dopily while he's miserable? Might as well make her feel as bad as he feels. Besides, then maybe his parents will notice him, even if it's just to give him a swat. At least a spanking means he has his parents' undivided attention for a few precious moments. Eventually Johnny may develop withdrawal symptoms and anxiety about asking for what he wants; unconsciously he tells himself, *I won't ask for anything again.* Or he may seek some unhealthy form of escape.

But imagine what would happen with Johnny if his parents stopped what they were doing and sincerely admired his picture. He might think, *I did a good job. My parents care about what I do. They like my work. I'm special to them. I can do things to please them.* How might he feel? Valued. Worthy. Special. Able. What might he do? He might draw another picture, confident that he could do a good job and bring pleasure to his parents. When he tackled some other task, he would have the assurance his parents would be interested in that accomplishment also. He would build on his successes and develop a positive attitude and a healthy sense of security. He could trust his parents to be there for him—supportive, encouraging, loving, and attentive. He would likely become that kind of parent himself.

Not only should we consider the issue of needs in a family context, but also in a cultural context. For example, when a little girl falls down and hurts herself, we take her in our arms and hug and console her, but if a little boy falls down we say, "You're a big boy. Don't cry; you'll be okay." Both need comfort, but culturally we respond differently to the boy. This carries over to our perception of men versus women. Culturally, we don't expect a man to shed tears or reveal his feelings.

How do we deal with the childhood pains and emotional hurts

we've accumulated over the years? How do we cope with our feelings of anger, sadness, and guilt? How do we keep negative emotions from destroying the very intimacy we're trying to build in our marital relationship?

## AN ANTIDOTE TO HINDRANCES: EMOTION MANAGEMENT

We learn time management in college and financial management in seminars, but tragically, few of us master the essentials of emotion management! Feelings such as anger and guilt are part of our God-given internal steering mechanism, but God never intended these feelings to accumulate inside of us. Guilt needs to be emptied through confession to God, and as appropriate, to others. Anger that has stagnated into resentment needs to be emptied through forgiveness. Scripture gives us guidelines: "Do not let the sun go down on your wrath" (Eph. 4:26). Why not? Because anger occupies a space inside you, and it needs to be dealt with or it grows into a deep root of bitterness, spreading its tendrils like seeds in rich soil. You know you're bitter when anger becomes generalized. Scripture is clear here too: Hebrews 12:15 tells us to "[look] carefully, lest anyone fall short of the grace of God; lest any root of bitterness springing up cause trouble."

One woman we counseled was angry with her father, so angry she was bitter against half the population in the world. She had no interest in marrying because as far as she was concerned men were no good and she wasn't about to waste her time on them. Unfortunately, her anger against one man—her father—was preventing her from seeing the potential of a meaningful relationship with any man. She will probably spend her life clutching her bitterness to her breast, never realizing the love she might have experienced had she not written off all men because of one.

### Understanding Your Emotional Capacity

One way we can better understand unhealed hurts is through the concept of "emotional capacity." Imagine you have a cup inside you that holds emotion. It's of limited capacity just as in the physical sense you can eat only so much food before feeling stuffed. You do, in fact, have a portion of your brain that handles emotion. When unresolved hurts, anger, and resentment accumulate, there is less room to handle emotional stress as well as less room to experience positive emotions.

When you married, you probably marched down the church aisle expecting your mate to have an empty cup that could be filled up with good feelings for you, but what you might not have realized was that maybe 90 percent of that cup already could have been filled with junk.

David Ferguson shares this illustration from his own life: "Teresa and I went through a time in our marriage for about two years when I would say, 'I love you,' and she would answer back, 'I just feel numb; I don't feel anything.' During those two years God burdened me with the question, *How does a person get like that—and how do you fix it?* The most important thing for me was realizing I had played a major role in hurting Teresa, and I had to deal with that first. After that, we helped each other heal hurts we'd brought with us into marriage.

"When I counsel someone who says, 'I don't feel as loving as I used to' or 'I just feel numb,' I know that person's emotional cup is filled with negative or unresolved emotions. You can't feel romantic and resentful at the same time. It's a human impossibility. Resentment will kill romance. So I tell that person, 'Let me work with you to help you get this stuff out of you. Then you can be free to decide what to do about your relationship.' Too many people fill themselves with negative emotions then decide they need to get rid of the relationship. So they leave it and find another partner, but since their emotional cup goes with them they still retain all those negative feelings."

## Hurt and Anger: Two Sides of the Same Pain

Take a closer look at what's in your emotional cup. Let's suppose your mate has rejected you in some way. You feel hurt, violated, saddened; you suffer a diminished sense of self, and you feel vulnerable to more pain. Your feelings of loss and vulnerability are so tender, you can't tolerate them for long, so you hide behind a protective wall of anger. That's what we mean when we say hurt and anger are two sides of the same pain. Your negative feelings become focused on another person rather than on yourself because it's easier to endure anger than pain.

### The Many Masks of Anger.

The anger from your unhealed hurts may exhibit itself in many ways. You may become impatient, quick-tempered, depressed, suspicious, jealous, or mistrustful. You may escape into your work, hobbies, children's activities, or church work. You may suffer from a variety of addictions or display passive-aggressive behaviors such as procrastination, avoidance, silence, or sarcasm. To be healed, you will need to confront your anger and work through it until you can release it through forgiveness.

### Hurts Involve a Loss to Be Mourned.

Whatever it is that has hurt you so deeply—whether it's rejection or neglect or some form of abuse—you need to allow yourself to feel that pain, then express it, sharing it with someone else who can validate and comfort you. In other words, you need to mourn . . . and experience the promised blessing of comfort. "Blessed are those who mourn, / For they shall be comforted" (Matt. 5:4). All unhealed hurts must be mourned. If you're also struggling with guilt feelings, you need to receive God's forgiveness and grant forgiveness to others who've hurt you.

## Does Your Cup Runneth Over?

You may recognize this as a moment when it is crucially important to pause and reflect on your own emotional capacity. Using the illustration of a cup as your reference, you and your spouse answer the following questions as openly and honestly as possible.

1. What symptoms do you see in your life that might indicate an accumulation of unresolved emotion? (For instance, I have a hard time sleeping. I'm depressed a lot. I'm impatient with the kids. I have no energy.) _____

_____

# EMOTIONAL CAPACITY
– Your "Cup" May Runneth Over! –

## Symptoms of a "Full Cup"

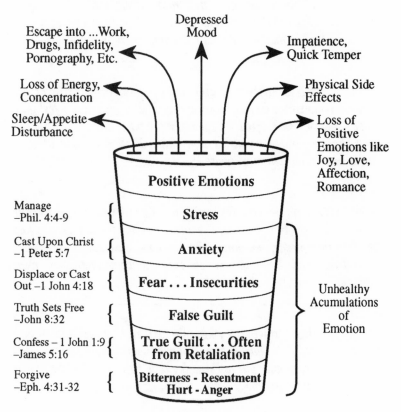

Depressed Mood

Escape into ...Work, Drugs, Infidelity, Pornography, Etc.

Impatience, Quick Temper

Loss of Energy, Concentration

Physical Side Effects

Sleep/Appetite Disturbance

Loss of Positive Emotions like Joy, Love, Affection, Romance

**Positive Emotions**

Manage –Phil. 4:4-9 { **Stress**

Cast Upon Christ –1 Peter 5:7 { **Anxiety**

Displace or Cast Out –1 John 4:18 { **Fear . . . Insecurities**

Truth Sets Free –John 8:32 { **False Guilt**

Confess – 1 John 1:9 –James 5:16 { **True Guilt . . . Often from Retaliation**

Forgive –Eph. 4:31-32 { **Bitterness - Resentment Hurt - Anger**

Unhealthy Acumulations of Emotion

## You Can Only Hold So Much Emotion

2. What hurts might there be in your emotional cup? *(For instance, I feel hurt over the way my spouse belittles me. I hurt from all the times my partner ignores my wishes. I feel hurt over the way my spouse rejected me when we were first married.)* _____
   _____

3. What anger and bitterness do you feel? *(For instance, I'm angry over the way my spouse uses sarcasm to put me down. I'm angry I never felt my partner's support in my career. I'm bitter I was pressured by my spouse to marry and was too young to enjoy my youth.)* _____
   _____

4. What feelings of guilt or regret have you experienced over how you've sometimes treated your spouse? *(For instance, I feel guilty over the way I've nagged my spouse in the past. I regret the accusing and abusive words I've hurled at my mate. I feel guilty that I haven't spent more time with my spouse.)* _____
   _____

5. What emotions do you find within yourself that relate to other relationships? *(For instance, I feel hurt that my friends want to focus only on their needs, not mine. I'm bitter my boss didn't give me the raise I deserved. I'm angry my children only come around when they want something.)* _____
   _____

6. What childhood hurts do you still carry in your emotional cup? *(For instance, I feel hurt that my parents ignored me as a child. I'm angry that my mother put my sister's needs first. I feel bitter that my parents never praised me.)* _____
   _____

When Jimmy and Marla Carlton answered these questions, they found that Marla filled in every blank with plenty of words to spare, while Jimmy had a hard time coming up with anything to say. "I'm not good at this emotion stuff," he admitted. When pressed about symptoms, he said, "Ask Marla. She'll tell you I'm moody, impatient, and quick-tempered. I suppose I escape into my work a lot, even though the insurance business is far from the ideal escape. Marla will probably tell you I run away from my feelings every chance I get. I don't mean to. In fact, I feel guilty that I can't respond emotionally the way she wants me to."

Marla was glad to hear that. "I feel better just knowing Jimmy would like to express his feelings more. I know I'm too emotional. Look at my list. I couldn't even write everything down. I'm angry that Jimmy keeps his distance from me and the kids and doesn't get involved in our lives. But I also feel guilty for making Jimmy settle down instead of staying on the road with the band. I feel depressed and I eat too much. I feel a ton of anxiety. What if Jimmy walked away from us someday? And I guess I'm bitter that our life isn't what I thought it'd be when we fell in love." Marla chuckled wryly. "Other than that, I'm fine!"

## UNPRODUCTIVE BEHAVIORS

David Ferguson met Marla's little jab of comical sarcasm with a sympathetic smile. Then he asked Jimmy and Marla, "How many negative feelings in your emotional cup can be traced back to your experiences as children?"

"Lots of them!" Marla exclaimed. "Jimmy and I both felt we could never measure up to our parents' expectations. We were always trying to earn their love and attention. Right, Jimmy? I know *I* felt pressure to perform and be the best."

### Performance Pressures

When David Ferguson remarked that both marriage and family life suffer dramatically when couples exhibit unproductive behaviors, which may result from pressure to perform, Marla gave a whopping amen. "I'm a walking testimonial," she said. "When love and acceptance are conditional, the relationship is unhealthy. It's the story of my life!" She went on to tell David what it was like in her family when she was growing up. The cycle of performing became an endless treadmill of doing things to gain affection, attention, or approval. "It was that way for my brothers and sisters too. We became human 'doings' rather than human 'beings.' My folks loved the arts and the theater and good music. I spent my childhood taking piano lessons, but I was never good enough. Even today, no matter what I do, I'm still not good enough. Sometimes I even feel that way with God."

David reminded her that God isn't interested only in behavior. "We're more than our behavior. God cares about each of us as a person. He didn't put us here just to *do*, but to *be*."

Performance pressure is contagious. *If I feel I must perform, then you must also perform!* While Jimmy and Marla Carlton came from very different backgrounds, both families suffered from the bondage of conditional love. In both Marla's boisterous, freewheeling household and Jimmy's staid, tight-lipped environment, the rule of thumb was selfish taking rather than unselfish giving. Personal responsibility for one's own attitude and behavior was replaced with justifying one's actions and blaming others. Usually in such homes self is exalted, the Spirit is grieved, and intimacy is lost—sometimes forever.

You may have come from a home like Jimmy or Marla's where you were expected to perform if you wanted love and acceptance. Your home may have been a highly demanding one or a neglectful one; in either case, the result was the same. Love was a rare commodity dispensed grudgingly or as a bargaining chip. Jimmy's parents demanded perfection of both themselves and him. After all, he was their only son so they had only one chance to get it right. But since perfection was impossible to achieve, Jimmy's parents were never happy with themselves or satisfied with his performance. Tragically, their demands took many forms in addition to perfectionism—a grab bag of unpleasant responses: constant criticism, inappropriate expectations, prideful superiority, endless rules, and lots of social pressure. Needless to say, his folks were aghast and nearly choked on their credentials when Jimmy married marvelous Marla.

Marla's family was anything but typical. Imaginative, whimsical, and impulsive, they could have stepped bag and baggage straight out of a 1940s Jimmy Stewart comedy. But with few rules or boundaries, and with each member so intent on doing his or her own thing, it became a neglectful home environment. Each of the five children had to fight for the parents' attention, and fight they did—tooth and nail—to earn some morsel of approval. No wonder Marla craved attention so deeply. She had given it her best shot for a lifetime and still felt anonymous in her family circle.

Homes like Marla's might include a workaholic, an emotionally closed parent, or a preoccupied, distant, or substance-abusing person as well as the selfish-narcissistic martyr. In each case the message to other family members is the same: "I'm so absorbed in other things, you're not very important to me!"

Children in such homes may seek attention through academics, athletics, popularity, or finally through disruptive behavior. Whatever they do, their cry is the same: *Please notice me . . . Care about me . . . I'm important!* To win applause, Marla, like Jimmy, had turned to the entertainment field and become an actual performer. But she admitted it never made a bit of difference to her folks. "I could walk into my parents' house carrying an Oscar or a gold record, and their response would still be the same: 'Shut the door, Marla. You're letting in a draft!'"

David sympathized with Marla and stressed a point we made earlier in this book: "The broad path of performance many families travel ends in destruction; the narrow path of unconditional giving that few families travel brings great blessing."

Unfortunately, both Jimmy and Marla had been caught in their family's performance trap, and because it was all they knew, they had carried over to their marriage the same expectations and behaviors they had been taught.

"Here's how healthy relationships work," David explained. "Be, then do. That order is essential."

"Come again?" said Marla.

"Intimate relationships are founded on first 'being' accepted, loved, and valued; then follows a desire to 'do' things consistent with that acceptance, love, and worth."

Jimmy nodded. "Doing stuff to win love is a hollow victory. You never know where you stand or whether you've done enough."

"Right," David agreed. "A much better motivation is gratefulness for having received love, approval, and acceptance. Secure in the knowledge we're loved, we feel a freedom to respond. We experience an incredible sense of liberty. It's the same principle in our relationship with God. Having received what we could not earn and did not deserve—that is, grace—we're free from the fear of never having it and the fear of ever losing it."

Jimmy whistled under his breath. "It kinda blows my mind. Here I can't get my own parents to accept me, but God does. Wow!"

"Trouble is," said Marla, "even though I know how lousy it feels not to be accepted by someone you love, I still find it hard to love and accept people unconditionally, even Jimmy and my kids. Does that make me a bad person?"

"No. Only human. But here's something we might all repeat to ourselves when we're struggling to love unconditionally: 'Why should someone for whom Christ died have to earn *my* acceptance? What gives me the right to withhold the love, acceptance, forgiveness, and comfort I freely received from Christ?' You might check out Ephesians 5:2 and 4:31–32, Romans 15:7, and 2 Corinthians 1:4 for backup Scripture."

"I agree with that all the way," said Marla, "but when you get down to the nitty-gritty of everyday living, it's awfully hard to keep that mind-set. Everything interferes with those good feelings. How can we keep showing unconditional love when dinner's burning or the toilet's overflowing or little Jeffy's just swatted Anna with his tennis racket or Jimmy comes home without the groceries I sent him out for? Know what I mean?"

"I do. And maybe the best way to help you deal with the nitty-gritty is to turn your spotlight, so to speak, on some more hindrances to intimacy—in the area of communication, for instance."

## Communication Patterns

"Oh boy, here we go!" said Jimmy, rocking back in his chair.

"What's that supposed to mean?" challenged Marla.

David interrupted. "How would the two of you characterize your communication?"

"Chitchat," said Jimmy. "Hi, how are you? How was your day? When's dinner?"

"That's for sure," said Marla. "Mainly factual stuff. Jeffy hit

Anna today. The car's out of gas. Our checking account's overdrawn. I'm too tired tonight!"

"You can say that again!" said Jimmy. "I hear that line in my sleep."

David smiled knowingly. "All right, think about this. How much of your conversation is *intimate*—where you feel free to share your dreams, hopes, feelings, and fears in an atmosphere of loving acceptance?"

They both laughed. "Last year maybe. I'm sure there was one time, wasn't there, Marla?"

"Don't ask me. I wasn't there or I'd have remembered!"

"Ahh, *an unavailable spouse?* That's one of the hindrances to communication. It takes quality time together to move past chitchat."

"You've got us both on that one," mused Marla.

"Another hindrance is *unhealed hurts.* It's awfully hard to feel intimate with someone you're mad at."

"I know. We've tried," said Jimmy. "It's a real downer."

"Here's another: *an unbridled tongue.* It's all too easy to wound each other when you speak before you think."

Marla rolled her eyes. "That's me, Foot-in-Her-Mouth Marla."

"I won't even try to touch that one," said David. "So last but not least, is *criticism.* It puts a real crimp in intimacy."

"Uh-huh," said Jimmy. "Nothing quenches that ol' fire of romance like Marla telling me I've got bad breath or my feet stink."

"Then brush your teeth and change your socks," she snapped.

"When you stop spreading that goop all over your face."

"What do you mean, *goop?*" She patted her cheekbones. "It's an expensive facial mask that keeps my complexion beautiful."

"Ha! It makes you look like King Tut—before they unwrapped him!"

David figured it was time to break in. "Whoa! We haven't finished with the hindrances to communication!"

"No problem. Jimmy and I already got 'em all down pat."

"But I think you'll really identify with this one. It's called *hiding and hurling.*"

"Sounds like a new dance step," said Jimmy.

"Let's just say it keeps you on your toes and at each other's throat.

Actually, it is a little like choreography. You dance around each other and make all the wrong moves but never really connect."

"Sounds interesting," said Marla. "So explain already."

### The Destructiveness of Hiding and Hurling.

We all tend to fit in one of these categories. We're typically either a hider or a hurler. We either hide our pain behind a wall of silence or we hurl an attack to make someone else hurt like we hurt. Either approach produces disastrous results.

"Well, there's no mystery here," said Marla. "I know I'm a hurler. And Jimmy's a hider. It's like we were born to play those roles."

"True enough. You probably settled into those roles as very young children."

"So what's wrong with being hiders and hurlers? It's natural. It's what we are. It fits our personalities."

### Hiders Don't Share the Truth.

"Tell me, Jimmy," said David, "when is the last time you told Marla, 'Nothing's wrong. I'm fine. It really doesn't matter'?"

"I dunno. I guess that's my stock-in-trade answer. It just sort of comes out automatically."

"Why?"

"Okay, I getcha. It's easier to say 'nothing's wrong' than to take a good look and admit what's really going on inside me."

"It all goes back to this thing with his dad, doesn't it?" said Marla. "He learned as a child to keep his feelings to himself and he's still doing it."

"Right. Now what about a 'hurler'? What does she do?"

### Hurlers Often Share the Truth, but Not in Love.

"How about it, Marla? You say you're a hurler. What have you 'hurled' at Jimmy lately?"

"You mean besides a frying pan? I'm just kidding!"

"NOT!" said Jimmy. "I've got the bruise to prove it."

"You do not! I never hit you!"

"She's right. I'm kidding."

"Boy, with you for a husband, who needs enemies!"

"That's one hurl," David noted. "Any more?"

"How's this? 'You treat the dog better than you do me! You never talk. The TV is better company than you! You're gone so much, when you came to the door I thought you were a traveling salesman!'"

"Okay, I get the idea," said David. "Now tell me, how could you have shared the same truths in a loving way?"

### Healers Share the Truth in Love.

"Wow, that's a tall order!" Marla said. Then she thought a minute. "I guess I could have told Jimmy, 'Sometimes when you're giving little Fido a hug, I wish it were me,' and 'When I married you, I admired you for being the strong silent type, but I love hearing what you're thinking and how you're feeling,' and, 'I know you have to travel a lot, but I really miss being with you.'"

"How does that make you feel, Jimmy?"

"It sure beats the first version. I'm ready to take my little bride home for some cozying by the fire."

## Sexual Struggles

"That's the last subject we're going to discuss today," David told Jimmy.

"Fire?"

"No, but it's something that can be just as hot and dangerous. Sex."

"I thought we were talking about hindrances to intimacy."

"We are. And when it comes to games people play, sex is high on the list. In fact, it's among the top four problems couples bring to a marriage counselor, right up there with communication, money, and kids."

"Just what are these games?" asked Jimmy.

"See? He's afraid he's missed something!" said Marla.

"Don't worry, Jimmy, you haven't missed anything. We're talking about hindrances to romance. Ways we sabotage those special times we could be having with our spouse."

"Right!" said Jimmy. "So what are they? I'm for anything that will break down barriers in that department."

"The numbers game, for one. Quantity is the most frequent complaint. Sadly, couples often define their sexual relationship in terms of numbers: How often they have sex, how many times one or the other reaches orgasm, how much foreplay occurred and how long it lasted. It's tragic when we take the God-designed plan for two becoming one flesh and reduce it to numbers.

"Nor should you negotiate these numbers—comparing your sexual frequency with the 'average' couple (whatever that is) or agreeing to 'trade' two more sexual encounters per week for twenty minutes of foreplay or one dinner date and cleaning the garage!

"The way you look at sex is important. If you view sex as something you *do*, then you'll evaluate it like other activities such as tennis or golf:

"How often?

"How long?

"How adept?

"Or if you consider sex something you *have*, then you'll see it as something to negotiate, trade, or conditionally share, just like money or other possessions:

" 'Not now.'

" 'Maybe later.'

" 'Maybe, if you would just do this for me . . .'

"Conflicts naturally follow when couples try to bargain or manipulate one another or when one partner goes on strike. So only by understanding where you *are* can you ever hope to get where you want to go, especially when it comes to your journey toward sexual oneness.

"Rather than sex being a *performance you do* or a *possession you have*, God intends sex as a *privilege to give*. Intimate sexual fulfillment comes as two close friends find themselves not taking from each other sexually, but mutually giving!"

We'll have more to say on this subject in the following chapters, when we examine more closely how you can gain freedom from the lies, pain, and games in your marriage.

CHAPTER

# 8

# Think Straight

WE HAVE FOUND the enemy—and it is us! All too frequently a major relationship enemy lies within us as our own thoughts hold us captive to fear, provoke us to retaliate, or prompt us to suppress our true feelings. Our fears prevent us from being vulnerable. Retaliation destroys opportunities for romance. And suppressing our feelings makes us overly self-reliant.[1]

Certainly the apostle Paul must have seen this same pattern as he observed the strained relationships among believers in Corinth. He wrote, "I fear, lest somehow, as the serpent deceived Eve . . . so your minds may be corrupted" (2 Cor. 11:3).

Epictetus, the stoic philosopher of the first century, remarked, "Men are disturbed not by things but by the *view* they take of them." Even in his generation he understood the importance of a person's thoughts.

Over the past three decades the counseling field has focused on this cognitive, or thinking, dimension in its approaches to therapy. More and more frequently, individuals are being viewed as thinking, feeling, and behaving (in other words, one's mind, emotions, and will forms his or her "soulish" self).[2] As therapists have recognized the dominant role thoughts play in affecting emotions and behavior, they have begun leading clients to explore what it is they are "telling themselves" (in other words, they have delved into the clients' self-talk) that keeps them emotionally disturbed. Unhealthy or irrational self-talk is then confronted or disputed, while more rational or healthy self-talk is emphasized. Amazingly, as a person changes his "self-talk," so he also changes his feelings and behavior!

Of course, psychologists aren't the only ones declaring the importance of our self-talk. God has been aware of the significance of our thoughts all along. He even spelled it out in His Word. Proverbs 23:7 tells us, "As he thinks in his heart, so is he." Romans 12:2 stresses the relevance of restructuring our thinking: "Do not be conformed to this world, but be transformed by the renewing of your mind." Paul made healthy self-talk a goal when he wrote, in 2 Corinthians 10:5, "casting down arguments and . . . bringing every thought into captivity." And he reminded us in Philippians 4:8, "Whatever things are true [and] . . . of good report . . . meditate on these things."

## RENEWING THE MIND . . . ESSENTIAL TO INTIMACY

David Ferguson helped Jimmy and Marla Carlton take a closer look at their own self-talk. "You both realize, don't you, that every marriage goes through a post-honeymoon stage where you're confronted with the reality of who you married rather than who you *thought* you married?"

When they looked at each other and laughed uneasily David knew he had hit a nerve. "There's a lot of unhealthy self-talk going on out there," he continued. "Many marriages are disrupted by the self-talk of perfectionism, which demands that everyone, including the spouse, must be perfect."

"Bingo!" said Marla. "That's Jimmy, all right. He expects himself—and me—to be perfect."

"Not perfect," argued Jimmy. "I just think we can do better in some areas, that's all."

"Me too," Marla shot back. "That's why we're here!"

David broke in discreetly. "Does this unhealthy self-talk sound familiar? 'If I'm vulnerable, I'll be hurt or rejected.' "

"Bingo again!" said Marla. "That's Jimmy too!"

"Hey, when are we gonna target Marla with some of this stuff?" demanded Jimmy, swiveling around in his chair. "All the buckshot's aimed at me!"

"Not so," David assured him. "When it comes to faulty thinking, we're all guilty.

"As we navigate through imperfect childhoods as imperfect people in a world filled with half-truths, each of us is destined to acquire some faulty thinking patterns," David told the Carltons. "It's a recurring source of stress in most families. In fact, dysfunctional family patterns are passed on to the third and fourth generations because the family members perpetuate unhealthy family self-talk. So you two aren't alone, not by a long shot."

"So how do we fight it—this bad self-talk?" asked Jimmy.

"You need to renew your thought patterns."

"How do we do that?"

"First, recognize your own faulty thinking. Let's consider some examples. Here's one: 'I shouldn't express my emotions to others.' This attitude might come from a home environment where emotion was kept inside or where expressing feelings was ridiculed."

"I hate to sound like a broken record, but that's Jimmy for sure," said Marla. "I get so frustrated when he doesn't understand how I feel. But how can he when he doesn't understand his own emotions?"

"A good observation," David noted. "What do you say to that, Jimmy?"

He chewed a moment on his lower lip. "Well, Marla's right, I suppose. I hate it when she gets all emotional on me, especially when the tears come. I can't stand all that blubbering. It makes me want to run like the dickens."

"Have you ever cried?" David asked.

"When I was a kid maybe. I don't remember."

"Did you feel it was wrong to cry?"

Jimmy's face reddened a bit. His eyes took on a glassy, distant look, as if he were recalling a painful memory. When David urged him to share it, he lowered his gaze and said, "I was just a little kid when my grandfather died, but I remember walking in my dad's room and catching him crying. I felt so bad for him, losing his dad and all, I just wanted to comfort him somehow. But when my dad spotted me watching him, he came unglued. Told me to get out and stop spying on him. It devastated me. I figured crying must be a shameful thing to do. I vowed right then and there no one would ever see me cry."

Marla reached out and touched Jimmy's arm. "I never knew."

"Didn't want you to. It was a terrible memory."

"But now I understand why you hate to see me cry."

"Here's another faulty thought pattern," David offered. "'Admitting I'm wrong is a sign of weakness and would be used against me.' Does that strike a responsive chord?"

Jimmy nodded. "I'll say it before Marla does. That's me. My dad was a stubborn man. Never admitted he was wrong. I'm the same way."

"So you're saying you came from a home where apologies were rare?"

"Nonexistent. But if you failed at something or made a mistake, watch out. You were in for heaps of criticism, and they'd never let you forget it."

"There was some of that in my home too," admitted Marla. "We were a big family and everyone was a taker, so we were always on the defensive. We were all good at rationalizing, making excuses, and blaming someone else."

"Do you see any of that in your home today?" David asked.

Marla smiled sheepishly. "I'm afraid so. For years I've blamed Jimmy for the problems in our marriage. But I make excuses for myself and rationalize that I'd do better if he were a better husband. I guess I should concentrate on cleaning up my own act first."

Jimmy's face lit up like a Christmas tree. "I swear, I never thought I'd hear those words from my sweet bride!"

David smiled. "Hold on. Here's another faulty thought pattern to consider: 'I deserve what I want.' What do you think?"

"We're all guilty," said Marla. "Every last one of us."

David nodded. "The media do a good job of bombarding us with a blitz of messages ranging from 'You deserve a break today' to 'You have a right to chicken done right!' We're all told we deserve the best and we should demand our rights. Look out for Number One. The only trouble is, it's a message that's incompatible with a happy marriage.

"Here's another one," David continued. "'I want it now!' Why is that a faulty thought pattern?"

"Easy," said Marla. "It's selfish and childish. It's what my kids said when they were little. They'd sit in the high chair and hammer the spoon on the tray and demand a cookie. If you think about it, that's what our whole generation is doing, isn't it? We're all hammering our spoons, wanting everything yesterday. Do you suppose that's why so many marriages are going down the tubes?"

"I agree that the 'I want it now' attitude is a serious problem, Marla, perhaps more in this generation than in previous ones; but it's a symptom as old as Adam and Eve. Of course, it thrives in our world of instant gratification and quick fixes, where we have everything from fast food and instant lube jobs to automatic tellers and quickie divorces."

"Right," said Jimmy. "If you're hungry, grab a burger. If you want entertainment, put a video in the VCR. If you need something, write a check or pull out your Visa card. Even the kids hear the message—If you wanna have sex, just put on a condom. It's as though we're being told we can have anything we want right now if we know the right button to push or have the right card in our pockets."

Imagine what happens when a couple conditioned with the "I want it now" attitude discovers family relationships don't work that way. Spouses don't change quickly, parenting takes more than an instant, and intimacy requires a lot of patient, selfless giving.

Often, in our marriages we think we can solve our unhappiness by getting our mates to change. *If my circumstances were different or if my mate were nicer, I wouldn't feel so angry or depressed or sad. If my mate would change, I'd have a better marriage.* Perhaps your relationship is so burdensome you don't enjoy it anymore. You may feel despair because you've dug a deep mental hole in the ground. You're so low down you have to look up to see bottom.

You may have traded the truth for a lie. In fact, where your marriage is concerned, you may have traded many truths for many lies. And now those lies are tearing your marriage apart. They may be tearing you apart as well.

To see the truth, you need to develop the mind-set of Christ. He has the perfect plumb bob (a lead weight hung at the end of a line to determine the depth of the water or the straightness of a wall). He is perfect truth showing itself in perfect righteousness. To move in His direction we need to take our thoughts captive to Christ until the truth takes over and becomes stronger than the lies.

It doesn't happen overnight or with just one try. During the Persian Gulf War, the American-Allied strategy to get Saddam Hussein out of Kuwait meant bombing the Iraqis unmercifully until they left. We need to do the same thing in our thought life—run thousands of bombing missions over it day after day. We usually run only one a week—going to church. You're kidding yourself if you think you can solve your marriage problems by making some lukewarm effort once in a while. Little ruts that over the years became gigantic trenches require time and effort to reroute. But it's well worth it!

How do the lies you tell yourself affect your behavior and produce negative consequences? Perhaps this story will illustrate: There once was a man named Sam who wanted to borrow his neighbor's lawn mower. As Sam walked down the road toward his neighbor's house, his thoughts went something like this: *Joe's a good neighbor; he shouldn't mind my borrowing his mower. Yes, sir, you can always count on Joe! And he's certainly borrowed enough things from me. Like my hedge clippers. They were dull when I got them back. I let him know it too. Come to think of it, he hasn't borrowed anything since. Maybe he's mad, holding a grudge. That'd be just like Joe—stubborn old codger. He'll probably come up with some excuse why I can't borrow the mower. It's not like it's brand-new or expensive, but the way he guards it you'd think it was gold. I betcha anything he's gonna tell me no, that selfish old tightwad. Well, just see if I ever lend him anything again!*

By now Sam is on Joe's porch and ringing his bell. When Joe opens the door and offers a welcoming smile, Sam thunders back, "Keep your old lawn mower! And just see if I lend you my clippers again!"

We smile as we imagine poor Joe wondering what in tarnation's got into his neighbor. Obviously Sam did a snow job on his own mind, convincing himself of a scenario with Joe that was completely false. We can easily see the folly and the fallacy in Sam's thinking. He was allowing one thought to lead to another and another and another, and each conclusion buried him deeper in a bog of lies. And because Sam acted on the lies he told himself, he damaged and perhaps even destroyed his long friendship with his neighbor.

This little story would be comical if it weren't so true of many of us in our marriages. We constantly tell ourselves lies that damage and perhaps even destroy our relationships with our partners. What are these lies? Let's take a look at a few and see how to defuse them.

## MAJOR MARITAL LIES THAT DISTORT REALITY AND HINDER INTIMACY

### "It's All Your Fault!"

Jay and Natalie knew they had a bad marriage, and they even agreed on the cause. Sort of. They both said, "It's all your fault!" They were both so eager to plead their own cause, Chris Thurman had to call a truce before he could hear their stories.

Natalie told her side first: "When I married Jay, I never dreamed he'd be the type to go out carousing. He's always out with his friends, drinking and gambling and who knows what all? Even when he's home he slouches around with a long face, letting me know he'd rather be out with his drinking buddies. Meanwhile, I stay home washing his clothes and fixing his meals and darning his darned socks, but does he even appreciate it? I knew marriage wouldn't be perfect, but the way I see it, Jay has all the fun and I have all the misery. The worst thing about it is he won't even admit it's his fault."

Natalie had hardly gotten the last word out before Jay launched in with his viewpoint: "I thought it would be fun being married to Natalie. We had a great time when we were dating, but after we got married everything changed. She thinks we should settle down and act like an old married couple, but I'm not ready for the rocking chair. Sure, I like to have fun. Natalie knew I liked to have a good time with my friends when she married me. Can I help it if she isn't good at making friends? When she nags me about staying home, I tell her, 'Get a life! Then maybe you'll stop harping at me all the time.'"

As soon as Chris could persuade Natalie and Jay to stop tattling on each other, he pointed out that marriages, good or bad, are usually the result of both partners. As that vintage song puts it, "It takes two to tango." Often, we're so intent on seeing the speck in our partner's eye, we fail to see the beam in our own. That's exactly what Natalie and Jay were doing. They were so busy blaming each other for their problems they failed to see their own negative contributions to the marriage.

"The truth is, you don't have control over how others behave, but you can take control of your own actions and reactions," Chris explained. "For example, Jay, what could you do to make Natalie feel better about your evenings with the guys?"

He shrugged. "I never thought about it before. I guess I could take her with me sometimes—but she wouldn't like it."

"How about it, Natalie? Would you like to go with Jay sometime?"

She was silent a moment; her mouth twitched a little as she thought. Finally she said, "Jay wouldn't want me going with him. He doesn't enjoy my company anymore."

"Is there somewhere the two of you could go together?" Chris asked. "Something you both like to do?"

"I like going to church, but I haven't been lately," said Natalie. "It's no fun going alone."

"I know that," said Jay. "Maybe I could take you to some of those church functions so you wouldn't have to go alone."

Natalie and Jay were beginning to see things from each other's viewpoint and realize that few marriage problems are all one person's fault. Imagine what marriage would be like if we could all see our own flaws objectively and work on improving them rather than condemning our mate for his or her faults!

## "If Our Marriage Takes Hard Work, We Must Not Be Right for Each Other"

Many of us enter marriage with a "happily ever after" mind-set. Christians are especially susceptible to this attitude. We may spend a lifetime praying that God will lead us to the right mate, the one person He has picked for us. Then, when our marriage runs into trouble, we panic and think, *Oops, this must not be the one God picked out for me after all!* Somehow, we have the mistaken idea God chooses someone for us who will make us happy when, in fact, God is more interested in our maturity level than our happiness. He wants to trim our rough edges, strengthen our characters, and make us more loving and Christlike. Happiness may be a by-product, but it's not the main goal.

Often, marriage struggles can reveal your faults and deficiencies and give you a chance to get your act together. Remember that you're still "under construction"; God isn't finished with you yet. If you demand a quick fix in divorce court, you don't give Him a chance to show what He can accomplish in the lives of two flawed human beings who surrender to Him.

Yvette and Martin were just such a couple on the verge of divorce. A petite brunette with a designer's taste for clothes, Yvette effused elegance and style. In contrast, Martin, wearing a casual shirt and jeans, looked as if he would have been more comfortable on the seat of a tractor or the back of a horse than in that overstuffed chair.

Yvette's voice rang with disillusionment; her visit to a marriage counselor was obviously a last-ditch effort. "I met Martin in Bible school, and we dedicated our marriage to the Lord right from the beginning. But now we both feel like the Lord's withdrawn from us. Why else would we be having such a hard time? Maybe Martin's not the one God chose for me; maybe it would have been the next man I'd met after Martin, someone more compatible. Now I'll never know."

Chris asked Martin to describe how he saw his marriage. "I feel about the same as Yvette," he replied, rubbing the palms of his hands nervously over his jeans as if he were itching to get back out into fresh air and wide-open space. "I fell head over heels for Yvette the minute I saw her, and I was counting my blessings when she said, 'I do.' But in the three years we've been married it's been an uphill journey all the way. We're as different as night and day. Doesn't matter what I want; sure as shootin' it's something she doesn't want. I like the outdoors; she likes being inside. I like the country; she likes the city. I like being alone; she likes crowds. I like hunting and camping; she likes parties and concerts. I want a wife at home raising the children; she wants a full-time career. I want a comfortable old ranch house; she wants a high-rise penthouse."

"How have you managed to get through three years together?" Chris asked.

"Compromise," said Yvette. "Our whole life is one big compromise. I work part-time as a legal secretary; Martin's a building contractor and spends most of his time outside. We live in a two-story house just outside the city; on weekends he goes camping with his friends while I go to the opera with mine. Sometimes he'll give in and go to a concert or I'll go camping with him, but we just do it to please the other. Neither of us has changed. I still hate camping; he still hates concerts. We both feel there must be someone out there we'd be happier with, and we feel it would be best to call it quits now before we have children."

"It sounds as if the two of you have already made some splendid adjustments in your marriage, considering you're such opposites," Chris pointed out. "Are you sure you want to throw all that away?"

"But it's been so hard," Yvette lamented. "We have to work at it constantly, every day. Marriage shouldn't be so much work!"

"That's just the point," Chris assured her. "Marriage, especially a good marriage, *is* a lot of work. You two sound like you're on the right track—compromising, doing things to please each other, and still making sure you both find ways to maintain your own individuality. You appear to have a very healthy marriage."

Yvette and Martin both looked astonished and, within moments, relieved. "You mean this is how a good marriage should be?" she exclaimed. "Hard work and compromise? I figured if we were right for each other it should be smooth going and everything should fall into place naturally."

"That's a fairy tale, and what we've got here is real life. The nitty-gritty. And there's no way to make it work without hard work. And the more hard work it takes, the better marriage you're likely to have."

It was obvious that Yvette and Martin were still very much in love. But they had bought into a common lie—that marriage is easy and couples who love each other shouldn't have to work at creating a successful relationship; it just happens. Once they realized even the best of marriages requires constant care and attention, they stopped feeling so discouraged, dug in their heels, and got to work. Now, though they're still opposites on an uphill journey, their marriage is thriving.

## "You Can and Should Meet All My Needs"

Just as there are no perfect marriages, so there are no perfect partners who will meet all your needs. Your mate can't—and shouldn't; he or she is only human, like you. As we've stressed before, God wants to meet your needs both directly and indirectly—first, through your relationship with Him, then through your mate, and also through family, friends, career, hobbies, and a variety of other healthy, appropriate sources.

Becky entered marriage convinced she and her husband Russell should meet all of each other's needs. A shy young woman who had a difficult time making eye contact, Becky described what she expected. "I don't feel comfortable around people, and I've never had any close friends," she admitted softly, "until Russell. When we started dating he became my best friend. I thought when we got married we'd be even closer. We could do everything together. All I want is to take care of him and be there for him. I don't need or want anyone else. Why can't he feel the same?"

Russell shook his head slowly as Becky spoke. When it was his turn, he tightened his lips, as if reluctant to speak his mind. Finally he said, "I love Becky, but she's smothering me. I don't know how long we can keep on this way. I knew she was needy from the beginning—starved for affection, you might say. But she was so generous with me, always putting my needs first, waiting on me, treating me like a king. I figured we'd have a terrific marriage."

"What is the problem as you see it?" Chris asked.

Russell heaved a sigh. "There's no easy way to say it. Becky's life is focused on me and nothing else. She doesn't work; she has no friends, hobbies, or interests. She won't go anywhere or see anyone. She wants to give me her full attention, and she expects me to do the same. It's too big a job for one man. I want out."

It took time to convince Becky that she was using her husband to fill the deficiencies in her own life. By making Russell the center of her existence she didn't need to stretch and grow and make friends and find personal areas of interest. She was hiding behind him, letting him protect her from the risks and uncertainties of an immense and complex world. No wonder Russell was rebelling; no person can act as a buffer against life, isolating and insulating another human being from pain and disappointments. Becky had completely unrealistic expectations, and Russell had unknowingly played into them until he was overwhelmed.

Gradually Becky realized a healthy marriage requires two whole individuals. She began taking small steps away from Russell— joining a women's Bible study, going shopping with a friend from church, even trying her hand at selling cosmetics door to door. "That's a real stretch for me," she admitted, "but Russell thinks it'll help me overcome my shyness."

As Becky developed new interests and became confident of her abilities, Russell felt the freedom to meet her needs out of love rather than coercion. Becky was quick to admit Russell was still her first priority, which was fine with him too. As she took pride in her accomplishments, he became her greatest encourager, and their marriage flourished.

## "You Owe Me"

Many couples who have otherwise healthy marriages develop an attitude of, "You owe me." In other words, everything I do deserves a payoff. We call this the "green-stamp approach." Remember the days when you'd purchase items and receive redemption stamps? You'd take them home, paste them in books, and redeem them for a variety of mundane household items. Two books got you a clothes hamper, four books earned a toaster, six books bought you a silver tea set. On and on it went. Some shoppers developed obsessive-compulsive tendencies over their redemption stamps, refusing to shop anywhere that didn't offer them, bartering for them with neighbors and friends, hoarding their completed booklets like pots of gold.

How does the green-stamp mentality compute in the marriage

arena? It tells you that everything you do for each other earns a certain number of mental green stamps. You're reared with the concept that marriage should be 50–50: Each partner gives an even 50 percent to the other and everything comes out fair and square. The only problem is, it doesn't work, because how do you put a numerical value on your actions? How many green stamps for washing the dishes? Taking out the trash? Picking up the laundry? Changing the baby? Watching your TV show instead of your mate's?

Chris and Holly Thurman played this game for many years. "The problem," said Chris, "was that in my mind what I did was always worth more green stamps than what Holly thought it was worth, and vice versa. When I tried to cash in my green stamps and asked Holly for something, maybe an hour of love and affection, she'd say it wasn't enough. Or maybe she'd tell me she cleaned house and took care of the kids all day; now I owed her a night out for dinner. We were always owing each other; it was a destructive lie.

"Where do we get the idea our partners owe us?" asks Chris. "To put it clinically, our partner doesn't owe us diddly. The only marriage equation that works is 100–100. Each partner gives completely to the other without any expectation of payment or reward. By accepting the premise that your mate owes you absolutely nothing for all you've done, you stop making demands and inflicting guilt. Then when your spouse does something for you it's because he or she chose to do it, rather than out of a sense of coercion or guilt. Think of the freedom that exists in such a relationship! By demonstrating such a generous spirit, in the long run you may actually get what you're after. And, of course, there's nothing wrong with 'asking' or honestly presenting your needs in a spirit of love."

## "I Shouldn't Have to Change"

Have you ever heard someone say, "I've been this way all my life, and I'm too old to change"? It's the "you-can't-teach-an-old-dog-new-tricks" mentality. We all fall into that familiar trap at times. And why not? Our society and the media have rubber-stamped this idea, so it's considered the gospel truth. How often have you heard, "Don't try to change him; he's a drinker just like his dad" or "She can't make her marriage work; she comes from a dysfunctional family" or "He can't stop his life of crime; look at the life he came from in the ghetto."

It's all too easy to excuse such behavior by saying, "I can't help it; I'm just like my dad" or "That's just the way I was raised" or "You knew I was like this when you married me." But the truth is you do have the capacity to change, and you need to be willing to make changes for the sake of your marriage.

We can almost hear someone protesting, "But I thought you said we should accept our mates unconditionally and not try to change them!" We did say that. But that doesn't absolve you—or us—of the personal responsibility to change your negative behavior. Just as you hope your spouse accepts you as you are because she loves you, so you must recognize the need to make changes to please her—because you love her. It's the same principle on a spiritual level. God loves us unconditionally. Out of our love and gratitude we seek to please Him. That means making changes in our lifestyles and attitudes.

Remember Becky and Russell? Once Becky realized her husband couldn't meet all her needs, she was willing to change both her attitudes and her behavior. She learned to look to other people and activities as sources of fulfillment. Instead of insisting, "I'm naturally shy and can't change," she forced herself to step out into situations that would help her overcome her shyness. As she made necessary changes, her marriage—and her character—grew stronger.

Often, one spouse's weaknesses prove to be the other spouse's strengths. One partner is outgoing; the other is shy. One's tactful; the other's not. One's a natural comic; the other's too serious for his or her own good. Each can learn something from the other—if both remain open and teachable. Why not learn from and move closer to each other for the sake of your marriage?

### "You Should Be Like Me"

Whether we admit it or not, we all privately think our own way is best—our way of thinking, living, behaving. If the rest of the world were like us, this would be an okay place. In fact, the American perception of the rugged individualist is echoed in Frank Sinatra's popular song, "I Did It My Way."

But when it comes to marriage, insisting on doing things "my way" can only spell trouble. People with this attitude generally see the world in black or white, right or wrong, all or nothing terms. There's nothing wrong with that if you're talking about biblical absolutes, but it won't work in marriage.

Remember Jimmy and Marla Carlton? Jimmy unconsciously maintained the belief that Marla should be his clone. Oh, he never would have uttered such an opinion aloud, but he showed it in little things he did every day. He thought Marla should keep a detailed budget just as he did and as his father had before him. She should mark off each item on the grocery receipt to make sure she hadn't been cheated. She should rinse dishes clean before loading them in the dishwasher. She should clip coupons and save something for a rainy day—neatly and in its place, of course. She should set the dinner table with silver, china, and cloth napkins and serve a large meal on Sunday afternoons.

That was the lifestyle Jimmy's parents had modeled, and it had become his way. When he married, he expected it to be Marla's way as well.

But Marla's style was entirely different. She didn't believe in budgets or checking grocery receipts. What were dishwashers for if not to toss in dirty dishes? Why waste time clipping coupons when there were better things to do? And why save stuff she would never need? Or if she did save it, she stacked it where she could see it and didn't mind the clutter. And where meals were concerned, Marla would just as soon eat on a TV tray and watch her favorite show. Forget huge Sunday dinners; Marla wanted Jimmy to take her out to a nice restaurant. There was obviously no way Jimmy could turn Marla into a carbon copy of himself. Even if it were possible, how long before he would have been bored out of his skull with an exact replica of himself?

That timeworn cliché is true: Variety *is* the spice of life, and it can be the salvation of many marriages. Variety can keep a marriage stable and in balance, with neither partner going too far overboard or spinning off radically in any one direction. Maybe Jimmy didn't need to be quite so compulsive about finances and household tasks; maybe Marla could exert a little more caution with the checkbook and care around the house. With time and effort, they found a happy middle ground that brought greater peace to their marriage.

## SEEKING THE TRUTH

In this chapter we've covered many of the ways we humans unwittingly lie to ourselves. No wonder we can't always think straight! In addition to the major distortions we described here, there are lots of little deceptions we tell ourselves.

Sometimes you fall into the notion that external changes will make a difference in your marriage. You'll buy a new house, remodel the old one, or take a vacation—and that will make your marriage better. You may feel better temporarily, but then reality returns.

Or you may have bought into the idea that the best way you can get your mate to change is through criticism, badgering, manipulation, aloofness, hatefulness, or coercion. No! The best way is to make changes in your own backyard and pray for your spouse's needs.

You may feel your spouse should be naturally capable of loving you. But the truth is, nobody naturally knows how to love; everyone's deficient in that area. Your natural self just wants to love *you*. It doesn't seem natural to die to self and put someone else first, but that's what marriage requires.

Possibly you think doing nothing to make your marriage better will at least maintain the status quo. But that's not true either. Doing nothing will make your marriage worse.

The worst lie you tell yourself is that you can have a healthy marriage apart from God. That's what Adam and Eve thought—and that was the end of paradise and the beginning of hell on earth.

By now you've probably surmised it's a constant battle between healthy and unhealthy thinking. Lies will enslave your marriage; the truth will set it free. Discovering your own marital lies and replacing them with truth is hard work, but the reward is immeasurable. All day long we punch prerecorded tapes inside our brains. What are your tapes telling you?

# CHAPTER 9

# Forgive Each Other

DAVID FERGUSON WAS selfish. He hadn't realized it when he married Teresa. He just figured a wife was supposed to follow the husband around picking up after him and waiting on him hand and foot. That's what Mom had done. Now here was Teresa, refusing to follow in his mother's footsteps. Here was Teresa calling him "spoiled" and "oblivious"! She'd actually had the gall to say, "David, you live with your head in the clouds. World War III could take place right in front of you and you'd miss it!"

But David was learning. Maybe there was something to what Teresa was saying after all. The issue came to a head one hectic morning when he and Teresa were rushing the family off to work and school. He tells what happened:

"I was always running late (it was another of my faults I hadn't wanted to deal with). I went bounding out the door, jumped into the car, and settled back in the driver's seat, wondering where everybody was. I thumped my fingers impatiently on the steering wheel. Finally Teresa came out the door with the dry-cleaning in her arms. She put it in the trunk and went back inside for the kids' lunch boxes, which she put in the backseat. Then she went back inside and got the car seat and put that in the car. Then she went back and brought out our young son and buckled him in. Finally she brought out our two daughters and got them in the car," David recalls.

You're getting the picture, aren't you?

"Teresa had made five or six trips between the house and the car, and it never once entered my mind, *Why don't you go help her, you jerk?* It never once dawned on me! In fact, what crossed my mind was, *If she doesn't hurry up, I'm going to honk!*

"So after the fifth or sixth trip, I noticed a look on her face that told me, *David, you've really blown it, boy!* And I thought to myself, *By the time she gets in this car, it's not going to be a pretty sight.* As I backed out of the driveway I figured I'd get World War III and really hear about it or I'd get the cold war. You know what that is—we're talking about *nothing* for weeks!

"But on that frantic morning a miracle took place inside my wife. She was nice. Normal. We drove to work and talked about the weekend, and her attitude was great.

"Of course, when a guy realizes he's blown it, he'd rather have his wife jump on him. Then he can rationalize why he treated her that way in the first place. The fact that Teresa didn't nag me made me feel worse. She dropped me off at the church where I was on staff—that's right, I was on the pastoral staff of a large church. In ministry! And all day long I felt guilty. Why? Because I *was* guilty!

"That's the day it dawned on me that I wasn't oblivious; I was selfish! Preoccupied with my own agenda and priorities. I knew then I'd missed a lot in my family; my wife and kids could be hurting, and I was just too selfish to see it.

"When I got home that evening, I took Teresa in my arms and told her I finally understood the depth of hurt I'd caused her. I told her I was wrong and asked her to forgive me. She did. And we began to see some positive changes in our family.

"Two weeks later I was downstairs pouring myself a cup of coffee and the thought went through my mind, *Why don't you pour your wife one?* I'd never had that thought before in my life. I didn't know you could carry two cups of coffee at once!

"A couple of weeks after that we were out with some friends. At the end of the evening my wife and daughters were going to go home in one car and my son and I in another. My normal thought pattern in the past would have been, *I'm in my car and I'm going home. Teresa's a big girl. She knows how to get there. If something breaks down she knows the mechanic to call.*

"But a new thought went through my mind: *Why don't you follow your wife home?*

"My son looked over at me and said, 'Daddy, what are we doing?'

"I said, 'We're going to wait and follow Momma home.'

"He said, 'Why?' (See what my selfishness was doing to him?)

"The truth is, I'd been a lousy role model throughout the early years of my marriage. But now, day by day, I was glimpsing areas of my life I could change and seeing positive actions I could take to restore the intimate connection with my wife and family."

Maybe as you've read through the first eight chapters in this book, you've caught a glimpse of changes you need to make in your own attitudes or behavior. Maybe you realize there are areas in your life that need to be confessed and forgiven. There are fences to be mended, bridges to cross, walls that need to be torn down.

With this chapter we've arrived at the midpoint of our journey. We've defined the potential of marital intimacy as you may experience it spiritually or in deep friendship or in passionate embrace. We've divided intimacy needs into four major "ingredients": affectionate caring, vulnerable communication, joint accomplishment, and mutual giving. As you walk intimately with your Creator and give to your partner out of an overflow of blessing, you experience intimacy in your marriage. But all too often, when the system breaks down, life overwhelms you with unmet needs, unhealthy thinking, unhealed emotions, and unproductive behaviors. Your hope is lost, your feelings go numb, and other alternatives look attractive—an affair, the divorce court, or other painful options.

Countless couples reaching this point begin searching for a means of restoration. But where does restoration begin? Ultimately, if it's to be lasting and life-changing, it has to go as deep as the healing described in this chapter. No surgery is successful without the temporary pain of probing instruments. Without this emotional surgery—seeking to free yourself from years and possibly decades of unhealed hurt, bitterness, guilt, and fear—your unhealthy thinking won't change, regardless of your effort; nor will your unproductive behaviors change, regardless of any new intentions. So take a deep breath, square your shoulders, hold your chin high—and get ready for the operating room!

## ASSESSING YOUR CONDITION BEFORE SURGERY

We've said it before; now we'll stress it again. When it comes to relationships, *hurts are inevitable*. People aren't perfect; relationships aren't perfect either. You will hurt each other, and it probably won't even be intentional. You don't get up in the morning planning how to hurt each other but, like dropping a bowling ball on your foot, it hurts the same whether you planned to do it or not.

So the issue isn't whether you will be hurt but what to do with the hurts. How do you heal them? If they're not healed, they'll accumulate and produce negative feelings, filling your emotional cup to the brim and overflowing with emotional pain, anger, bitterness, and resentment. No wonder you don't feel like sharing your hopes and dreams! All positive feelings such as love, affection, and romance have been crowded out.

And if you throw life's daily stresses into the mix of your negative emotions—hurt, anger, bitterness, resentment, worry, anxiety, doubt, guilt, insecurity, and fear—you begin to observe symptoms. It's hard to sleep, or maybe you want to sleep all the time. You have no appetite, or you want to eat all the time. You turn to drug or alcohol abuse to numb the pain. Even work can be a form of escape to keep you from dealing with your hurts.

You may not even realize all these negative feelings are there inside you. You just know you've felt depressed lately, or you don't have much energy, or you've felt impatient and out of sorts. Or maybe it's just been a long time since you've experienced positive emotions such as love, joy, or romantic feelings. Since you can hold only so much emotion before your cup is full, maybe it's time to empty the cup so it can be refilled with positive feelings.

We can almost hear you saying, "How can I empty my emotional cup when I don't even know what's in it?"

Glad you asked. The questions below will help you identify some of the unhealthy accumulations of emotions in your cup. If you can empty them out, your painful symptoms may go away and you'll have the capacity to experience positive emotions. So answer each question as honestly and thoroughly as you can.

1. **Hurts:** In what *ways* and in what *relationships* have you felt wounded with words or actions?

<table>
<tr><td></td><td>Ways</td><td>Relationship</td></tr>
<tr><td>a.</td><td colspan="2">_____</td></tr>
<tr><td>b.</td><td colspan="2">_____</td></tr>
<tr><td>c.</td><td colspan="2">_____</td></tr>
</table>

2. **Anger:** Who do you avoid, reject, criticize, ignore, or otherwise retaliate against?

   a. _____

   b. _____

   c. _____

3. **Bitterness/Resentment:** Who do you wish harm on? Talk evil of? Or strive *not* to be like?

   a. _____

   b. _____

   c. _____

4. **True Guilt:** What have *you* done that would hurt, reject, wrong, wound, or otherwise show contempt or disrespect to another?

   a. _____

   b. _____

   c. _____

Did you notice that some of your negative feelings started long before you met your spouse—perhaps from your earliest days of childhood? If you're like most of us, you didn't grow up learning how to resolve, or empty, your emotional pain, so you brought it with you into marriage. Then, instead of a hope chest, you may have unpacked a Pandora's box of anger, heartaches, and assorted unresolved hostilities. And here you thought you entered marriage empty-handed![1]

As you examined your own emotional baggage, you may have wondered where anger left off and the hurt began. Think of it this way: Wherever you find anger, underneath you find hurt. It just depends on which direction your emotions take you—anger at the other person or sadness for yourself.

## THE HURT-ANGER-FEAR CONNECTION

Keep in mind that three of the most harmful emotions you can have are anger, sadness, and fear. Here's how the three interrelate: When you reach out to your mate and he or she rejects you, you feel hurt, tender, and vulnerable. You experience a sense of loss. But to protect yourself, you immediately cover the hurt with anger. At the same time you confront fear. The next time you think of reaching out to your mate, you remember what happened last time. So you feel anxious, reluctant to reach out, fearful of being hurt again. Beneath the fear lies hurt.

You may notice that when some minor irritation occurs it taps into an unresolved reservoir of anger inside you. When a car recklessly cuts in front of you on the highway, you lay on the horn and utter a few choice words of contempt. When someone makes a thoughtless remark, you see red and strike back with a barrage of cutting retorts. Later you realize those incidents shouldn't have provoked such an extreme response. You wonder where all the anger came from. In rare moments of insight you realize the anger was there all along, simmering beneath the surface like a kettle of soup on a low fire. But the minute the heat is turned up a little, the pot boils over.

When you keep your anger inside, forcing a lid on a bubbling pot, you begin to feel depressed. With so many hurts to deal with, your emotions begin to congeal into a muck of negative feelings similar to John Bunyan's "Slough of Despond" in *The Pilgrim's Progress*. Anxiety, panic attacks, and phobias spring from deep fears, which often spring from deep hurts. When you resolve the hurts, the anger will go away and the fear will diminish.

You may also have noticed some obsessive-compulsive tendencies in your behavior. They, too, are related to emotions that haven't been healed. Here's how it works: In your brain you primarily do three things: You think things, you feel things, and you choose to do things. This is your mind, your emotions, and your will. If your emotions get stopped up or blocked, input goes through two channels instead of three. So your thinking and doing go on overload, becoming obsessive (always thinking) and compulsive (always doing). You find it hard to relax; you have to keep busy.

Perhaps, as you've examined ways you've been hurt or ways you've become angry, bitter, or resentful, you've dredged up some serious problems in your marriage such as lack of communication, an adulterous affair, or verbal or physical abuse. Sadly, hurts don't simply go away. Time doesn't spontaneously heal resentment, and trying harder doesn't compensate for guilt. In most troubled marriages, human nature has joined with unhealed hurts to make you forget your spouse's needs and think only of your own. On the other hand, you may find yourself blaming your spouse for everything that goes wrong; in fact, you may become an expert at detecting your mate's faults and errors.

David counseled one woman who announced she was itching to die so she could go to heaven and squeal on her husband. She insisted he was a dirty dog, a no-good bum, and a lazy, rotten louse. David gently burst her bubble, reminding her it was irrational to suppose God didn't already know what a jerk her husband was. More to the point, she would never stand before God and give an account of someone else, only of herself.

## THE HEALING POWER OF CONFESSION

According to David Ferguson, "Confession is one of the most misunderstood issues in the Christian life. What is real confession? Our flesh doesn't want to hear it; nothing in our humanness wants to hear it. But what God wants us to do in the quietness of a reflective moment is to say the same thing about our wrongs as He says. For example, that morning when I waited for Teresa in the car and later realized my selfishness—God wanted me to confess that selfishness was wrong.

"If we could only grab hold of the reality that we have a personalized Christianity. God would have let Christ die for me if I were the only sinner! He died not for some vague concept of sin, but for *my* sin, personally. Christ died for my selfishness, for my sarcasm and verbal abuse. He died because I rejected this one I declared I loved. Isaiah 53:5 says He was wounded for my transgressions, bruised for my iniquities. He took my chastisement upon Himself.

"Here's the bottom line. We had a part in killing Christ, and we don't want to accept that truth. It makes us feel remorse, sadness, guilt, sorrow. Yet we need to feel broken. Godly sorrow leads to repentance—and changes in our lives." (See 2 Cor. 7:9–11.)

"We must let God produce this sorrow and tap into our sense of regret so we can experience His forgiveness," David continues. "Yes, we'll feel remorse and brokenness, but we'll also feel gratefulness and exhilaration that God has forgiven us." (See 1 John 1:9.)

What does a good confession look like? "It's not what Teresa and I did for so many years," says David. "I confessed her faults and she confessed mine."

A good confession names the wrong, acknowledges that it was wrong, and asks for forgiveness without trying to explain away or justify the deed. After you've confessed to God and received the forgiveness available through His Son, next comes confession to your spouse. (See James 5:16.)

The day David apologized to Teresa he said, "I'm beginning to understand how deeply I hurt you by my selfishness. I see how wrong it was. Will you forgive me?"

In apologizing David followed these three important steps: "I named the wrong (selfishness), acknowledged the fact it was wrong, then asked for forgiveness. That put the ball in Teresa's court. She had to make a choice whether to forgive me.

"Don't just say you're sorry," he cautions. "That doesn't accomplish anything. Don't say, 'I'm sorry it bothers you' or 'If I've hurt you, I'm sorry.' Say what you've done and admit it was wrong."

He adds, "Your natural tendency is probably to say it was wrong, then offer excuses. Every part of your flesh wants to explain it away. Instead, just say, 'I was wrong, period!' When you start explaining, you're justifying yourself. If you take away the power of the confession, you'll never get healed.

"Suppose I say to Teresa, 'I realize I've neglected you and it was wrong of me. I wouldn't have done it if you'd just been more affectionate to me.' Did you feel that? I got close to an apology, then flipped it around. Instead of healing the hurt, I just blamed her for my sin!"

When it comes to forgiveness, David has this advice: "During that vulnerable time when your spouse asks for forgiveness, reach over and touch him and tell him you forgive him, period; it'll take an act of your will. Don't say, 'I'll forgive you as long as you promise never to do it again.' What if God did that to us? He knows we may do it again and forgives us anyway!

"The beautiful thing about forgiveness is that it's a divine reality, a divine commodity. When your mate asks you to forgive him, his real question is, 'Will you share with me some of the forgiveness God has already given you?' It's a matter of stewardship. I've received forgiveness. Will I share it? Or will I selfishly say I got it from God but I won't give it to you!"

Ask yourself: *Who needs to hear a confession from me?*

Do you realize the power of a sincere apology?

We recently counseled a couple who were having trouble with their fourteen-year-old son. Aaron kept sneaking out of his bedroom window to join his friends for a night of mischief and neighborhood pranks. What concerned his parents most was Aaron's refusal to accept responsibility for his actions.

His mother said, "We want him to see the wrong of his actions and apologize for the worry and sleepless nights he's caused us."

But Aaron wouldn't budge. "Only thing I'm sorry about is I got caught," he grumbled.

During one session we asked him, "Aaron, when is the last time someone apologized to you?"

Dead silence. His parents squirmed. Finally he muttered, "Big people don't have to apologize; only kids!"

Aaron didn't have the slightest idea what an apology looked like. His parents had not role modeled a genuine apology to him or to each other. Example is the best teacher . . . for good or bad.

If, like Aaron's parents, you find it hard to apologize, you're not alone. Ninety-five percent of the people we counsel consider themselves Christians; almost 70 percent are church leaders—pastors, missionaries, elders. But surprisingly, they're locked into a justify-rationalize-blame cycle: *I wouldn't have done that if you hadn't done this . . . I wouldn't have said that if you didn't say this . . . I'd do better if you'd do better.*

The beauty of an intimate relationship comes when two people willingly give an account of themselves to God (Rom. 14:12) and focus on their own responsibility for their problems. Have you done that? Take a good look at your marriage. What has each of you done to make the problems worse? What can each of you do to make the problems better? Healing takes place when you confess how you've hurt each other and begin thinking first of your spouse's needs. The pattern of examining your own behavior instead of your spouse's must become habitual. Behavior won't change with just one attempt. It requires consistent openness to God's scrutiny, bringing the brokenness of a godly sorrow which produces repentance (change).

## HEALING HURTS THAT HINDER ONENESS

You've taken a general look at the hurts, anger, bitterness, and guilt filling your emotional cup—feelings derived from relationships with your parents, siblings, mate, children, or friends. And we've talked about what genuine confession looks and feels like. Are you ready to begin the process of personally confessing and forgiving your own marital hurts? We suggest you and your spouse begin by taking a *personal inventory* of ways you have hurt each other and your marriage.

## IDENTIFY THE HURT

### 1. Alone: List Ways You Have Hurt Your Spouse and Your Marriage

Start with each partner taking two blank sheets of paper. At the top of one page write, "Ways I have hurt my spouse and my marriage." At the top of the other, write, "Ways I have been hurt by my spouse and our marriage." Now make your lists separately and privately, identifying each hurt that comes to mind. (You may want to go to separate rooms to compose your lists.)

Here's an example of hurts that might be listed: selfish, critical/negative, insensitive, disrespectful, verbally abusive, unsupportive, ungrateful, unfaithful, wrong priorities, rejecting, unforgiving. (Put down specific hurtful events, fights, arguments, or "scenes" that need to be confessed. Use extra paper if necessary.)

Need more hints? Do you husbands remember the time you walked in the house and found your wife crying? You knew she was hurting, but instead of comforting her you barked, "What's wrong with you now?"

Wives, remember the time your husband came home so down he looked like he'd been hit by a steamroller? You knew he wanted some encouragement and a hug, but you were right in the middle of your favorite TV show. Besides, where was he the last time you needed comfort? Let him see how it feels to be ignored!

Got the idea? Once you get the hang of it, you should have no trouble coming up with plenty of material for your lists.

Jimmy and Marla Carlton had no problem coming up with a long list of ways they had been hurt, but it was another story when it came to composing a list of ways they had inflicted hurt on the other. Marla remarked, "It shocked me. Until I started putting down my gripes against Jimmy, I had no idea how deeply entrenched my negative feelings were. My list was a mile long! I've been blaming Jimmy for everything that's gone wrong since our wedding. No wonder I didn't have any positive feelings left!"

"Same here," Jimmy admitted. "I couldn't wait to write down all my complaints against Marla, and believe me, I had a healthy list! But when I started putting down ways I'd hurt her, I saw things from her point of view. Looking back at my own list, I realize how one-sided I was being!"

## 2. Confess to God and Receive His Forgiveness

*All unresolved hurts—anger, bitterness, and resentment—require forgiveness.* Follow the admonition of Ephesians 4:31–32: "Let all bitterness, wrath, anger, clamor, and evil speaking be put away from you, with all malice. And be kind to one another, tenderhearted, forgiving one another, even as God in Christ forgave you."

*Unconfessed guilt from either active or passive retaliation also requires confession.* First John 1:9 tells us, "If we confess our sins, He [God] is faithful and just to forgive us our sins and to cleanse us from all unrighteousness." It's a matter of personal responsibility. I must give an account of myself to God (Rom. 14:12), not to others. Otherwise I live in a world of rationalizing, justifying, and blaming: *I wouldn't do this if you wouldn't do that . . . I had a right . . . it's all your fault!*

Here's how you might pray: "God, I have deeply hurt You and my spouse by my _____ *[use one of your answers to Item 1, above]*. These actions are wrong, and I ask You to forgive me. Thank You for doing so as I receive the gift of Christ's death in my behalf. I ask You to change me into the kind of person I need to be."

Notice how we recognize our *accountability to God* when we admit that hurting our spouses also hurts God and needs His forgiveness. In fact, isn't it sobering to realize that our selfishness or unloving attitude or demeaning words were exactly why Christ had to die for us!

Consistently confessing to God and receiving forgiveness was a whole new concept for Jimmy and Marla. "I've been a Christian since I was a child," said Marla, "but I've taken God's forgiveness for granted. Sometimes I'd pray, 'Forgive me for my sins,' but I'd rarely spell them out or feel real sorrow for them. For the first time I see the connection between the wrongs I do and Christ's death on the cross. Now, when I picture Him dying, I see Him carrying *my* sins. And when I do something I know is wrong, I stop myself and think, *Hey, Marla, you're adding another sin to what Christ had to carry.*"

Jimmy admitted he had never given God much thought. His parents were nominal Christians who considered church-going more a patriotic duty than an opportunity for worship. As an adult Jimmy made infrequent visits to church—on Easter or when the children were in the Christmas play or being baptized. "I went only when Marla insisted. I never thought about a personal God who loved me and wanted me to love Him. It's like all the puzzle pieces were out there scattered around, but I never put them together before. I admit it's still new to me—the idea that I need a Savior and that I have a God who loves me enough to give His Son to die for me. It blows my mind to think God cares about what I do. I'm not ready to start confessing my sins to God today, but I can see the need to confess them to Marla, and I'll even give some thought to accepting Christ as my Savior. Maybe it's just what I need. Marla prayed with me the other night. I never felt so close to her—or to God—in my life."

### 3. Together: Share Your Lists and Request Forgiveness

James 5:16 says it very well: "Confess your trespasses to one another, and pray for one another, that you may be healed." Notice it doesn't say, "Confess your spouse's faults."

Here's an example (let's say it's the husband's initiative): "Honey, I've seen that I've hurt you deeply by being _____ *[use one of your answers to Item 1, above]*. I have been very wrong. Will you forgive me? The word *confess* means to 'agree with' God, and God says these things are wrong."

Notice that it's not enough just to say, "I was wrong." *Requesting forgiveness*—actually saying the words, *"Will you forgive me?"*—is a vital part of the process. The vulnerability of this question conveys a sense of humility and challenges your mate with the responsibility to forgive.

## CHOOSE TO FORGIVE

In response to her husband's confession, a wife will, we hope, recall how freely God has forgiven her. Then she will reach over and touch her husband and say, "I forgive you." Remember, *forgiveness is a choice, not a feeling!* The question is not, "Do you *feel* like forgiving?" but *"Will* you?" The admonition in Ephesians 4:31–32 to put away "bitterness, wrath, anger . . . forgiving one another" is a command to *choose* to forgive (release, turn loose of). Will you release the hurt? Then new feelings will come! Be sure to seal this choice by actually verbalizing your forgiveness—"I forgive you."

At this point, the husband might ask, "Are there other hurts I've not seen that need my apology? Share them with me so I can seek your forgiveness."

Once all of her husband's wrongs have been confessed, the wife shares her list and receives her husband's forgiveness.

Jimmy and Marla spent a weekend away from the children to share their lists. In a cozy rented cabin at the lake they revealed their hurts, confessed their mistakes, and received forgiveness.

"It was so different from our usual vacation trips," said Marla. "In the past we each came with our own expectations, and when something went wrong we'd be at each other's throat. But this time we were both careful of the other's feelings. Of course, we were both really nervous too. When I started telling Jimmy how he'd hurt me, I thought he would turn cold and distant like he used to, but he didn't. He sat and listened. I had his undivided attention, and it was wonderful! But even better, Jimmy was really sorry for his mistakes. Knowing he felt real sorrow and wasn't just saying the words made all the difference."

"What got to me," said Jimmy, "was when Marla said I hurt her by shutting her out and acting like I didn't love her. When she'd do something I didn't like, I'd turn this stony face on her and act like she was invisible. It wrenched something inside me when she described how that made her feel. I saw myself feeling the same way when my parents withheld their love from me. And here I was, Mr. Tough Guy, making her hurt the same way I'd been hurt," he said.

"But Jimmy wasn't the only one guilty of dishing out hurt," said Marla. "If Jimmy could kill with a look, I could do some pretty serious damage with my tongue. I'd lash out at him with enough words for both of us. I was wrong to criticize and condemn him. I was wrong to complain about him to the kids so he'd look bad and I'd look good. I asked him to forgive me for playing the wounded martyr and always painting him as the bad guy. He forgave me and I forgave him. I know we still have a long way to go, but our marriage will never be the same!"

"Thank goodness!" chuckled Jimmy. "Or, I guess I should say, thank God!"

## 4. Exchange Lists—and Then Tear Them Up!

*Let new memories begin replacing old ones.* Philippians 3:13 suggests that we forget what lies behind and press forward to what lies ahead.

Start the forgetting process with this new memory of forgiveness. Exchange the lists you've made and destroy them. Tear them up, burn them, or bury them! After this special time of confession and forgiveness, experience the *intimacy and oneness of praying together.* Hold hands and pray (silently, if you wish), thanking God for forgiving you, changing you, and healing your marriage.

"This part was easier for Marla than for me," said Jimmy. "Oh, I didn't have any trouble tearing up those lists. In fact, we tore them in little pieces and scattered them in the lake. But I'm not comfortable praying. I tried praying silently and let Marla do the talking aloud to God. She's good at it, no matter who she's talking to."

"I felt so close to Jimmy when we were praying," said Marla. "It wasn't just a spiritual thing; it was physical too. I never thought the two had any connection, but after we prayed I just wanted him to hold me tight. It's the first time I really understood what the Bible means about two being one."

"Amen to that!" said Jimmy with a smile. "One thing led to another . . . and all I can say is I wouldn't mind prayer meetings that ended like that one!"

### 5. Begin the Ephesians 4:26 Habit: "Do not let the sun go down on your wrath."

*If you want to maintain intimacy in your relationship, you must develop a habit of confessing to God and those you hurt as well as forgiving those who hurt you.* Otherwise, your "emotional capacity" (your emotional cup) begins to fill again with painful emotions.

We can already hear some of you expressing questions and concerns. "Does this process really work?" "It's too hard for me to admit I'm wrong." "If I tell my wife my faults, won't she just use them to clobber me the next time we have a fight?" "Will my husband really have the capacity to forgive me? I'm afraid he'll get mad when I tell him what I've done wrong."

We understand your reservations. It's not easy to admit you're wrong and humble yourself enough to ask for forgiveness. It's something we rarely see in our society, but imagine what our world would be like if this were the norm!

We gave Marla and Jimmy this advice: The best way to keep from reverting to old patterns of hurting and blaming is to concentrate on giving to each other. Make a habit of confessing, forgiving, and sharing the truth in love. The keys to success are in these three principles:

1. Confess your own faults as they hurt your spouse, and forgive your spouse's faults as they hurt you.

2. Express your needs to your spouse in a positive, loving way rather than focusing on his or her negative behaviors.

3. Minister to your spouse's needs while you trust God to meet your own needs, either directly or as He works through your spouse.

David and Teresa put these principles into practice on an evening that could otherwise have spelled disaster for their marriage. "I'd had a long, exhausting day of counseling," explains David. "I'd gone in early and stayed late. A coworker hadn't done his job, so I had to tie up loose ends. I hated covering for his half-hearted efforts. Of course, there was no one there to vent my anger on and no one to notice or praise my extra effort, so I stewed about it all the way home through bumper-to-bumper traffic from a university basketball game that ended just as I finally finished work.

"Arriving home so late, I expected Teresa to be in bed asleep. (She's a morning person, not a night person like I am.) But when I walked in the kitchen door, there she stood, putting the finishing touches on my favorite dinner. She turned to me and said lovingly, 'Well, it looks like you've had a hard day, Sweetheart.'

"Irritably I snapped back, 'Yeah, if you'd had the kind of day I had, you'd look bad too!' (This is called displaced anger. Angry at my coworker, I took it out on my wife.)

"Obviously I had hurt Teresa by my response. Now what was she going to do about it? Stuff it or spew it? Attack or hide? She could have gone to either extreme, both incorrect. She could have taken my supper and thrown it to the birds in the backyard—along with all my personal possessions! She could have hurled a retort such as, 'A lot of thanks I get for staying up late cooking your dinner, you big jerk! Next time, fix your own dinner!' She could have stomped off, leaving me standing alone and rebuked. Certainly she would have conveyed her hurt, but not in love. Spewing her anger, hurling, or attacking could have set the stage for a battle royal.

"Or Teresa could have put my dinner silently on the table and pretended not to be hurt, telling herself it was no big deal. 'Stuffing' or hiding her emotions would have kept the peace, at least temporarily. Then, while I ate, she might have escaped to the bedroom and cried herself to sleep or lay awake, seething in anger. A day or two later I might have noticed a certain coldness and distance. 'What's wrong with you?' I'd ask, and she'd reply in her chilliest voice, 'Nothing's wrong. I'm fine!' Not so.

"Here's what Teresa actually told me after I'd snapped at her so condescendingly: 'Sweetheart, I really can see that you've had a hard day, and I'd like to help if you'll let me. Yet I feel like you're taking it out on me, and that hurts. Can we start over again?'

"Ouch! Deathly silence. Now who had the ball? By sharing the truth in a loving way (as Ephesians 4:15 exhorts), Teresa helped me see what I was doing without condemning me. 'You're right,' I replied. 'I'm sure that did hurt you. That was wrong of me. Will you forgive me?'

"She said, 'Sure.' We touched, held each other for a moment, then sat down and had our dinner."

A potentially divisive incident was healed by:

Speaking the truth in love: "You hurt me."

Confessing: "I was wrong. Will you forgive me?"

Forgiving: "Yes, I forgive you."

Learning to handle hurts productively and speaking the truth in love will not only resolve conflicts but strengthen family ties and encourage peace in your home. It's God's plan for restoring that intimate connection!

# Reject the Games Couples Play

"CAN YOU FIX my husband?" Sherry wasn't joking. A Bette Midler look-alike with the saucy impertinence to match, she was dead serious. "I've heard you fixed other husbands. So how about it? Mine needs it badly."

David Ferguson looked at Mark. He reminded David of a disgruntled and much-put-upon Kevin Costner. He sat beside his wife, looking as if he'd been hog-tied and dragged into the counseling office. "What seems to need fixing, Mark?"

"Well, I guess you could say—"

"He's cold," Sherry interrupted. "Cold as snow in January."

"I assume you're not talking about temperatures—"

"No, sir! I'm talking about the way he treats me. He expects me to be a loving wife, but he treats strangers better than me."

"Mark, does this problem involve your sexual relationship?"

"No," he said in a soft voice. "Sherry shut that down years ago. Actually, the problem—"

"Why wouldn't I shut it down?" she countered. "What woman wants to have sex with a man who treats her like a stranger, who avoids her whenever he can, who acts like he doesn't even care what she has to say?"

David looked back at Mark. "Why did you agree to come in for counseling?"

He stole a furtive glance at Sherry. "I was kind of hoping to rekindle things in the bedroom, if you know what—"

Sherry sat forward, gripping the chair arms. "What right does he have to make sexual demands when he doesn't value me as a person? First things first, I say."

"Mark," David asked, looking him directly in the eye, "how does it feel to be interrupted in midsentence by your wife?"

He managed a little grin. "Well, to tell you the truth, it really gets on my—"

"He knew I liked to talk when he married me," Sherry protested. "It wasn't a problem then; I don't see why it should be now. Mark just needs help warming up his personality. Then we'd be happy."

David sat back for a moment of contemplative silence. Then he directed his question to Sherry. "I wonder if your husband's coldness might be related to his anger over your interruptions."

She looked aghast. "That's impossible. Mark's always been the quiet one; I'm the talkative one. He's never complained about it before."

"But have you ever asked him? Have you ever really listened to him?"

"Of course I do," Sherry insisted. "Don't I, Mark?"

"Well, actually I can't remember you ever really listening to what I—"

"That's nonsense! I'm a wonderful listener! Ask anyone!"

"What about it, Mark? Has she ever let you finish a sentence?"

He grinned, as if pleased to finally win a round for once. "Not that I recall," he said. "It's awfully hard to have warm feelings toward someone who never gives you a chance to say how you feel."

This was a moment of revelation for Sherry. As much as she wanted her husband's warmth, it had never occurred to her she herself was sabotaging their relationship. The two of them had much to work through as they identified and healed their hurts and stopped playing the "blame games" that had brought them so much grief. Gradually, as Sherry found the freedom to really listen to Mark he warmed up and they developed a new closeness that included sexual intimacy.

## GAMES COUPLES PLAY

What about you? What games are you playing in your marriage? Games couples play—knowingly or unknowingly—can promote or prevent marital intimacy. This chapter will focus on those games that turn a potentially healthy marriage into a destructive, self-defeating relationship. See if you recognize yourself in any of our examples.

## Let the Games Begin!

Some games are harmless and even fun as a couple learns to laugh off minor irritations. One couple agreed on a game to handle the wife's nagging. With a little smile, her husband would turn his gaze upward, as if watching a leaky ceiling. Thus, without speaking a word he reminded her of Proverbs 27:15, which compares a nagging woman to dripping rain!

Some games can actually encourage closeness. When your wife dabs on that certain perfume or slips into a flimsy negligee, you know it will be an evening of moonlight and romance. When your husband surprises you with flowers or candy or leaves a love note on your pillow, you know he's telling you you're special. These games add fun and romance to a relationship and draw a couple together. But, unfortunately, other games disrupt and destroy.

## Games that Hinder Intimacy

When it comes to destroying intimacy, couples find a full spectrum of games to play. Not that they consciously want to ruin their relationship; they just become so starved for intimacy they begin expressing their behavior in weird ways, doing whatever it takes to get their needs satisfied. When a partner's need for attention and appreciation goes unmet, he or she may turn to games that *manipulate*. When a partner's hurts remain unhealed, he or she may rationalize his or her behavior and begin the *blame game*. When transparency and openness give way to fear, couples may find refuge in games that help them *avoid* and *hide*.

Couples who come for marriage therapy have often fallen into the trap of one or more of these unhealthy games. Many originated in childhood. David Ferguson shares these examples from his own marriage:

"Teresa grew up in a home where her father could fix everything that broke. So she began our marriage with a mind-set, a belief system, that said, 'If my husband loves me, he will fix everything in our home that breaks.'

"Let me tell you, that put a real damper on our intimacy because in our house I don't fix anything! It took Teresa awhile to stop believing a loving husband has to be Mr. Fix-It, but after I'd messed up enough jobs, she learned not to call on me. Now the toolbox belongs to my wife!

"Of course, Teresa wasn't the only one who carried over preconceived ideas from childhood. I grew up in a home with a sometimes-rigid father. Because of his military background, we often had bed inspections when Dad would pop quarters on the sheets. If the quarter didn't pop high enough, my dad reached over, pulled the covers off the bed, and threw them on the floor. Then I had to make the bed all over again. In my mind as a child, making beds was a big deal. You could spend your life in the bedroom making beds.

"By the time Teresa and I got married, I'd had enough bedmaking for a lifetime. I figured, from here on it's her job! But imagine the conflict if I'd begun to pop quarters and inspect her bed-making! In fact, if Teresa had insisted I be a jack-of-all-trades and I had demanded she make beds that passed my father's rigid inspection, any intimacy between us would have gone right down the drain."

Often, the games we played with our parents are the same ones we play with our mates. One man who grew up with a complaining mother who harped constantly about his irresponsibility married a woman who played the same game. He had just exchanged one "harpist" for another!

A woman who had grown up with an unavailable father learned to expect that men could not be counted on. She ended up in a bad marriage, living out the same disappointments she'd grown up with.

Behavioral games are often rooted in faulty thinking patterns developed in childhood. A boy who grows up believing "women are always telling you what you haven't done" may be overly sensitive and resistant to his wife's suggestions. Unresolved emotions such as anger at a parent may become displaced on a spouse.

## BEHAVIORAL GAMES COUPLES PLAY

Couples develop games as a substitute for closeness when they fear dealing with their inner thoughts and feelings—but they still need something to talk about! Games emerge as a manipulative, non-vulnerable way to seek attention, appreciation, approval, or empathy. When marital and childhood hurts aren't healed, these unresolved emotions can promote destructive games. Let's take a look at five of the most "popular" games couples play.

### The Complainer-Procrastinator Game

Over the years Arlene and Rudy had become experts at playing this game. Each knew his or her role perfectly and never missed a line. Arlene would make a request: "Rudy, would you please take out the trash?" Rudy would agree: "Sure, Dear, I'll do it later." But he never followed through.

After asking over and over with no results, Arlene would turn into the *Complainer*, "nagging" while Rudy continued to postpone his commitment and became the *Procrastinator*. Here's how the game usually played out:

Complainer: Rudy, would you change that light bulb?
Procrastinator: Sure, Sweetheart, after this TV program.

*Later that afternoon.*

Complainer: Rudy, I thought you were going to change the light bulb!
Procrastinator: I will when it's convenient, okay?
Complainer: I can't count on you for anything!
Procrastinator: I'd do it if you weren't such a nag!

You may ask, What are the benefits of playing such a game? The Complainer may want to "prove" her spouse can't be counted on. Why? To gain attention as the *martyr* spouse or to reinforce her own sense of *self-reliance*. Or she may desire to justify certain *retaliatory behaviors*, such as overspending, an uncontrolled temper, or refusing sex.

Why does the Procrastinator continue to play this game? He may want to "prove" his spouse is a nag and thereby justify his own actions. He may desire to show his wife he can't be controlled by a woman, or he may be trying to ease his own fears by showing her how much she needs him.

How does a couple disengage from the Complainer-Procrastinator Game?

Arlene, the Complainer, might make her request with a *specific time requirement*. For example: "Rudy, would you stop and pick up some milk on your way home from work tonight?" If Rudy agrees but doesn't follow through, Arlene could lovingly point out that he hasn't complied with her request and give him a *"final" time frame:* "Rudy, if you would like milk for breakfast, you'll need to pick up a half-gallon on your way home from your bowling league tonight."

If he still doesn't follow through, Arlene should *implement another plan.* She could *do the task herself,* driving to the store for the milk (but she'll have to guard against feelings of bitterness and retaliation!); she could *hire the task done* ("Bobby, I'll give you a dollar if you'll ride your bike to the store for some milk"); or she could *leave the task undone,* especially if the consequences will affect her spouse: "Goodness, Rudy, there's not a drop of milk for your breakfast. I guess you forgot to buy some."

How can Rudy, the Procrastinator, disengage from this game?

He could simply *finish the task* he had agreed to do, or he could *honestly share his intentions* up front: "Arlene, I won't have time to stop at the store after work. I've got bowling league tonight. Could you possibly get the milk yourself . . . or send Bobby?" He might also answer truthfully, "I'd like to help, but I just don't think I can with the tight schedule I've already got."

How about you? Are you and your spouse caught up in the Complainer-Procrastinator Game? If so, take a close look at your underlying needs. Do you Complainers crave more attention or yearn to feel more secure, or are you trying to prove your spouse's love for you? Do you Procrastinators need to be needed and appreciated, or are you compelled to keep your spouse "needing" you? If you examine your motives and answer these questions frankly you may find you and your mate no longer need to play these destructive games.

## Hooked on "Nothing's Wrong"

Tami and Norman had their routine down pat, but neither had the slightest idea how dangerously predictable he or she had become. All Norman knew was when Tami got angry she turned as silent and cold as an Alaskan glacier; and if you asked Tami she'd say she was married to a Neanderthal who thought empathy was something you could catch.

Take her birthday, for instance. Norman thought he'd do something nice and bring home fried chicken. Tami planned on a night out at her favorite restaurant instead. When Norman came in with his bucket of Original Recipe, Tami looked shocked; then her countenance plunged.

Norman said, "Surprise, Baby! Look what I brought home for your birthday! You like the colonel's chicken, right?"

Tami sputtered a moment, then regained her composure and said with a hint of sarcasm, "Of course, Darling. It's just what I always wanted."

"You sure, Hon?" he asked. "You don't look too thrilled."

Tami removed two plates and slammed the cupboard door. "I'm fine, Norman, just fine." But she was thinking, *You low-life! What planet were you raised on?*

"Maybe you think chicken was a bad idea," Norman persisted.

"It's a brilliant idea," she murmured under her breath, "just like all the rest of your wacky notions."

"Go ahead, tell me. You didn't want chicken for your birthday, right?"

"No, it's fine, Norman. Don't worry about it." But privately she thought, *You've just wrecked my entire birthday, that's all, you idiot! But a lot you care! Toss me a few bones—chicken bones—and you figure you've done your duty. If only I had a man who really appreciated me!*

For the entire meal, Tami and Norman ate their crispy chicken amid a verbal Ping-Pong match.

"I suppose you wanted to go out tonight," he said accusingly.

"Norman, it doesn't matter." *It only meant the world to me!*

"You never mentioned going out."

"Don't worry about it." *What was I supposed to do—write it across the sky? Tattoo it on my chest? Beam it over our satellite dish?*

"Tell the truth. Are you mad at me for not taking you out?"

"I'm okay, Norman. Really." *Considering this has been the worst birthday of my life!*

"You are mad."

"No, I'm *not* mad." *But I'd like to boil you in oil or dunk you in wet cement, you cretin.*

After that sizzling dinner, Tami excused herself and skulked off to bed. For two days she moped around, sullen and silent. Norman urged her to tell him what was wrong, but she insisted it was nothing, nothing at all. Finally Norman gave up, musing, *Women! Who can figure 'em?*

Norman and Tami had just played a deadly round of the Nothing's Wrong Game—a classic way of drawing attention to unmet needs without being vulnerable. One partner conveys by facial expression, body language, attitude, murmuring, or door slamming that *something is definitely the matter!* When asked about it, Tami's "nothing" response invites further questioning and her partner's full attention. He's "hooked" now as he persistently tries to pry information from his "nothing's wrong" mate. This childish game often erupts with anger if the Hooked spouse begins to feel used or the Nothing's Wrong spouse is ignored.

What are the supposed benefits of this game? The Nothing's Wrong player gains attention from a spouse by indirectly prompting him or her to pry out important facts or needs. This is much less risky than making an effort to talk things out or vulnerably share real needs. This player remains in control since the game is played on her terms.

The Hooked player often benefits from this game. He can remain his insensitive, irresponsible self until his partner begins the game; then he can plead innocent, claiming he didn't know anything was wrong. Because he often lacks an awareness of his own needs, he remains oblivious to others' needs as well.

How does a couple stop playing the Nothing's Wrong Game? The Nothing's Wrong player can disengage by thinking through what her real need is (appreciation, help with the kids, time alone with her spouse); then she can choose the right time to express it ("Darling, now that we're alone and relaxed, I need to tell you how I feel about . . ."). Bingo! The game is over!

Her Hooked partner can disengage by sharing the truth in love when he notices the game beginning: "Your tone of voice tells me something's wrong. Will you tell me what you're feeling?" He can express his support and availability ("When you feel like talking, let me know"), and he can listen attentively and respond lovingly. Then, before you know it, the game is over!

### The Performer/"Yes, But" Game

Debra and Joseph were in business for themselves. Both accountants, they had rented a little office space and opened up their own tax service. In a rocky economy they were just making ends meet; they were better at tax estimates than estimating the toll the business was taking on their personal lives. It had come down to a power struggle. Joseph was certain he knew what was best for their future, but Debra couldn't agree.

Joseph said, "We need to expand, rent double the office space, hire more help; then we'll draw in more customers. They'll see us as a successful, growing organization."

"Yes, but what if we can't manage the overhead?" Debra protested. "We could lose what we already have."

"Then we'll stay where we are but hire more help."

"Yes, but what if we get someone who botches the job?" Debra continued.

"It's that or spend more time in the office ourselves."

"But we're hardly ever at home as it is," Debra argued.

"Then we'll have to cut down our work load."

"But we won't be able to make ends meet and the business could fail."

"Then what do you suggest we do?"

"I don't know."

"I give up! We'll let things muddle along as they are!"

This game is a common one with couples in a power struggle. As one gives suggestions, the other shoots them down. It's often played by couples who are anxious about closeness; they play the game to avoid intimacy and personal responsibility. The "Performer" (in this case, Joseph) becomes frustrated and angry while the "Yes, But" person (Debra) feels unimportant and martyred. Each player often escapes into other priorities—work, kids, church, or hobbies.

What are the apparent benefits of playing this game? The Yes, But player may be seeking attention for unmet needs without actually wanting the needs met, for if the needs were met she fears her spouse's attention might be withdrawn. The Performer plays out of a need for approval and appreciation. Unfortunately, this game obscures and leaves unmet a couple's real needs.

How does the Performer stop this game? He can lovingly reassure his spouse he wants to help find a solution and then give a maximum of three options. The spouse is responsible for making her choice. The Yes, But person can listen to the suggestions and either pick one or suggest one of her own, focusing on positive aspects of the choice rather than negative.

Debra and Joseph came to realize Debra's vacillation about the business resulted from her need to spend more personal time with her husband. Joseph was willing to work on the problem. "We can temporarily down-size a little," he suggested, "or maintain our present operating level and hire an assistant, or we can begin expansion in small increments and hire several office workers. Any of those choices should give us more time together."

"I can't ask you to do that," Debra protested. "The business comes first."

"No, our relationship comes first. Which of the three choices do you prefer? Pick one, or if you've got another solution I'm willing to listen."

Debra was impressed. "You're really serious about this, aren't you—about our spending more time together? I don't know what to say. I'm pleased! Maybe—maybe we should maintain our present level and bring in an assistant. If that goes well, we can think about expanding next year."

As Debra and Joseph invested more time in their personal lives and got their relationship back on track, Debra felt free to offer a more assertive voice regarding business decisions. And Joseph was relieved to have a fully functioning partner again—both at home and at work.

## Outdone by the Sweet Martyr

Kyle fell in love with Clara because she was the sweetest girl he'd ever met—pretty, soft-spoken, friendly, sincere. When they married, he was sure he'd found the perfect wife. But not long after the honeymoon he discovered Clara had more tales of woe than he could ever keep up with. No matter what his problem or dilemma, Clara could always go him one better. For example:

Sweet Martyr (Clara): How was your day, Dear?

Outdone (Kyle): It was terrible, one of the worst I've had.

Sweet Martyr: I know what you mean. The toilet overflowed, and I had one of my sick headaches.

Outdone: At least I signed the deal on the Smith account.

Sweet Martyr: Really? I spent the day cleaning house—in spite of my headache. Did you notice?

Outdone: Yes, it looks great. I think I'll relax awhile.

Sweet Martyr: You look tired.

Outdone: I am. I could sleep for a week.

Sweet Martyr: I'm exhausted too. And I broke three nails scrubbing the floor. And look at my knees!

Outdone: You shouldn't work so hard. Let's relax a little.

Sweet Martyr: I can't relax with this throbbing headache. What if it's a tumor? Maybe I'm terminal!

Outdone: I'm sure it's just a migraine. Now sit down and rest. I'd like to tell you about my day.

Sweet Martyr: Can't. I've got to start dinner, though I'd hoped you'd take me out to eat to make up for my miserable day.

Outdone (in exasperation): Okay, get your coat on. Where do you want to eat?

This game is played by a self-absorbed spouse overwhelmed by her own neediness. She turns every conversation back to her own abundance of needs. Not as skilled at verbalizing his desires, her partner is outdone in every way as his needs, hurts, and hopes are topped, minimized, or ignored. He will likely grow weary of trying to meet Sweet Martyr's needs, and eventually he may become angry, withdrawn, or seek attention elsewhere.

How can a couple disengage from such a game? Sweet Martyr can express her wishes directly without beating around the bush; she can give undivided attention to her partner's needs and lovingly help to meet them. Outdone can be lovingly assertive when he gets the Sweet Martyr treatment: "It hurts when you don't seem interested in my day." He can also learn to express his own needs in a loving way. And finally, he can look for creative ways to meet his partner's needs.

### Frustrated by "Never Enough"

Sonja and Robbie were successful baby boomers determined to make their mark in the world. Both professionals, they owned a custom-built home and sent their children to the best schools. But no matter how much wealth and prestige they amassed, it was never enough for Robbie. The more dissatisfied Robbie became, the more frustrated Sonja felt, until their relationship was nearly on the rocks. Their conversations usually went like this:

Never Enough (Robbie): I wish we had the money to put in a swimming pool. Every house on our street has one except ours.

Frustrated (Sonja): My overtime schedule starts next week. We could save the extra money for one.

Never Enough: You know I don't want you working so much. You should be home more with the kids.

Frustrated: My boss said I can get off early for the kids if I work a couple of nights at home.

Never Enough: I don't want you bringing your work home. I hardly see you as it is.

Frustrated: We've got tonight. Why don't we go to that little restaurant we like on Seventh Street?

Never Enough: That place? Last time the food was lousy.

Frustrated: I give up! You're never satisfied!

This game isn't much fun for either player. Both are overly needy and insecure. Never Enough may be seeking to meet his needs through his partner's performance, but he fears she won't give without constant reminders of his dissatisfaction. The underlying message is: *I need you around to keep trying!* But no matter how much she does, he's never satisfied.

The only way to stop this game is for Never Enough to focus on what he already has to be grateful for and express his appreciation to his spouse when she does fulfill specific wishes. Frustrated can express her commitment to her spouse, share her own needs with him, and show her appreciation for his efforts.

## EXPERIENCING THE INTIMATE CONNECTION

Our world has emphasized achievement and performance to the exclusion of emotional development. Young children do well learning to tie their shoes and count to ten, but who helps them identify their feelings? School-age youngsters begin the treadmill of endless activities . . . scouts, dance, sports, piano . . . but how do they learn to deal with normal rejections, fears, and disappointments? Adolescents focus on athletics, academics, popularity, and dating, but how skilled are they at healing the hurts from normal tensions at home?

Most of us were never taught how to communicate our emotions or how to respond properly to another's feelings. Without developing an adequate vocabulary to express feelings, most adults enter marriage hopeful of deep emotional closeness but unable to achieve it. The friendship dimension of intimacy suffers as their feelings of love, romance, and affection diminish. A couple tries to cope with this loss, but eventually they drift into separate worlds, the man becoming absorbed by business or hobbies, the woman escaping into the world of the supermom or of other endless activity. They may also become resentful, overly self-sufficient, or fearful of abandonment or rejection.

For many couples, this coping existence is made even more tragic by its contrast with their religious expectations. They fall into a pattern of pretending what happens at home matches what they proclaim at church. When a person's home life is dramatically different from his or her spiritual values and teachings, feelings of inadequacy, guilt, and condemnation may be added to the previous pain of loneliness, rejection, fear, anger, or bitterness.

## Developing the Skill of Emotional Responding

To develop closeness with your mate, you must learn the skill of *emotional responding*. How does it work? When he or she shares an emotional hurt or need with you, respond with your own emotions, saying, in effect, *If you hurt, I care . . . If you have a need, I care!* Learning this seemingly simple but profound principle can greatly enhance your relationship. Any other response—logic or facts, criticism or complaint—undermines your intimacy, and you'll begin to tell yourselves, "We just can't communicate!"

Sounds easy enough, you say? Maybe so. But you also need to be aware of how *not* to respond. Four classic unproductive responses are guaranteed to miss the target in healing hurts.

Stan tried all four of these responses. He and Renée were well on their way to developing a communication gap after their first Christmas dinner with his family. A remark Stan's mother made hurt Renée deeply, but Stan compounded the problem with his inept reaction.

First, he tried *facts, logic, or reasons:* "Really, Renée, you know that's just the way my mother is. She speaks her mind. She didn't mean anything against you personally when she said she wished I'd married my old girlfriend."

When that didn't work, Stan tried *criticism:* "Boy, Renée, you're sure sensitive! You get all bent out of shape over nothing. You're being a real drag. Come on, lighten up!"

Then he tried *complaints (his own hurts/needs):* "Well, I'm hurt, too, you know. You embarrassed me in front of my folks with your sulking. How do you think I felt when you spoiled the party?"

Finally he tried *neglect:* "Okay, if that's how you're going to be, let's just drop it. I'll talk to you later. I've got other things to do."

What Stan didn't realize was that the wedge driven into his marriage at the family dinner was now a chasm because of his hurtful responses. This unfortunate incident could have been turned around to benefit his relationship with Renée if he had *responded emotionally* to her pain, like this:

"I can see you're really hurting, Renée, and it makes me hurt too. I want to understand how you feel and make it right. I'm committed to you, Darling. I love you and I'll see you through this, whatever it takes."

No matter how Renée has been hurt by people or forces outside her marriage, she knows she will receive support and understanding from her husband; the intimate connection is firmly established.

*Emotional responding always includes understanding, empathy, gentleness, and reassurance, and it may also include confession.* Take note of these examples of productive emotional responses when you've been a part of causing the hurt:

"Can you share with me how I've hurt you . . . and how it made you feel? I want to understand and make it right."

"I see now that I hurt you by my _____. That was wrong of me. Will you forgive me?"

And note the other productive emotional responses below:

- "I can really see you're hurting (or _____)."
- "I don't like to see you hurting."
- "It saddens me to see you so fearful (or _____)."
- "I deeply care about you and love you."
- "I'm committed to go through this with you."
- "I genuinely regret my part in hurting you."

David Ferguson was a master of the unproductive response in the early years of his marriage. "If at the end of a long day I came home and found Teresa in tears over one of life's inevitable hurts, I might say, 'What's wrong with you *now?*' (criticism), or 'Well, next time handle it differently' (giving "logic" or advice), or 'What a great homecoming! I should have stayed at work!' (sharing complaints). None of these was very comforting or conducive to marital harmony.

"After several years of this, I began asking myself, 'What does *God* feel for Teresa in her pain?' The answer was clear: He feels sadness for her; He hurts for her. So maybe it's okay for me to feel sad for her too. Maybe she just needs me to tell her, 'I can see you're really upset and I hurt for you because I love you.'"

Teresa, too, had to learn the art of emotional responding rather than blaming, criticizing, or complaining. When David worked late several nights in a row and came home exhausted, she was likely to respond, "You've worked late every night this week, and I'm sick of it!" But as she learned to speak the truth in love, she changed her approach. One night as they were lying in bed, she reached over and took his hand and said, "Sweetheart, I can see how hard you've been working this week, and at the same time I've really been missing you."

Teresa's loving expression of her needs prompted David to respond in kind. He said, "You're right. I've been overdoing it at the office lately, and it was wrong of me to be away from you so much. Will you forgive me?"

We all have a choice in our marriages. We can learn to speak the truth in love and respond with empathy to our mate, or we can resort to manipulative, destructive games and unproductive responses that break the intimate connection.

Many of the lies we believe and the games we play derive from unresolved childhood issues. Couples who haven't emotionally "left" their parents find it nearly impossible to "cleave" to each other. Our next chapter will help you determine if you've really left your mother and father to become one with your spouse.

# CHAPTER
# 11

# Leave Your Childhood Home

JIMMY CARLTON WAS telling a story, and he was as close to tears as anyone had ever seen him. "It was the middle of winter and my dad and I were driving home on a country road. I was about six or seven. I don't know where we'd been, but it was dark and cold and snow was falling. I remember thinking the angels in heaven were shaking their feather pillows. The heater was on and the radio was playing, and I felt real safe and secure beside my dad.

"Suddenly we hit a patch of ice and went spinning every which way. I screamed and grabbed my daddy's arm, and the next thing I knew we spun off into the snow and crashed into an old oak tree. We weren't hurt, but the car wouldn't work and it was too cold to walk anywhere.

"I started crying and my dad told me to stop. I was so scared I started shaking, so my dad put his arm around me and held me close against his chest. He'd never held me before, and I can still remember the feel of his scratchy corduroy jacket against my cheek. We must have sat there for an hour in that car waiting for someone to spot us and send help, and all the while my dad talked to me. I don't remember anything he said, but his voice was low and steady, like the hum of an engine. I stopped shaking and crying, and even though I was numb with cold, I was happier than I'd ever been in my life because I had my dad all to myself and he was paying attention to me.

"Later, after we were rescued and back home again, I remember going up to my dad and putting my arms around him. He pushed me away and said, 'You're home safe now. Big boys don't need hugs.'

"He never hugged me again except politely and distantly. And I never stopped wishing I was back in that freezing-cold, crashed automobile safe in my daddy's arms."

Tears ran down Jimmy's cheeks now, but he made no effort to stop them. He was sitting forward in his chair, his elbows on his knees, his gaze fixed on his large, clasped hands.

Marla reached over and slipped her hand between his. "I never heard that story before, Jimmy. I really hurt for you. I'm sure your dad cared, Honey. He just didn't know how to show it. Just like my folks."

David Ferguson then invited Marla to reflect on something she might have missed out on in her growing-up years. She didn't need to be coaxed. "I was in junior high and had the lead in the school musical. I felt like Doris Day or Debbie Reynolds from those old movies on late-night TV. I worked so hard on my part and I couldn't wait for my parents to see me perform.

"But my little brothers were in grade school and had open house the same night, so my parents went there because there were two of them and only one of me. I remember standing on that stage singing my heart out and looking out into that dark sea of faces to see if my folks had come after all. They hadn't. Even the kids with walk-on parts had parents there.

"When I got home, I hoped my parents would ask me all about the play, but all they talked about was how well my brothers were doing in school. I decided then and there I'd never ask them for anything again, but of course the next time I was in something at school I hoped like the dickens they'd be there. I don't recall if they ever came to anything else or not; it was that junior-high musical that was so important to me. I vowed someday I'd do something worthy of their attention."

While neither Jimmy nor Marla Carlton would typically be labeled as "abused children," they did miss out on significant intimacy needs as they grew up; they entered marriage profoundly undernourished emotionally in key ways. Jimmy hungered for the affection and closeness he missed from his dad. Marla yearned for the attention and approval her parents rarely gave her. Both were pulling around a trailer full of unhealed childhood pain. It was that pain David had to address in counseling.

David reminded them that to be human is to *hurt*. It's not *if* we'll be hurt but *When? How much? By whom?* Trying to eliminate or minimize our vulnerability to pain simply makes us impersonal and cold. The more invulnerable we are, the more machinelike we become. Machines don't hurt; people do. God created us that way—with needs that produce pain when they go unmet.

The issue is, What have you done with that pain? Have you resolved it, minimized it, or denied it?

In healthy families marriage partners heal and resolve pain rather than retaliating or ignoring it; the functional family provides an approachable environment in which needs and hurts can be shared. Parents practice open confession for inevitable wrongs and encourage their children as they grow up to do likewise. As parents focus on sensitively giving to their children out of the nurturing love they receive from their relationship with God and each other, children grow up conceiving of a caring, giving heavenly Father in whom they can begin to trust at an early age.[1]

On the other hand, the dysfunctional family resembles that childhood game where you cover your eyes, ears, and mouth and chant, "Monkey see no evil, monkey hear no evil, monkey speak no evil." Change "evil" to "pain," and you've got the dysfunctional family. Not only do members refuse to deal with pain, the rule seems to be, Don't feel, don't trust, and don't talk, especially about problems or needs.[2]

What else do we know about the dysfunctional family? Parents fail to respond in a consistent, affectionate, satisfactory manner, so real intimacy rarely develops. Families lacking intimacy demonstrate little cohesion and lots of conflict, including arguments, disruptions, isolation, and even role reversal (the child takes on responsibilities ordinarily performed by a parent, causing overresponsibility later in life). Survivors of such families commonly have problems with trust, fears of abandonment, and difficulty with intimate relationships. Children from incestuous families have all these problems, plus troubles with secrecy and shame. Children from divorced homes as well as physically abused youngsters commonly exhibit anxiety, social isolation, and distrust; they have few or no models for healthy intimate relationships.

Couples often ask how the impact of their childhood environment relates to the fact they are now "new creations" in Christ. The connection goes something like this: Research consistently shows that a major portion of our thinking, feeling, and behaving is shaped before we are even six years old, before most of us accepted Christ! At our new birth, at whatever age it occurred, our spirit was made alive to God (Titus 3:5), but our thoughts still need to be transformed (Rom. 12:1-2), and our emotions may still need to be healed (Eph. 4:31-32, 1 John 4:18-19) and our old habits broken. Thus, God's sanctifying work in the "soul" realm of thoughts, feelings, and choices continues as long as we walk in this world. We need to look back at our childhood family so we can understand what happened to us in those early years.

## FAMILY INTIMACY OR DYSFUNCTION?

### The Barrenness of a Busy Life

It takes time to build close relationships, and the more relationships involved, the more challenging it becomes. With three, four, five, or more family members, it requires planning and commitment even to have everyone consistently sit down to a meal together. As children get older, the challenge is even greater.

Being dysfunctional doesn't necessarily mean a family is alcoholic, incestuous, abusive, or even neglectful. High on the list of contributing factors is a lack of consistent quality time together. There are late nights of work, committee meetings, social activities, church functions, P.T.A., children's sports, tutoring, studies, and gymnastics. Add your own commitments to the list and you'll notice there's not much time for a family to simply be . . . a family. Feeling the pressure not to miss out on worthwhile programs and opportunities, parents feel the *false guilt* to let their children do more than they got to do as children. Older children and particularly teenagers succumb to the pressures of overinvolvement, seeking to belong to all the "in" groups and clubs. All of these obligations contribute to the family's lack of intimacy.

Sociological studies frequently have addressed the extraordinary amount of parent-adolescent conflict in Western culture. Why does America have such major parent-teen struggles? A classic study of 1939 identified *rapid change* and a *fast-paced society* as elements that increased parent-youth conflicts.[3] Imagine how much truer that is in these reckless, mad-dash nineties! Rapid change and fast-paced living foster insecurity, reduce crucial family time together, and heighten differences between generations.

As counselors, we have asked many adult children how they knew, as they grew up, that their parents loved them—only to be told, "My parents worked hard" or "They provided for us" or "We had everything we needed." We have heard these words time and again, and every time we've felt the hollow emotional depths from which they came.

We ask those we counsel to think about their families of origin in relation to four specific questions: How did your family give attention? How did your family give affection? How did your family give empathy? How did your family handle conflict?

## 1. How Did Your Family Give Attention?

We all crave attention from those we love. Not just polite, surface attention, but genuine, focused involvement. One mother shared how she had become adept at carrying on her own projects while her small children chattered on about their interests. She took a certain adverse pride in being able to accomplish her tasks and "listen" at the same time, even uttering yes-or-no answers when appropriate. But she was smitten with guilt one day when she realized her preschooler had excitedly spieled off an entire story, and she hadn't heard a single word! She decided her children deserved better than that. The next time one came running to her with a story, she stopped what she was doing, looked him in the eye, and listened to every word.

Giving attention means to take thought of another and convey interest; more importantly, it means *to enter another's world*. Christ left

His world and entered ours to demonstrate His love. How often are you willing to show your love by entering another's world? Do you have the slightest idea *how* to enter a loved one's "world"? David Ferguson shares this illustration of Doug, a frustrated father, who was complaining that his three-year-old son, Jason, was out of control. He kept banging his head and kicking holes in walls. I suggested they spend some time together in the playroom while I watched from the observation room next door.

As Doug sat down in a chair, he spied a Velcro dart board on the wall. "Jason, go get those darts," he said. For several minutes Dad threw the darts while Jason retrieved them.

Eventually Jason got bored and wandered off. Spotting a set of Ninja Turtles on the floor, he cried, "Daddy, Daddy, look at the Ninja Turtles! Let's play on the floor with Leonardo!"

Dad said, "No, let's play darts."

Jason grew red in the face and clenched his fists. "No, Daddy, I wanna play Ninja Turtles!"

"I'm playing darts, Jason."

Jason began to kick and scream. In desperation Doug took hold of his son and pleaded, "Come on, Jason, it's going to be okay. Don't get all upset. If you'll be a good boy, tomorrow I'll take you to a University of Texas basketball game. You'd like that, wouldn't you?"

Jason quieted down and the session ended. I'm sure that father felt he had spent quality time with his son, thinking, *We played darts together and we're going to a ball game.*

But the truth is, that father never entered into that little boy's world! He never got down on his knees and played what his son wanted to play. Who enjoyed the dart game? Who was the basketball game for? Not the child. The father. The child missed his dad's genuine, undivided attention and it was coming out dramatically in the boy's behavior.

What about your family? Did your dad pay attention to you? Did your mother enter your world and share your interests?

## 2. How Did Your Family Give Affection?

Did your parents communicate caring and closeness through physical touch and verbalized love? Were they expressive of the powerful verbalized words "I love you"? Did they give hugs freely? Did they kiss you good night? Touch conveys two significant messages: *I'm here. And I care!* Touch also communicates feelings no words can match.

Teresa Ferguson admits that for many years of her adult life she feared affection so much that it became a problem in her marriage. "I was reared in a large family of six children, where Mom showed her love by cooking our favorite food and Dad showed his love by going to work. We didn't do much hugging and kissing. Verbalized love was rare to nonexistent. David was raised in a very affectionate family, so he expected lots of hugs and kisses from me. When he'd come home wanting affection, I'd make him a pot roast or bake him a pie. That's what affection meant when I was growing up. It was hard at first, but with God's help and David's patience, I learned how to show my affection directly with loving words, caressing touches, and kisses.

### 3. How Did Your Family Give Empathy?

When something went wrong, did your parents give you a pep talk? "Come on, don't let it bother you. Keep a stiff upper lip. Things will be better tomorrow." Sound familiar? If that's what you remember of empathy, your parents may have short-changed you in the comfort department. Comfort means to come alongside with sympathetic words, feelings, and touch; to console with tenderness. Empathy is primarily an emotional expression of loving care and concern.

Many parents who aren't in touch with their own feelings may resort to blaming, giving advice, becoming a martyr, or denying the significance of your pain. When you turned to your mother or father for understanding, what response did you receive?

- "It's your own fault. You should have known better!"
- "I tried to tell you. Next time do it this way."
- "All I do for you and you're still not satisfied!"
- "Don't be such a baby. You've got it a lot better than the rest of the world."

Any of these responses would have left you feeling worse than before. What you wanted was someone to listen to you, feel your pain, and offer comforting touch with reassuring words.

Was your father a source of refuge? Was your mother a haven of comfort? Empathy comes from a sense of feeling connected to another person—bonded, attached. Did you experience that sense of oneness with your parents? Do you experience it with your mate?

## 4. How Did Your Family Handle Conflict?

Because marital conflict is universal and inevitable, it's a factor in every child's life. Your parents likely fit into one of these four major conflict styles. Check the one that reflects your childhood home:

_____ **Open-Abusive Conflict:** These households are often tense, angry, and explosive as parents resort to verbal or physical assaults. The child may feel forced to take sides, and he or she may feel a sense of worthlessness and despair.

_____ **Open-Triangulated Conflict:** This pattern usually involves the child in the parents' conflict; child abuse may be the result. A parent may demand that the child take the parent's side, causing feelings of alienation, isolation, and a sense of being used. One or both parents may project their hostilities onto the child, causing the child to feel profound rejection and anger. His or her need for nurturing and affection remains unmet as he or she struggles with self-doubt and fear.

_____ **Submerged Conflict:** These parents develop covert methods of dealing with marital tension—fathers becoming workaholics to maintain some control over their lives; mothers controlling their children by smothering them with excessive attention. A parent may turn to alcohol to control his or her family by forcing them to deal with his or her addiction. These overt symptoms mask deeper unresolved issues. Children of such enmeshed relationships are often spoiled but insecure, fearful, and dependent. Covert fighting is, by nature, less than truthful and founded on manipulation techniques. Children reared in this environment may have difficulty with honesty, be manipulative in their relationships, and be reluctant to accept personal responsibility.

_____ **Balanced / Resolving Conflict:** In a positive, healthy manner, a couple diffuses marital strife by balancing personal needs with the needs of the family unit as a whole. Rather than leaving emotional wounds untreated or ignored, the spouses openly admit and resolve their hurts—an approach requiring personal responsibility, mutual giving, open communication, and humility. Parents in such homes communicate to their children genuine love, fair and consistent discipline, a positive example, and supportive leadership. Their reward is very often respectful, cooperative children and a warm, secure home atmosphere.[4]

Which of these approaches struck a responsive chord in your own mind and heart?

When you were born, you began a journey away from your parents. The umbilical cord was cut, and your separation began. There were many "firsts" in your life: first babysitter, first night in your own bed, first grade, first night away from home, first boyfriend or girlfriend, first apartment, first job, first home, first child.

Usually the last phases of leaving your parents involve resolving unhealed childhood emotions, trusting God to meet your intimacy needs directly or through your spouse rather than your parents, and finding freedom to give emotionally to your parents rather than expecting to receive from them.

What about you? Have your really left your father and mother? In what ways have you left? In what ways are you still painfully connected?

In our next chapter we'll show you how to grieve your childhood losses and receive comfort from your spouse.

CHAPTER

# 12

# Mourn Your Childhood Hurts

YOU HURT. YOUR childhood pain is still with you, wrapped around everything you do, like a heavy, oppressive cloak.

Maybe you didn't even realize until now how much you're hurting. Maybe you've spent years denying your feelings or rationalizing them away: *It was all so long ago . . . You can't undo the past . . . Time heals all wounds, doesn't it?*

Many of us find ourselves trapped between an unchangeable past and fear of change in the present. The issue isn't how long ago the pain occurred but rather, is the pain still alive within us today?

Time is a necessary ingredient for healing but not a sufficient one. More is needed. Ask yourself this: For years and years has the sun gone down on your anger (Eph. 4:26)? Has your fear—which was *not* from God—been erased (2 Tim. 1:7, 1 John 4:18–19)? Have you found freedom from inner shame and condemnation? Have you allowed the God of all comfort to comfort you in your hurt (Rom. 8:1, 2 Cor. 1:4)? God in His abundant love wants to remove the sting of anger, fear, shame, or hurt from your memories (John 10:10). Once you do this, you can truly leave your childhood homes.

## BLAME IS NOT THE ISSUE—FREEDOM IS!

You may feel anxious about reviewing your past for the unfinished business of healing your emotional pain. Part of your anxiety may come from feeling that to recognize your pain is to blame another . . .

your parents, stepparents, siblings, spouse, child, another relative, former spouse, or friend.

Let's make it clear: Your goal is not to accuse, and then to try and condemn someone else for your perceived pain. Instead the issue is truth—the truth about your pain and the feelings associated with it. If the truth is you're angry, then it needs to be "put away" (Eph. 4:31–32). If you're experiencing guilt, you may need to confess to God and possibly others (1 John 1:9, James 5:16). Your fear can be cast out by perfect love (1 John 4:18–19). Your shame can be overcome by the wonder of who you are in Christ (Rom. 7:25), and you can be comforted in your hurt by one who weeps as you weep (Rom. 12:15). The Great Physician wants to heal and free you as only He can!

## HEALING CHILDHOOD EMOTIONAL PAIN

[The Lord] heals the brokenhearted
And binds up their wounds. (Ps. 147:3)

Jehovah-Rapha is our healer God. Just as the apostle Paul prayed for the Christians at Thessalonica that God would "sanctify you completely . . . spirit, soul, and body" (1 Thess. 5:23), the Great Physician desires to heal your soul. James 1:21 speaks of this present-tense, ongoing work in the life of the believer: "Receive . . . the implanted word, which is able to save your souls." God is at work through the Word to heal your mind, emotions, and will. Healing past hurts requires active work in each of these dimensions . . . mind, emotions, and will, as we see in the three-phased therapeutic approach described next.

### Hurt, Understand, Forgive: All Three Are Essential

Healing your emotional pain doesn't mean that you simply dismiss your past. Healing is not some spiritual amnesia! Trite pronouncements such as "Sure, it's all forgiven" don't work. Your emotions need to be freed to feel the hurt. Your mind needs to be renewed to embrace the truth about your hurt, and your will needs to choose to forgive the hurt. In Chapter 9 we walked you through a process to forgive your spouse. Now we'll give you the process we use to help couples forgive people who have hurt them in the past.

## The Order Is Essential

Again, you must begin with your hurt. There's no way around it. You can't forgive something you refuse to acknowledge. You can't "put away" your anger or bitterness if you don't admit it exists. Before you can forgive, you must see what it is you're forgiving.

Don't get caught in the trap of thinking you must understand your hurt before you can acknowledge and feel it. You might say, "That's just the way people were back then" or "I had it better than a lot of others I know." Such ill-timed understanding, no matter how true it is, will only minimize your hurt and hinder healing.[1]

## A Biblical Model

Pause for a moment and consider Christ's example as He faced His crucifixion.[2] Picture the man—real flesh and blood, muscle and sinew, sweat and tears—a man who could feel, who knew the gnawing of hunger and the soft betrayal of a kiss. He felt an anguish so intense it pulsed blood into His very sweat. See the sun-browned man with tousled hair, Golgotha's dirt under His fingernails, the weight of a roughhewn cross straining His back. Taste the vinegar as His parched tongue drew back in revulsion. Catch the hysteria of the crowd; smell the closeness of jostling, jeering humanity surrounding the cross. Hear their shrieks and taunts bombarding the God-man suspended between earth and heaven.

Think of how Scripture describes Him: "Despised and rejected by men, / A man of sorrows and acquainted with grief" (Isa. 53:3). Christ said, "My soul is exceedingly sorrowful, even to death" (Matt. 26:38). Have you ever hurt so badly you felt you were on the verge of dying? Christ has. But He *faced His hurt*. He didn't deny it, minimize it, or spiritualize it. He confronted His pain on His knees in Gethsemane, and He *understood the truth*. From the cross He declared, "They do not know what they do" (Luke 23:34). He knew the human heart inside out—blinded and in bondage, "like sheep have gone astray" (Isa. 53:6). Even as the nails tore His flesh, the spear pierced His side, and the weight of His own body cut off His air, Christ uttered the words, "Father, forgive them." In the midst of their offenses, He *forgave His offenders*, setting the example for us to forgive one another as He has forgiven us (Col. 3:13).

Christ didn't avoid His pain; He didn't pretend everything was fine; He didn't spiritualize the pain with a glib response. Rather, He faced it head on.

Think about your own pain. What emotion do you associate with it? What emotional memories do you have of incidents that brought you grief? Allow yourself to feel them now. Do you feel sad? Angry? Like weeping?

## Establish What Is to Be Forgiven

Christ's lonely hours in Gethsemane brought His pain into clear focus. As He agonized in prayer, sweating great drops of blood, He knew He had been:

—not honored, but despised

—not accepted, but rejected

—not supported, but forsaken

—not appreciated, but ridiculed

—not "prioritized" —but neglected

Healing begins at this very point . . . establishing and facing your pain. Ephesians 4:31 says, "Let all bitterness, wrath, anger, clamor, and evil speaking be put away," but you can only "put away" what you've admitted you feel. Set aside a quiet, reflective time to begin *journaling* some of your reflections, drawing from the items suggested below. You may find it a struggle to put your pain into words, but be as specific as possible. Avoid explaining or minimizing your hurts.

- Were you despised? Rejected? Abandoned? Ridiculed? Neglected?
- What intimacy needs—such as attention, appreciation, affection, and empathy—went unmet?

- Honestly name and face the pain you experienced in each of life's cycles: Birth, childhood, adolescence, and adulthood. This may be an ongoing process; you may peel back one pain and find another.

### Grieve the Loss Associated with Your Pain

Jesus said, "Could you not watch with Me one hour?" (Matt. 26:40). Feel the loneliness, anguish, and loss in Christ's words! He wasn't giving a sermon on the priority of prayer; He was speaking transparently out of His own pain.

To grieve is to focus on the emotions behind your loss—just as you would grieve over the loss of a loved one. Continue your quiet reflection and begin journaling your *feelings*.

- What do you **feel** about being despised, rejected, abandoned, or neglected?
- What do you **feel** about the unmet needs you've identified— the fact that you missed out on affection or encouragement or attention?
- What do you **feel** about the pain you experienced over your life—the fact that you were abused, used, ignored, or ridiculed? Check the emotions below that describe your feelings.

| | | | |
|---|---|---|---|
| ____ lonely | ____ sad | ____ afraid | ____ neglected |
| ____ hurt | ____ unloved | ____ unworthy | ____ bitter |
| ____ unimportant | ____ used | ____ rejected | ____ insignificant |
| ____ abandoned | ____ angry | ____ anxious | ____ humiliated |

### Receive Comfort for Your Pain

The promise is yours: "Blessed are those who mourn / For they shall be comforted" (Matt. 5:4). In the Garden of Gethsemane, as the disciples slept, the God of all comfort comforted His Son. He also desires to comfort you in your grief . . . and He may use other people to bring you comfort as well.

Identify a special "journey mate" to share in your grief. Our approach with married couples is to involve each partner as this special journey mate. If a wife, for instance, had a totally uninvolved husband this journey mate might be your pastor, a counselor, or a special woman friend within the body of Christ. Allow this special one to journey with you in sharing your grief and ministering comfort. You might:

- Plan to read your journal descriptions concerning your hurts and unmet needs out loud to this person.

- Mention what you will need from your journey mate: "I have something I'd like to share with you about some of my hurts and feelings; as I read, I just need you to listen and maybe comfort me."

- Talk about your feelings concerning what you missed and what you felt.

- Receive comfort from someone who cares, allowing him or her to feel genuine sadness for your hurt and what you missed.

Experiencing such comfort is the blessing promised in Matthew 5:4!

As you reflect on the hurts of your past, you may want to write a "therapeutic" letter to particular individuals who were a part of your pain, expressing your feelings and emotional wounds. Don't actually mail the letter; instead, its purpose is to help you clarify your pain, encourage you to feel your pain and then to share the letter with your journey mate.

## HEALING CHILDHOOD HURTS WITH THERAPEUTIC LETTER WRITING

To aid you in composing your letter, we've drawn up the following model:

Dear Dad (Mom, stepdad, brother, ex-spouse, etc.),
I've been reflecting on my relationship with you—how I felt and some of what I missed.
From some of my earliest memories, I've often felt . . .

I know I really often missed . . .

It hurt me so much when . . .

I now often feel . . .

It would mean so much to me if . . .

I wish I could hear you say to me . . .

Your Son (Daughter, sister, etc.)

David Ferguson encouraged the Carltons to write letters to their parents. Marla agreed, but Jimmy was reluctant. "It's silly," he insisted. "I've never written my dad a real letter. Why should I write one he's never going to see?"

"It's for you," said Marla. "It'll help you put your feelings down and get in touch with your hurts."

"I've already spilled enough feelings," protested Jimmy, "and I don't need a letter to remind me of my hurts."

Marla was frustrated that Jimmy wasn't more willing to explore his pain. "How can I comfort him if he won't even tell me how he hurts?"

David had an idea. "When we're dealing with 'non-feeling' spouses, the key is often for the partner to express empathy *first*, which helps 'free' the non-feeling spouse to feel his or her pain."

The next time David talked with the Carltons he asked Marla, "Can you imagine some of the significant needs Jimmy had growing up that he missed out on from his dad?"

"Sure. His dad was almost never around, and he took little interest in Jimmy's life. He acted more like a drill sergeant than a dad, barking orders and expecting complete obedience. Jimmy tried like crazy to please his dad. He did great in high school—got good grades, started his own band, even found time to play football and baseball. He was the perfect all-around guy. You should see all his pictures in his high-school yearbooks."

"Did it make any difference with his dad?"

"No, he never went to any of Jimmy's games, never heard his band play. Come to think of it, he never even went to your high-school graduation, did he, Jimmy?"

"No." Jimmy cracked his knuckles noisily. "Dad went hunting overseas with some big clients. He even made a joke about it. Said he was after big game, and he didn't mean elephants. He said he hoped I understood. Graduating from high school was no big deal. Everyone did it. He said, 'When you graduate from college, that's when I'll be there, boy! It's a promise!' I vowed then and there I'd never graduate from college because I wasn't about to hold him to his promise."

"Marla, can you imagine what Jimmy must have *felt* as he played football, then baseball, week after week, wishing his dad were there to watch him, but he wasn't? And what do you suppose Jimmy felt when his dad wasn't there to see his band play or see him march down the aisle at his high-school graduation?"

"I think Jimmy was real hurt. He must have felt rejected, like he wasn't important to his dad. Maybe he even felt embarrassed or lonely."

"Now, Marla, this is very important. As you sit here and think about Jimmy growing up feeling hurt or rejected, wishing his dad had been at his games or graduation—as you imagine him feeling lonely and embarrassed and less important than his dad's clients or hunting—what do you *feel* for your husband?"

Marla looked over at Jimmy. He was staring down at the floor, his jaw rigid, his face expressionless. There was a catch in Marla's voice. "I feel very sad for Jimmy. He missed so much. It makes me hurt inside to think of him playing football so hard every week and his dad not caring enough to be there."

Marla blinked back tears. "But what hurts me most of all is picturing him as a little boy in that car with his dad when they crashed into that tree. I keep seeing Jimmy trying to hug his daddy and his daddy just pushing him away."

"How does that make you feel?"

"I feel a lump in my throat and an ache in my chest, like I want to cry all the tears Jimmy would never let himself cry."

"So you feel very sad for Jimmy. You hurt for him, Marla. Why would you feel so sad and so hurt?"

"Because I care about him. I love him! It hurts me to think of him hurting."

"Marla, let's reflect on what you've shared with me. You feel very sad for Jimmy because he missed so much, and you really hurt for him because you love him, and it hurts you to see him hurt. Is that right, Marla?"

"Yes, that's right."

"Now, Marla, while I leave you and Jimmy alone for a few minutes, I'd like you to comfort him. Turn and talk to Jimmy. Sit close, maybe hold his hand. Look him in the eye and simply tell him what you've told me.

"And, Jimmy, as Marla shares her comfort with you, simply let yourself receive it. Just let her hug you and hurt for you. Let yourself feel your hurt, then maybe tell her thanks for caring."

Jimmy looked a little quizzical, but he was game. And Marla had years of comfort stored up, ready to share. When David returned a little later, there wasn't a dry eye in the house, and Marla and Jimmy looked happier than he had ever seen them. Jimmy had indeed entered into the blessing of Matthew 5:4.

The Carltons set aside time the next week for Marla to read her letter aloud to Jimmy, giving him an opportunity to share his comfort—holding her, hurting with her, reassuring her of his love. Over their next few visits as their childhood hurts were comforted their inner pain began to subside. Jimmy's hurt, which so often revealed itself in fearful avoidance and aloofness, soon gave way to more openness and transparency as he shared his feelings and needs and became much more sensitive to Marla. Marla's hurt, which so often erupted in the anger of a sharp tongue and demanding ways, soon gave way to a gentle spirit and more selfless giving.

Both the Carltons were finally beginning to put their pasts behind them. They had begun an important emotional "leaving" of their parents. The trailer full of hurts they had pulled into their marriage was beginning to be emptied. Now they were ready to experience more of what falling in love was meant to be. Would this be possible day after day, year after year, once their counseling sessions were over? Only as they continued to tap into the power to practice true intimacy. There would be other times of reflecting on newly remembered or experienced hurts, and receiving the blessing of a partner's comfort as they continued discovering who they really were and could be—in Christ.

# 13

# Understand Who You Are

HAS THIS EVER happened to you?

You wake in the middle of a deep, dark night, your mind still dream-fuzzy. Lying stone-still, you stare into shadows, listening to your mate's steady breathing beside you. Your own heartbeat blends with his or her rhythm; your chests rise, then fall with a clockwork precision. Through the window, moon glow spills across the planes and angles of that familiar face. You know those sleep sounds as well as you know your own voice.

You have shared your being and your bed with this person, your mate, for so many years your lives are entwined like vines spreading over a garden wall. Little evidence remains of the separate selves you once were. As the Bible describes, you are one.

And yet . . .

And yet, in the razor-sharp moments of clarity that stab your mind in the middle of a deep, dark night, you know with an aching certainty that you don't know this person at all.

And worse, your mate really doesn't know you.

Greg and Ellen were like that. On the morning of their twenty-fifth wedding anniversary, she rolled over in bed and studied his slumbering form—the athletic torso softened and rounded a bit with age, the thickening jowls and graying temples, and in his face the childlike, unguarded expression of sleep. But she knew, without consciously forming the thought, that when he awoke the scowling mask would be back in place and he'd resurrect his usual defenses like a shield. Keeping her out. Locking himself in. It was a familiar, bitter stalemate. They had spent years relentlessly sharpening their adversarial skills until they had their roles as worthy opponents down pat.

And while their two children planned a gala anniversary party to celebrate their twenty-five years together, no one guessed how often the idea of divorce loomed in their minds.

Or did people guess? Ellen could never be sure how well they hid their true feelings from family and friends. Did their children sense how long ago adoration had turned to animosity? What irony! The qualities they had loved most about each other were now the traits they most despised.

If anyone bothered to ask Ellen what went wrong—which no one did—she would probably only shrug and shake her head. Yes, a great deal was going on in her marriage, but most of it was beneath the surface, beyond words. Surely no mere words could capture and contain the complexity of feeling, the geysers of anger, and the whirl-pools of pain she experienced, living with Greg. And by Greg's si-lences and sullen expressions, one would guess his pain went as deep as Ellen's.

Let's imagine we're able to tap into their minds and hear their stories in their own words. What might we hear?

Ellen might tell us, "Greg was the most romantic guy in the world when we were dating. We met at the end of the hippie movement in the late sixties, and Greg called me his little 'flower child.' He liked it that I was different from other girls, not all caught up in my looks and clothes and money. He said I intrigued him. I was such a free spirit—this elfin girl with love beads and waist-length hair, full of the protests and causes of the Woodstock generation—while he was this down-to-earth, Ivy League guy who didn't want to ruffle anybody's feathers. He liked it that I could talk to anybody anytime anywhere and never run out of things to say, while he got tongue-tied giving a waitress his order. He thought it was great that I was involved in so many causes . . . saving the seals, the earth, the environment, what-ever. He said I had a heart of gold, and he made me feel so wonder-ful, so appreciated. It was as if he saw all these special things inside me no one else took time to notice.

"We were magic together . . . until after the wedding. Then for no reason at all Greg did a complete turnaround. All he could think about was transforming me into a carbon copy of himself. Well, no way! One of him is more than enough for this world."

And what would Greg say if he were invited to speak his mind?

In a somber voice, with his brows knitted together over troubled eyes, he might reply, "Ellen and I have been at cross purposes for our entire marriage. It's like she's frozen in time—the same little featherbrain she was when we dated. Sure, it was cute then to see her in her crazy outfits trumpeting a new cause every week. And I admit I admired her spontaneity and exuberance. She has a real gift for gab, while I get uptight about making small talk. Trouble is, since the day we got married she hasn't shut up. If I ever had anything to say, I've long since forgotten what it was.

"She knew when she married me I was serious about carving out a solid career for myself. Back then she said she admired my determination and confidence. She liked a man who was going places, and she wanted to go with me. But after the wedding she decided I was inflexible, cocky, and self-centered, and we've been going in opposite directions ever since. While I've tried to give our family some stability, she's out taking up everybody's cause except mine. She's a patsy for every wheeler-dealer who comes along. We've tried marriage conferences and romantic vacations to rekindle the marital flame, but let's face it: You can't start a fire without a spark. All the warmth I ever felt for Ellen has turned to ice. And with the cold shoulder she gives me, I know she feels the same."

It doesn't take a psychologist to see that Greg and Ellen have major problems in their marriage. They're both consumed with what they think they should *get* from their partner, not on what they have to *offer* each other. They're like ticks on a dog, with the disastrous attitude, "I'm here to take from you." But, as author Larry Crabb would describe it, what we find in such a marriage is that we have *two ticks and no dog!*[1]

For all of us, our only hope for a truly successful marriage lies outside ourselves and beyond our limited human resources. We can't do it alone. You see, to sustain a genuinely intimate relationship, we would need an unending source of love, acceptance, comfort, and forgiveness. None of us can manage that on our own. But there's good news. Such a source is available. His name is Jesus . . . and He calls His divine contribution *grace*.[2]

## GRACE, THE POWER BEHIND TRUE INTIMACY

Let's explore more fully how you can experience God's grace in your relationship. By doing so you can enjoy an abundance that goes beyond what you could possibly think of or ask for (John 10:10, Eph. 3:20).

God's grace is often described as *manifold*, meaning "many-sided." This word might describe a beautiful, multifaceted diamond—the more points to the diamond, the more its value. So it is with God's grace. The many aspects, or sides, define a rare and beautiful gift the Father has given to His children as part of their inheritance as joint heirs with Christ (Rom. 8:17).

As we think about our own intimacy needs, we begin to see a clearer picture of God's grace. He has met our needs for acceptance, comfort, forgiveness, and love. And because He loves us He also extends to us admonition, exhortation, encouragement, and rebuke. Each is a facet of His manifold grace.

Tragically, stewardship is most often thought of only in terms of money. In reality it's the blessing of God's multifaceted grace that cries out for our own stewardship. Since we've received an acceptance that's unconditional and permanent, stewardship prompts us to *accept others*, such as our spouse and children, as we've been accepted by Christ (Rom. 15:7). More and more we come to see that many of our relationship problems are rooted not in a lack of God's provision but in our own poor stewardship. As joyful stewards we need never lose the grateful wonder that we've been undeserving recipients of God's marvelous grace.

When David Ferguson shared these concepts with Jimmy and Marla Carlton, Jimmy admitted he still didn't know God very well; God was like a faceless grandfather in the sky. "This stuff you're saying blows my mind. I can't figure why God would deliberately become a man and put Himself in a position of being ridiculed, rejected, and murdered. It doesn't make sense."

"Because He loves us," said Marla. "We couldn't go to Him, so He came to us. He entered our world to show us His love."

Jimmy was silent a moment, thinking. "I always had this feeling—like something was missing in here." He tapped his chest. "I figured someday I'd stumble onto something that would fill that empty place, give me peace. I can't keep fighting it. I think this is it."

"A God-shaped vacuum exists in every heart," David reminded him. "No substitute can fill it. People try to force everything else under the sun into that space—fame, fortune, careers, power, or pleasures—but nothing else fits. Only Christ will do."

"You're talking about this 'born again' thing, right?"

"To be born again is to experience intimacy with our Creator. Since the Fall in the Garden of Eden human beings have had a hunger for intimacy with God. We may not always recognize it, but it's there. When we receive Christ as our Savior, He fills the emptiness and we begin experiencing the intimacy with God that was severed by Adam's sin."

"And somehow this all ties back to our marriage," said Jimmy, looking at Marla. "I can't love her the right way until I know God's love. I guess I've been realizing that more all the time."

"That's right, Jimmy," David agreed. "Marriage without God is a closed system that's destined to collapse, with two bankrupt partners both taking from the other. Each partner has only a limited and flawed supply of love, mercy, and forgiveness to give; when it's gone, so is he or she. In fact, codependency describes just such a 'taking' system—two people overwhelmed with their own neediness, each trying desperately to take from the other. If one gets tired of being taken from, he or she leaves the relationship and finds a new victim.

"The only real solution is an open system, where we tap into God's unlimited supply—God is the God of all comfort, God is love, God is rich in mercy—and we share from His abundance with our spouse. And as God forgives us, we forgive each other."

"That has to be better than the way we were living," said Jimmy, "always blaming and criticizing each other. But I gotta admit, it still sounds too good to be true. Is it really possible to live that way?"

"Good question, Jimmy. Let's find some answers. Just as Joshua declared, 'As for me and my house, we will serve the LORD' (Josh. 24:15), we agree it's a worthy intention. But turning the intention into reality is the challenge—for all of us. Sometimes we get bogged down by people trying to shame us into living our good intentions. They'll say, 'If you really wanted to do better, you would' or 'If you really loved me, you'd act like it.' Those shame games never work."

"That's for sure," said Marla. "I tried them all on Jimmy."

"The message here is, 'confront and exhort my behavior and attitudes, but don't judge my intentions and motives.' There's a better way to empower good intentions."

"I'd sure like to hear it," said Jimmy.

"Remember Joshua's bold declaration to serve the Lord? He was obviously secure in who he was, in what mattered in life, and in who he intended to please. He showed a healthy indifference to what others did; he was free from peer pressure; and he was certainly not codependent—basing his actions and attitudes on the approval of other people!

"Insecurity, fear, and low self-esteem are at the root of countless marriage struggles," David noted. "People get so busy searching in others for their identities they never discover who they really are. They wander in confusion, tossed to and fro."

"Like feathers in the wind," mused Marla, waxing poetic.

"Feathers, smeathers! You said we'd find some answers," urged Jimmy, sounding a trifle impatient. "What's the bottom line?"

"Here's your 'bottom-line' answer," said David. "The life we live in Christ Jesus gives us a secure identity. He tells us who we are, where we're going, and how we're to live. That's the foundation for our lives—and for marriage intimacy."

## WHO ARE YOU?

"The Bible is like a mirror," said David. "It reflects who you really are, not just who you think you are."

"That's not exactly comforting," said Marla. "Sometimes I look in the mirror and think, *Ah, the ol' girl don't look so bad.* Other times

I look in the mirror and cringe. I'm afraid I don't think of a mirror as my friend."

"Really?" mused Jimmy with a wink. "The time you spend looking in it, I'd have figured a mirror was your best friend."

Marla gave him a playful nudge with her elbow. "And just when I thought you were doing so well in therapy, Sweetheart!"

David signaled a truce to their little repartee. "What you need to keep in mind, Jimmy and Marla, is that, humanly speaking, the way you see yourselves is subject to the whims of emotion and circumstance. Sometimes you think you're okay; other times you may feel like the scum of the earth. The way you define who you are is so subjective you can never depend on it."

Marla nodded. "I see what you mean. If someone looks at me cross-eyed or criticizes something I do, I start downgrading myself. Pretty soon I generalize the feeling to cover everything about myself, and I end up feeling worthless and depressed."

"Right," said David. "That's what most of us do, because our self-perception is always changing. One day we're up; another day, we're down. So you see, security comes when you see yourself through the mirror of a truthful, unchanging standard."

"You mean the Bible?" said Jimmy.

"Exactly. You can trust what it tells you about yourself."

Jimmy sat forward, eying David intently. "Okay, Doc. Just who does it say I am?"

## Scripture Tells You:

*You are* one who was especially fashioned by God, your Creator; You are a unique individual with special gifts and talents (Ps. 139:13–14).

*You were* someone who was separated from your Creator by your independent nature and sinful choices (Rom. 5:8).

*You have become* a new person in Christ as you acknowledged your sin and your helplessness and in simple faith received Him; His divine nature now prompts Christ-like living in you (2 Cor. 5:17).

*You begin* this new life as a spiritual babe; you need the nourishment of God's Word (1 Pet. 2:2).

*You have become* a vital participant in God's plan for this world, an ambassador for Christ, an extension of His presence, an expression of His character (John 15:5).

## WHERE ARE YOU GOING?

"Okay," said Jimmy, "I get the idea of who I am, but where am I heading with all this? I have to make dozens of choices every day. How do I know I'm making the right ones?"

Marla smiled. "In other words, what's our destiny, Doc?"

"I can't tell you that, but I can assure you the Word of God will shed a light on your pathway. Take a look at Psalm 119:105. The brevity of life calls for priorities that can stand the test of time; your decisions will impact the present and shape your future. God knows that. He won't let you wander alone in the darkness of confusion."

### Scripture Tells You:

*You are prompted from within* by God's Spirit to seek Him in His Word and to live out what He teaches (Ps. 119:2).

*You live in a troubled world* where man's independent nature strives against God; God's Word guides you through your daily temptation and tribulation (Ps. 119:9).

*You can be "adequate"* to deal with every life situation as His Word teaches and trains you; adequacy removes fear and insecurity (2 Tim. 3:16–17).

*You're being conformed* into Christ's likeness as His Spirit works in you (Rom. 8:29).

*You will forever* be God's child; having been made an heir of His and declared a saint, you're securely headed toward heaven (Rom. 8:17).

## HOW DO YOU LIVE?

"All right, so if I'm a Christian I'm eventually going to heaven," said Jimmy. "Terrific! But how do I live in the nitty-gritty here and now? I need help with the basics. Sure, Marla and I are doing better these days. We should. We're in therapy. But what about when we're on our own again? Is God really going to be around then? Is He going to help me understand my wife? Is He going to help her put up with me? I still have lots of questions. How do we train our children? How do I handle my dad's rejection? It's easy to know *what* I want to do, but not *how* to do it."

"Let's go back to Psalm 119:105, 'Your word is a lamp to my feet,' " said David. "The Bible not only lights your way, it guides your steps. That's the truth. But to discover it for yourself, you'll have to put it into practice in your daily life."

## Scripture Tells You:

*You experience* a deep gratefulness and gain valuable insights as you consider God's handiwork—the wonders of creation and the miracle of human life (Ps. 111:2).

*You can receive nourishment* from God's Word to motivate and direct your living (Matt. 4:4).

*You can separate yourself*—your thoughts, values, attitudes, and actions—from the world's ways as you yield to Christ's Spirit within you (2 Cor. 6:17).

*You can share* in the life of Christ—His living His life through you in this world—as you embrace the truth of His Word (John 20:31).

*You experience* an inexpressible joy and excitement in seeing yourself on a divine mission, extending Christ's presence and message into your world (2 Cor. 5:20).

"Jimmy, not only do we have the Scriptures to light our way in the darkness," said David. "We also have Christ Himself as a source of light. Remember what I said about His experiencing all our humanness, yet without sin? As I come to know Him, I come to know myself. He was the divine 'man' through the incarnation. He identifies with my humanity, and through His resurrection I can partake of His divine life.

"The Creator of the universe said about Jesus, 'This is My beloved Son, in whom I am well pleased' (Matt. 3:17). Because we have our identity in Christ, God says the same thing about us: 'You are my beloved child in whom I am well pleased!' Even in our pains, temptations, and trials, Christ identifies with us and sympathizes with our struggles. We're not alone! Whenever we wish, we can approach God's throne with boldness and receive mercy and grace. Hebrews 4:16 tells us so. What better security could we have than that?"

"I just don't know," said Jimmy, rubbing his chin thoughtfully. "Isn't the Christian life filled with an awful lot of rules and regulations? I'm a carefree sort of guy. I hate to get bogged down in a long list of dos and don'ts."

"As with any relationship, Jimmy, intimacy develops through caring encounters with your loved one. It's the same way with Christ. Some Christians become so obsessed with religious rituals and routines they forget the reason behind the practices. It's a shame we turn privilege and opportunity into obligation and duty. We sternly tell Christians you must pray, read your Bible, and go to church every Sunday when what we should be saying is, 'As a Christian you have the opportunity to share yourself transparently with God, get to know Him intimately through His Word, and share His love with others in the body of Christ. You also have the privilege of being His representative and offering His love to a hungering, needy world.' What more can we ask for? We have *security* in being personally acquainted with God and a special *identity* in knowing we're the object of His love."

"We're back to what you said in the beginning," said Jimmy. "I need to know Christ and what He did for me—how He came to earth as a man and suffered and died—"

"And how He rose from the dead. Don't forget the power of His resurrection and what that means for you today," said David. "When you know Christ as your Lord, Savior, and sympathetic Friend, you have the power of His Holy Spirit to depend on in every area of your life, including your home and family."

Jimmy Carlton was thinking about everything they'd talked about; David could almost see the little wheels turning in his brain. Jimmy wasn't the sort of man to jump impulsively on anybody's bandwagon, and David wasn't about to push him into decisions he wasn't ready to make.

After a minute he crossed his long legs and wiped a streak of dirt off the toe of his cowboy boot. Then he sat back expansively and spread his elbows over the arms of the chair. "Okay," he said matter-of-factly. "I'm ready."

"Ready for what?" asked Marla.

"I'm ready to accept this Jesus of yours into my life."

"I'd be glad to pray with you," David offered.

"Okay, let me just say something first," said Jimmy, sitting forward now and speaking confidentially. "I'm sure you know I didn't want to come here in the first place. I never figured I'd be looking for answers from a shrink. It's no secret Marla dragged me here kicking and screaming. I came because my marriage was ready to bust up, and I figured, what've I got to lose?

"Well, now Marla and I are getting things patched up pretty good. Not that I'll ever understand women, but I sure understand Marla a lot better than I ever did before. So we did good coming here. I think we're going to make it okay.

"But what I didn't expect was finding out how God plays into all this. Like I said, I figured if God was around at all, He was just a big old granddaddy in the sky, a glorified Santa. I never took Him seriously, and I never knew He took me seriously—until now."

Jimmy's voice softened. "You know, you can ignore a God who sits in some ivory tower off somewhere in the clouds, a God who pays you no mind, who's off polishing harps or counting angels on a pin-head.

"But I can't ignore a God who became a flesh-and-blood man and walked in my shoes, who let Himself be spit on and nailed naked to a cross and murdered for me. If He'd come to this earth only as God and gone through the motions but stayed above it all—you know, 'I'm here and I'm God and I'm going to save you but don't think you can touch Me because I'm insulated from you.' But He didn't do that. He made Himself as vulnerable as any of us; He let Himself feel all the raunchy stuff we all feel—the pain, the wretched loneliness, the bitter disappointment.   I can't ignore that. I want a God like that in my life."

Jimmy put his face in his large hands and began weeping quietly.

Marla leaned over and put her arms around her husband and they held each other for a long moment.

Once Jimmy accepted Christ into his life, David encouraged him to seek fellowship within the body of Christ. Marla was already a Christian and attended church sporadically, but now she, too, was eager to pursue righteousness, faith, love, and peace with those who call on the Lord with a pure heart (2 Tim. 2:22).

David challenged the Carltons to think of themselves as Christlike reflections and walk as children of the Light (Eph. 5:8), to prevent the darkness of sin from overtaking them (John 12:34-35). He pointed out that just as the Bible and Christ Himself are the Light in a needy world, so they, too, reflecting His glory, "are the light of the world" (Matt. 5:14) as they show His compassion and concern for others.

"But don't underestimate the importance of fellowship with other Christians," David reminded them. "You'll be encouraged to see how God is at work in their lives just as they'll be encouraged to see God at work in you. There's no greater feeling of joy than knowing God has used you to bless someone else's life or bring someone to Him."

David closed the session by talking about gratitude and its importance in the believer's life. "Gratefulness to God is an important element of worship. It's amazing how quickly you can slip out of an 'attitude of gratitude' into a complaining, critical spirit. But as long as you resolve to keep a grateful heart, you won't find yourselves constantly complaining. Somehow, you just can't be grateful and negative or grateful and judgmental at the same time—thank God!"

David suggested that Jimmy and Marla might want to start a "journal of gratefulness" as an ongoing family project. Each page would include the date, the family member who had been blessed, how he or she had been blessed, and how that person had shared his or her appreciation. "Naming your blessings and expressing appreciation helps seal the reality of the blessing in your heart and gives you a chance to bless others," David told them.

Marla liked the idea. "It's a terrific way to help Jeffy and Anna see how God is working in our home. In fact, I've already got a long list of blessings to write down, starting with Jimmy coming to Jesus!"

Your family may want to start its own journal of gratefulness. Use the sample format below to get yourselves started.

| Date | Family Member | How We've Been Blessed | How We Shared Our Appreciation |
|------|---------------|------------------------|-------------------------------|
|      |               | *Look for God's interventions, expressions of family member's love, answered prayers, and special people, events, blessings, and happenings.* | *Say thanks.* *Write a note.* *Take a gift.* *Give testimony.* |

# Practice Intimacy Disciplines

WHEN DAVID FERGUSON married Teresa at age sixteen he had no idea what a husband did to please his wife. "I just figured you did what my dad did, which was to buy her things and take her places. That's how you pleased 'the little woman.'"

If you'd asked Teresa how a wife showed her husband she loved him, she would have said, "You cook for him. That's what my mother did for my dad. She had dinner ready every day at 5:00 P.M. sharp."

So when they married, Teresa buried herself in the kitchen cooking, setting dinner on the table at 5:00 P.M., even though David was never there until 7:00. Meanwhile, David obsessively bought Teresa things she didn't want and took her places she didn't care to go. Neither of them appreciated what the other was doing because it wasn't what he or she needed.

To make matters worse, David and Teresa came from entirely different backgrounds. "I came from a small family," said David, "just my folks, my brother, and myself. And Mother was very affectionate, always hugging us and expressing her love. So when I got married, the only role model of a woman I'd seen was someone who hugged you, kissed you, and told you she loved you. I thought that's what women did.

"But Teresa came from a very large family and never saw Mom and Dad hug or express their love. So she didn't spontaneously express her love either.

"For years I hid the fact that it bothered me she wasn't more demonstrative and affectionate, until finally I exploded and said,

'Teresa, you treat the dog better than you do me!' And we didn't even have a dog! Naturally, my attack didn't motivate Teresa to be more affectionate. Just the opposite!

"Throughout the early years of our marriage, Teresa and I were on a treadmill, trying to whip each other into shape. It seemed logical; if we didn't keep the pressure on, the other one might never change. How wrong we were! Instead of positive changes, our efforts brought only bondage. Neither of us was free to be ourself or change the things that needed changing."

Like many couples, David and Teresa were on a crash course to destruction, each selfishly taking from the other until their marriage was ready to collapse. But God had a better plan. He showed them true love is an unconditional commitment to an imperfect person, and marriage is to be a living example and testimony of Himself. Their marriage flourished as they made these vows to each other:

> My darling,
> I will trust God to direct and change you.
> I will make it my priority to meet your needs.
> I will empathize with and help heal your hurts.
> I will share the truth of my needs with you in love.
> I will share the truth of my hurts with you in love.
> I will treat the truth you share with me
>     confidentially, as *our* truth.

Out of their own hard-won trials and experiences, David and Teresa Ferguson and Chris and Holly Thurman have developed the principles of Intimacy Therapy they've shared in this book. We've talked about the ingredients of intimacy. Now we will look at the disciplines necessary to keep intimacy alive in your marriage.

You may be asking, "How do my spouse and I turn lofty principles and 'disciplines' into natural habits of thinking and behaving in our daily lives?"

To illustrate we'll show you how Jimmy and Marla Carlton implemented intimacy disciplines into their lifestyle. At first, they were both concerned their renewed closeness might be just a fluke. "How do we know we won't revert to our old selves once we stop seeing a counselor?" Marla asked.

"Because Intimacy Therapy has a divine basis in Scripture," David reminded her. "I'm not making up these principles off the top of my head. I'm drawing from God's master plan. He has a stake in your marriage. He wants it to honor Him and be a living example of His love to the world. His Spirit within you will enable you to love each other with His own unconditional love. The power comes from Him and His Word."

Jimmy nodded. "That makes sense. But what about these intimacy disciplines you mentioned? *Discipline* sounds a little heavy and, uh, distasteful. My dad was big on discipline. It conjures up images of rigid rules and toeing the mark and orders like, 'snap to, boy!' It's not one of my favorite words."

"Don't worry, Jimmy," David assured him. "The disciplines I'm talking about are simply practical ways of keeping your marriage on track, of turning temporary behaviors into permanent habits to last you over the long haul. These disciplines are tools you can use to encourage spiritual intimacy, friendship intimacy . . . and affection and sexual intimacy."

"This is sounding better all the time," said Jimmy.

"Let's look at them one by one," David suggested.

Jimmy grinned. "How about sexual intimacy first?"

"I thought we might start with spiritual intimacy," David said with a smile.

Jimmy shrugged. "So we'll save the best for last, huh?"

Marla nudged Jimmy. "Honey, if we get these disciplines down pat, it'll *all* be the best."

He reached for her hand. "So what are we waiting for?"

## DISCIPLINES TO ENCOURAGE SPIRITUAL INTIMACY

"You can't foster real spiritual intimacy until you've developed the confession/forgiveness habit," David reminded the Carltons. "We've already talked about the importance of apologizing as you realize you've hurt each other. And if you don't realize you've hurt your spouse, he or she will lovingly let you know, so you can apologize. This beats hiding your hurt or hurling attacks. A habit of confessing and forgiving will keep the sun from going down on your anger, hindering your closeness."

"But is that the same as spiritual intimacy?" asked Marla.

David turned the question back to her. "What do you think?"

"I think having a good sex life and being good friends is a lot easier to pin down than being 'spiritual' with your mate. Even though Jimmy's a Christian now, we still feel self-conscious talking about God or praying together."

"Ideally, spiritual closeness comes from two individuals each getting closer to God, only to find they feel closer to each other as well."

"So where do we start?"

## Couple Prayer Times . . . Begin Silently

"Jimmy and Marla, did you ever stop to think that prayer is the greatest untapped source of power in the world? Yet surveys often find fewer than 15 percent of church-going couples pray together. Still, it's one of the best ways I know to draw you closer spiritually," David said.

"Whoa! I'm just beginning to get the hang of this God business," Jimmy protested. "I wouldn't know what to say, and I sure as shootin' can't pray like the preacher. Or even like Marla. And believe me, she'll let me know if I sound dumb."

"Hold on, Jimmy," said David. "I was about to suggest the two of you pray together *silently* at first."

"How? Just sit down and close my eyes? Marla'll think I'm nodding off. It doesn't sound natural to me."

"But you can make it a natural part of your time together. Spend a few minutes talking about things that matter—family concerns, hopes, dreams, or fears. Or maybe your kids, work, money, feelings, or future events. Then, Jimmy, you take the initiative and reach for Marla's hand; bow your head, and the two of you pray silently for a short two or three minutes. If you become comfortable praying aloud, fine; if not, that's fine too. After you've prayed you'll sense a new closeness; when you're on your knees together the masks fall off and you're more open and vulnerable. In fact, praying together will likely lead you to greater emotional and physical intimacy as well."

"Okay, if we pray aloud how do we know what to say?"

"Start with short conversational prayers, speaking just as you would to a close friend. Pray for specific things. And be brief. Long, pious prayers can become drudgery."

"It sounds almost too easy," said Jimmy. "There must be more to it than that. We're talking about talking to God!"

"Well," David noted, "prayer does usually include adoration, confession, thanksgiving, supplication, and petition."

"I knew it!" Jimmy exclaimed. "It's as complicated as a jigsaw puzzle with half the pieces missing!"

"Not at all," David assured him. "Those are just big words for praising and thanking God, confessing your sins, and asking for the things you and others need. And remember the promise of Matthew 18:19, that if two agree on earth about anything they ask for, it shall be done for them by our Father in heaven. There's no more powerful 'two' praying than a husband and wife who, in God's eyes, are already one!"

"What else do we need to do to develop spiritual intimacy?"

### Devotional Life of Scripture Study, Memorization, Meditation, Using God's Word as the Foundation for Spiritual Oneness

David asked Jimmy and Marla to read John 21:15–17, where Jesus speaks to Peter about feeding lambs and sheep within the body of Christ. "Did you notice that the lambs are fed 'predigested' food as the mother provides them with milk? Mature sheep feed themselves with solid food. Spiritual food works the same way. We receive 'predigested' truth from preachers and teachers, but it's still 'milk.' It stimulates our growth so we can feed ourselves by studying the Bible on our own."

Jimmy looked a bit skeptical. "You make it sound like Bible study is an absolute necessity. Is it really that important?"

"Let's see what God says about that, Jimmy. Second Timothy 3:16–17 tells us all Scripture is inspired by God and profitable for 'doctrine, for reproof, for correction, for instruction in righteous-ness, that the man of God may be complete, thoroughly equipped for every good work.' That covers a lot of territory, doesn't it?''

"Sure does," Jimmy admitted. "How does it do all that? Does it happen just by reading a few verses every day?"

"We can maximize the Bible's impact on our lives in five ways: *Hear* the Word from others; *read, study,* and *memorize* it on our own; and *meditate* on it. Check out Joshua 1:8, Acts 17:11, Revelation 1:3, Romans 10:17, and Psalm 119:9. They'll tell you the same thing."

"To tell you the truth," said Marla, "for a gal whose main reading diet is recipes, dime novels, and women's magazines, I feel a little intimidated by the Bible. I haven't even been to junior college like Jimmy. I'll give it a try because I know I should, but I'm not sure how much I'll get out of it."

David assured Marla she wasn't alone in her feelings. "Many peo-ple jump in cold and quickly get discouraged when they don't un-derstand what they're reading. The secret is to be prepared. Have the right equipment—study tools such as a concordance or Bible dic-tionary, and an accurate but easy-to-read translation, such as the New King James or the New American Standard or the New Interna-tional Version."

"Okay, so we escape all those *thees* and *thous,*" said Jimmy. "But where do we start?"

David suggested Jimmy and Marla take any passage of Scripture that interested them and follow this sequence:

**Hear** what the author has on his heart as you put yourself in the situation, time, and setting of the original "hearer." Be aware of who the author is, when he wrote the passage, to whom he was writing, and for what purpose.

**Read** the passage *for what it says.* Observe and write down impor-tant ideas you want to remember.

**Study** what the passage *means* and what it *means to you*—two steps involving *interpretation* and *application.* A Scripture will usually have only one interpretation but many applications as the Holy Spirit min-isters the truth to individual hearts.

**Memorize** key verses or an entire passage, hiding God's Word in your heart *that you might not sin* (Ps. 119:9) and that in *whatever you do, you may prosper* (Ps. 1:1-3).

**Meditate** on these memorized passages, turning them over in your mind and visualizing key truths in word pictures so God may bring forth *the mind of Christ* (1 Cor. 2:16) and have victory in your thought life (2 Cor. 10:3-5).

"I'm not so good at memorizing things," said Marla, twisting a strand of red hair around her index finger. "In school it was all I could do to remember the names of presidents and history dates."

"Same here," said Jimmy. "Although, come to think of it, I wasn't so bad with dates. In fact, I *made* a little history!"

"Jimmy, be serious!"

"I *am!*"

"If you're interested, I have some suggestions to help you develop a *Scripture memory program*," said David.

"We've come this far," said Jimmy. "No sense turning back now."

"Good attitude. Start by choosing a consistent time every day to memorize."

"Every day?"

"If possible. Early in the morning or late at night will probably be your best time."

"Early for Marla, late for me," said Jimmy. "I'm a night owl; she's an early bird."

"Maybe we can compromise—early one week, late the next."

"Once you've settled on a time, look up the verse and read it in context for clearer understanding. Read the reference and verse several times, then memorize it by phrases."

"That's it? Sounds easy enough."

"Not quite. Write the verse down from memory and check yourself to be sure it's letter perfect."

"Aha, the real test! Have I memorized or not memorized!"

"Don't try to overdo it. Two to five verses a week is a good pace; it takes several days or even weeks to really memorize one. Then the key is to *review*. Use 'wasted' time while driving, waiting, or walking, but keep going over the verses until they're permanently lodged in your mind and heart."

"Earlier you mentioned meditation," said Marla. "I know you don't mean the kind they do in New Age religions. But I'm not sure how you meditate on the Bible."

"I can tell you in three words—*memorize, personalize, and visualize.* Memorize passages that speak directly to needs in your life; personalize the verses by adding pronouns to express your own desires and emotions. God delights in hearing His own Word repeated in our prayers, especially when it's spoken out of our deepest feelings. Finally, visualize His Word by building mental pictures of God's truth. Dwelling on these scriptural pictures will help give you victory in your thought life."

"Victory in my thought life?" echoed Jimmy. "Now that's something I could use."

"You start with your thoughts. Welcome them as opportunities to be tested, exposing them to God's Word and claiming specific principles and promises. Cast down wrong thoughts, focusing instead on 'victorious' Scriptures. Learn to turn your thoughts into conversations with God. You'll begin to realize the real temptation is not wrong thoughts but the desire to think independently of God. You might want to study several excellent verses on this subject—James 1:2, Romans 12:2, and 2 Corinthians 10:4-5."

Jimmy looked over at Marla. "Babe, all this talk about God helping us and all, my head is swimming! How about yours?"

She laughed easily. "I feel free as the wind, Jimmy. Think of it! We're not alone anymore. No more stumbling in the dark or muddling through the mess!"

Jimmy rocked back in his chair. "Man, oh man! Who would have thought Jimmy and Marla Carlton would be on a first-name basis with the Almighty!" He blinked back sudden tears. "I don't usually get choked up about things—just ask Marla—"

"Right. He used to be Mr. Rock of Gibraltar—the great stone face with the emotions to match—"

"But I gotta say—" Jimmy paused, composing himself.

Marla reached over and took his hand. "Go on, Honey."

"I told you before about my dad, how I never could talk to him, never felt he had time to talk to me. But now I've got a new Daddy and He wants me to share everything with Him, no holds barred. That kinda blows my mind—a great big Holy God wanting to know my little itty-bitty thoughts. I got me a whole lifetime of thoughts to share with Him—and with you, too, Marla."

"Same here, Jimmy. I want us to be . . . best friends!"

"I'm glad you feel that way," said David, "because that brings us to the second set of disciplines—those that will help you become intimate best friends.

## DISCIPLINES TO ENCOURAGE FRIENDSHIP INTIMACY

### Marriage "Staff Meetings"

Have you ever tried holding a marriage staff meeting with your spouse? Companies, corporations, and all sorts of organizations hold staff meetings to air concerns, solve problems, and review new ideas to keep the company healthy and on the cutting edge. Doing the same thing in your home can help you keep your marriage fresh and up to date and your communication lively and productive. Use some of the following questions and comments in your staff meetings to deepen intimate communication with your mate.

1. Since it's important to feel accepted unconditionally rather than feel you're "on trial," how can I better communicate my unconditional love to you?

2. You know I love you, and I want you to feel it too. What are some seemingly little things I can do to really make you feel more loved?

3. How can I better communicate to you the positive aspects of our marriage?

4. I've just recently been reminded of how much I appreciate you for _____ (identify an important character quality such as sensitivity, diligence, loyalty, truthfulness, etc.). A recent time

I was reminded of this was when you _____ (cite a specific memory that was special to you).

5. What are some things you've been concerned or worried about lately? I'd like to work toward helping to eliminate them.

6. What should I do next time I'm about to become irritated with you over _____?

Take turns with your answers. And keep in mind that while these questions promote intimacy they also expose vulnerabilities, so be careful not to let your responses inflict wounds. At all costs avoid being negative or critical! Typical responses might include:

- I really feel good when you remember to call and just say you love me.
- I'm looking forward to the time when you're more comfortable initiating affection. That will really mean a lot to me.
- It would mean so much to me if I could hear you express your appreciation in words.

## Scheduling Time

"Becoming intimate best friends requires time—one of the commodities most often lacking in our chaotic, fast-paced world," David Ferguson told the Carltons when he first suggested marriage staff meetings to them. "But the external pressures of work, carpools, child rearing, and checkbooks don't have to take their toll on closeness if couples join forces to manage family events before they 'manage' you."

"What kind of time are we talking about?" asked Jimmy.

"Are you wondering how *little* you can get by with or how *much?*" asked Marla with a wry little smile.

"How *much*, Sweets, naturally!"

"I suggest setting aside about two hours each week to get together and talk. Schedule a time; don't leave it to chance."

"When is the best time?" asked Marla.

"Whatever fits your schedule: lunch on Thursday, Tuesday night after the children are asleep, Saturday-morning breakfast. Or if the time has to change each week, schedule it routinely each Sunday evening. The key is to give the time you've scheduled your top priority. It'll encourage your mate. I know one wife who cried with joy when her husband remembered their staff meeting and turned down a golf date."

"We should write 'staff meeting' right on our calendar," said Marla. "It sounds so official, who would dare interrupt?"

"That's a good point, Marla. You'll want to protect your time together from interruptions and distractions, so try to meet somewhere away from home and office, or in a quiet place at home without phones or visitors, if possible."

"I hate to say this," said Jimmy, "but what are we supposed to talk about at these 'staff meetings'?"

Here's a typical agenda David suggested:

### Calendar Coordination.
What's planned for the coming week? What child is going where? Who's working late? What social activities are scheduled? Be sure to plan your next "dates" as a couple and your next family outing. You may even find it of great value to pencil some possible lovemaking times!

### Discuss Family Goals.
Write down your annual goals for your family; then break them down into quarterly or monthly target dates. During staff meetings monitor your progress. For example:

Does the budget look tight this coming week, and how can we all help to set spending limits?

What's our next planned major household expenditure, and how can we all better contribute to bringing it about?

Are our family vacation plans scheduled? Reservations? Itinerary?

Have we decided on new couples whose friendship we want to cultivate this year?

How are our personal goals progressing—reading, diet, exercise, hobbies—and how can we encourage and support one another?

### *Parenting Plans.*

Remember, if you don't present a united front, your kids will divide and conquer! Discuss significant discipline issues, what seems to be working and what doesn't.

Plan family times together plus quality times with each child. Mom and daughter may want to shop; Dad and son may play golf.

Discuss and agree on parenting responsibilities and schedules for the next week or more. In other words, who needs help? Who needs a break without the kids?

What goals seem reasonable for your child this quarter in the areas of behavior, attitude, and responsibilities, and how can you work together to achieve them?

### *Listening Times.*

One or the other may just need to talk:

Sharing stresses at work or with friendships,
Sharing hopes and dreams,
Sharing feelings and insights about recent moodiness,
Sharing concerns and fears about family, money, the future.

Remember, you can't argue when one is sharing and the other is listening. Give undivided attention, empathy, support, and eye contact.

### *Productive "Criticism."*

Lovingly share hopes for the future. Avoid "you" statements and generalities such as, "You never spend any time with me" or "You always take the kids' side against me." Use "I" and "me" statements with specifics, speaking positively: "I sure miss being alone together and hope we can plan a date together soon" or "It would mean a lot to me if we could stay in agreement in front of the kids and discuss our differences privately."

### *Appreciation.*

Show appreciation for who your spouse is and what he or she has done. Use your weekly staff meeting as a reminder that your partner is a blessing to you. Focus on his or her good qualities and express your gratitude: "Thanks for your help with the kids this week" or

"I appreciate the way you got things done around the house" or "Thanks for cheering me up when I was down."

## GOAL SETTING . . . WITHOUT A VISION, FAMILIES PERISH

"We don't seem to be getting anywhere! I don't think we're accomplishing anything!" Marriage counselors often hear complaints like this. They can usually be traced to a deeper concern. People have no idea where they're going or where their marriages or families are headed, so they have no idea whether they've arrived.[1]

The Hebrew word translated *perish* in Proverbs 29:18 in the King James Version of the Bible is also translated "go unrestrained . . . each to his own way." What a tragic but fitting description for many marriages and families. Husbands and wives frantically pursue their own crowded agendas; children are left to fend for themselves or, at the other extreme, are overextended in their own busy but barren existence.

Family time consists of watching an occasional TV program together. Meals together are a rarity. Parent-child interactions spell conflict rather than quality time. Family members go through the motions in quiet desperation, wondering why life seems so empty—all signs of a family perishing!

King Solomon, the author of Proverbs, was wise indeed when he said, What's needed is a vision, a sense of direction and destiny, a guiding framework around which we can make our decisions with distinct objectives toward which we can stretch. The contrast is clear: perish or flourish; wander aimlessly or reach ahead purposefully.

### Three Key Ingredients in Goal Setting

A goal needs three elements in order to stir one's vision and give purposeful direction:

#### What.
What do you want to see accomplished? Make your goal measurable and observable by being as specific as possible. Don't say

vaguely, "I want to be more spiritual"; say, "I will begin a daily prayer time for my family's needs."

### How.

How will you go about accomplishing your goal? Devise a plan or method that will work for you.

### When.

When will you achieve your goal? If it's a daily or weekly goal, you'll need to allocate time in your schedule. If it's not a recurring goal, set a realistic completion date.

A word of warning! Before you proceed, realize goal setting can be harmful to your health. Consider these "don'ts": *Don't* use goals as a guise to criticize your spouse. *Don't* criticize a mate who's not as excited about goal setting as you are. *Don't* fall into the trap of condemning yourself or others for unfinished goals; instead, adjust your time frame and proceed. Above all, *don't* let goals be a substitute for emotional relationships with God, your partner, and others.

Invite your spouse to join you in answering the exploratory questions below. Then use your answers to guide you in identifying specific goals for your family in the year ahead.

1. In what two key ways would you like to see me grow personally in the next year?

2. How would you most like me to pray for you in the next few months?

3. What recurring concern do you have about each of our children?

4. What is an important area you'd like to see emphasized in our romance?

5. What do you see as two of the most important challenges we face this coming year?

6. What improvements or changes would you most like to see around our home?

## Benefits and Blessings of Goal Setting

Vision is not without cost. You'll have to give generously of your time and energy to accomplish your family goals. You'll have to make sacrifices. But there can be big payoffs in benefits and blessings:

### A Basis for Marriage and Family Oneness.

How can two walk together unless they be agreed (Amos 3:3)? Agreeing on where you're going is essential to oneness in relationships. You may start by agreeing that neither husband nor wife makes a time commitment involving the other without first discussing it. Consider weekly family nights, household-improvement plans, or vacation ideas that encourage "walking together" as a couple or family.

### A Framework for Decision-making.

Life consists of countless pressing decisions—where to invest your time, effort, and money; which activities to participate in; which projects to support. Without established goals, confusion and conflict abound. Simplify your choices by using family goals as a decision-making framework. If saying yes will further accomplish a family goal, then proceed; if not, decline!

### A Reminder of Important Priorities.

"Good" things are the worst enemies of the "best" things. Careers may crowd out home life; materialism can quench eternal priorities. Goal setting reminds us of our accountability to priorities that matter most.

### A Sense of Accomplishment and Security.

Checking off completed items on your "things-to-do" list brings a sense of accomplishment. You have that secure feeling your life isn't haplessly out of control; rather, you've taken charge of your destiny. Marriage and family goals have this same potential, multiplied many times over, for bringing a deep and meaningful sense of accomplishment and security to each family member.

### Example and Witness to Others.

We live in a time of a "leadership vacuum" in every area of life. People are searching desperately for individuals or families who know where they're headed. One of today's best avenues of evangelism and witness is through the goal-directed example of a Christian home with a vision.

## Examples of Positive Goals

You may be saying, "I want to set positive goals for my family, but I'm not sure what realistic, workable goals look like. Can you give me some hints?"

We'll do better than that. We'll divide goals into eight practical categories and list some examples in each area.

### Spiritual

Read through the Bible this year.
Memorize one Scripture verse each week.
Spend thirty minutes daily in devotions.
Listen to teaching tapes on the way to work.

### Family

Establish monthly contact with "distant" relatives.
Eat five meals together at home per week without TV.
Begin weekly family fun nights.
Father take daughter on annual "date."

### Financial

Develop a family budget.
Eliminate all credit-card debt by end of year.
Begin systematic giving to church work.
Draw up a family will.

### Personal/Social

Exercise fifteen minutes each day.
Lose a specific amount of weight.
Learn a foreign language or take piano lessons.
Eliminate one irritating habit.

### Marriage

Participate in a Marriage Enrichment Seminar.
Schedule dates together, alone, twice monthly.
Identify and enjoy two new hobbies or interests.
Praise your spouse at least once each day.

### Household

Purchase a home security system.
Clean out the garage or attic for a garage sale.

Wallpaper the bathrooms and kitchen.
Landscape the backyard.

## Career
Complete an advanced degree in your field.
Reorganize the office for greater efficiency.
Attend a time-management seminar.
Apply for a job transfer or new position.

## Ministry
Volunteer as a Sunday school worker.
Spend a week of vacation doing mission work.
Begin a Bible study at work or at home.
Witness to three family members or friends.

## Emotional Responding

When we ask people to think about the things they know their spouses missed, they give answers such as:

"As I have come to know my husband, I know he missed a close relationship with his dad."

"As I've come to understand my spouse, I can see he's been terribly hurt by his former wife."

"I've come to see that my wife was victimized by her older brother and still carries the emotional scars."

"I realize my spouse desperately missed encouragement and affirmation from her father."

Now, in the privacy of your own thoughts, pinpoint who or what has hurt *your* spouse. What has he or she missed? What scars is he or she still carrying?

Develop the discipline of emotional responding on a daily basis. Life will inevitably bring its ups and downs; when your spouse is down, be there to care! The down time may come from work-related stress, a boss's lack of appreciation, a friend's insensitive remark, or a child's disrespect. Or your mate may feel physically "under the weather." We repeat, whatever the hurt, be there to care!

## DISCIPLINES TO ENCOURAGE AFFECTION AND SEXUAL INTIMACY

Roxanne and Dwight insisted they had a perfect marriage except for one thing: sex. The good news was they agreed on the problem; the bad news was that Dwight thought a good marriage offered limitless sex; Roxanne's idea of a good marriage meant *no* sex!

"Whenever we have a fight," said Roxanne, "Dwight's answer is to have sex—as if that solves everything. He doesn't understand that's the last thing on my mind. How can I have sex when I'm still mad at him?"

Dwight was equally insistent his way was best. "When we quarrel, I know what will fix it. We'll make love and everything will be fine again. But Roxanne won't give it a chance. She acts like, *Not now—and maybe not ever!* I think if we never had sex again, she'd be perfectly happy!"

Roxanne agreed. "Sometimes Dwight hits me over the head, figuratively speaking, with the Bible verse that says a wife shouldn't withhold herself from her husband. I've tried to obey that verse. Some nights I lie there gritting my teeth, telling God I'm doing this for Him, but it has never made me like sex any better. I guess I'm just what they call frigid."

Chris Thurman assured Roxanne that wasn't necessarily the case. If no medical problem was involved, the trouble probably stemmed from her thoughts or feelings, or from her husband's approach. "Sex to a man is first physical and then emotional," Chris explained. "For a woman it's first emotional and then physical. Roxanne, you may be holding a lot of hurts and anger inside—things that haven't been talked about and resolved, so you're feeling resentful. You can't be romantic and resentful at the same time."

Roxanne admitted she did resent Dwight's preoccupation with sex. He countered with, "I wouldn't be so preoccupied with it if I got some once in awhile!"

Chris told Dwight he understood, but added, "We must always look beyond our mate's behavior to her emotions. What is going on inside? What thinking may be faulty? What needs exist in her life? It's crucial you learn to do this on a regular basis. It'll affect how you relate as husband and wife. You need to understand this person. That means coming to understand what needs are vital to her."

"Well, sure," said Dwight. "I guess that makes sense."

"For example, consider the area of feelings. Unresolved feelings can extinguish desire, especially anger and fear. Is she angry with you, or her father, or an ex-spouse? Does she have deeply rooted fears of being vulnerable and trusting? Those feelings will interfere with sexual intimacy. After all, 'Letting go' sexually is one of the most vulnerable, trusting things a woman does.

"Another problem area may be faulty thinking. Some grew up in a culture that said sex is wrong; it's bad or dirty. Or maybe you grew up in a home environment with a negative attitude toward sex; the message was, *No, not now. Don't touch me there. That's all you think about; do I have to tolerate that again?* We've never grabbed hold of the divine concept of sex, the fact God thought the whole thing up—and He liked it! He's not upset about sex; He doesn't think it's bad except when it's used out of context. He considers sex a wonderful way for married couples to express their oneness and share an intimacy that was meant only for them."

As Chris Thurman talked Dwight and Roxanne through some important principles of oneness, he urged each one to come to certain truths. These were Dwight's truths: (1) I would enjoy it if Roxanne and I could share more physical affection; (2) and yet I don't want to pressure my wife; (3) I want to trust God to work in my life and my wife's to give us the kind of affectionate relationship He wants us to have.

When Chris talked with Roxanne, these were her truths: (1) I want to be affectionate with my husband; (2) I want God to work in our lives as He wishes to give us this kind of relationship.

At this point Chris asked Dwight and Roxanne if they would like to hold hands and pray and express these requests to God. They agreed and bowed their heads. Dwight prayed, then Roxanne. Their prayers were the same; they were experiencing oneness!

Chris noted that God is more concerned in drawing a couple together in oneness than in which one of them "wins" an argument. That's true in all aspects of a marriage. The choices aren't as important as a couple's arriving at God's oneness in their decisions.

But developing oneness was just the beginning of renewing the courtship in Dwight and Roxanne's marriage. To become close they needed to spend time together having fun, enjoying each other, and building special memories. Chris suggested dozens of simple little things they could do to stir the flames of passion in their relationship.[2]

You may feel your own marriage could benefit from some of the following "passion-prompters."

## Keep Courting Alive!

### Date Again.

Return to some of the "little things" you enjoyed while dating: sit together, hold hands, wear his favorite perfume and her favorite aftershave, give each other a back rub, listen to "our" song, go to your favorite restaurant. "Capture" your spouse for a surprise picnic or candlelight dinner at home alone, for a sumptuous evening of fine dining, or for an overnighter at a romantic hotel.

### Develop Common Interests.

Take turns picking something fun to do—sports, a hobby, an outing, church activity, or a civic or cultural event; learn to enjoy being together.

### Thirty-Second Phone Calls.

When apart, call your mate just to say, "I love you and I was thinking about you." David Ferguson shares how he came up with this idea accidentally some fifteen years ago:

"I was rushing around at work and picked up the phone to dial a friend, and I dialed the wrong number—my home number. I didn't want to talk to Teresa, but what was I going to do? So I faked it. I said, 'Hi, Sweetheart, how you doing?'

"Teresa, being rather blunt, said, 'What do you want?'

"I couldn't think of anything to say, so I faked it some more and said, 'I just called to check on you, Sweetheart.'

"Married to me fifteen years, Teresa knew better. She said, 'No, you didn't. You've never done that.' Twisting the knife a little deeper, she added, 'In fact, the only time you ever call me is when you want me to do something for you!'

"Sad, but true. Shame-faced, I resolved to change my selfish ways. I initiated my frequent thirty-second phone calls to tell Teresa how much she meant to me and that I was looking forward to being with her again."

### Initiate, Initiate, Initiate!

Express your love in words, hugs, touch, verbalized appreciation, love notes, and sexual sharings. You might say, "Love notes? Are you kidding? Why write to someone I live with?" Such is the questioning of the overly logical and rational mind—but such questioning chills romance!

It's the little reminders that warm the heart and convey emotional messages that build closeness. They say, *I was thinking of you. You're important to me. I trust you with my heart!* Finding a handwritten note in a coat pocket, purse, or lunch box can bring your spouse an inner joy guaranteed to last all day. A little love note on a mirror, a car seat, or a counter top brings pleasant thoughts that linger till you meet again.

### Welcome Home.

Greet your mate when he or she arrives home; don't just call hello from another room. Stop what you're doing, go to the door, and initiate contact. Smile, offer a hug, a kiss, or a touch, and express in words, "I'm glad to see you!"

## Understand the Power of Human Touch

Touch is one of the most powerful of our five senses, but too often couples deprive themselves of this pathway to closeness. Described below are three "touch exercises" you might try to increase closeness through nonsexual touching:

### Hand Massage.

With palms up, lightly begin tracing your partner's palm. Trace each finger all the way to the tip, touching each fingerprint in a light circular motion. Trace the inside of each finger, pausing to move back and forth in each finger "crevasse" where two fingers join at the palm.

### Foot Bath.

Take turns washing and bathing each other's feet. Sit in a chair with your feet in a warm pan of water; close your eyes as your partner swishes the warm water over your legs, ankles, and feet. Don't talk, just relax; the purpose is not "washing" but relaxation and enjoyment. Use water or suds; use your hand or try a sponge. Linger, don't rush!

### Synchronous Breathing.

Lie facing each other and look into each other's eyes, close enough to feel each other's breathing rhythm. Soon you'll find a common rise and fall in your inhalation/exhalation. At other times alter this pattern by fitting like spoons . . . her back against your abdomen. After your breathing is synchronized, close your eyes and just relax, savoring the physical sensations of being close.

## Enhance the Passion

As we said before, sex isn't all in your head, but a great deal of it is! Many couples enhance their passion by letting their minds wander over pleasurable thoughts of their spouse, perhaps beginning in the morning after a tender and affectionate parting, during an afternoon bubble bath, or during a relaxed reading of *Solomon on Sex* (Dillow, 1977). A balanced relationship will include touch in three ways:

### Spiritual Touching.

Holding hands to pray communicates spiritual agreement. Touch in church, embrace each other at times of great joy, and hold hands as a family during prayer at mealtimes.

### Soul Touching.

Embrace each other as you depart and reunite. Take a walk holding hands; walk arm in arm through the mall. Sit close to each other in the car; "claim" each other through your occasional touch or embrace when you're out in public.

*Sexual Touching.*

Soft, gentle touching or caressing the skin is much preferred to grabbing or mauling. Many wives have been turned off by the "me-Tarzan, you-Jane" approach. Tenderness and sensitivity are the key. Brush kisses on her neck, shoulder, or back; try a body massage with lotion or baby oil. Fabrics accentuate touch, so try satin sheets or silk nightwear.

## Overcome Hindrances to Sexual Intimacy

### Self-Talk and Your Love Life

Because your mind is one of your most sensitive and powerful ingredients in a passionate and fulfilling love life, your thoughts (or self-talk) can work for you or against you in your sexual expression. Anxiety (based on fear or anger) is the single most prevalent factor in sexual dysfunction. Individuals with the most severe anxiety mentally quench even the first stirrings of sexual interest. Negative self-talk may cause low sexual desire, sexual avoidance, or even an aversion to sex. What mental messages concerning sex were communicated during your childhood? Were the messages positive or negative? Tragically, childhood sexual abuse is a major contributor to low sexual desire in adults.

Here are other examples of common problematic self-talk: "Sex is something you tolerate." "All touching will lead to sex." "Nice girls don't enjoy sex." "You're being used when you have sex." Such negative thoughts need to be disputed, and underlying emotional issues must be dealt with. In some cases counseling is essential.

### Other Hindrances to Sexual Intimacy

- Letting the sun go down on your hurts will let anger quench romance and affection . . . heal your hurts as they happen.
- The bedroom is the worst place to discuss changes you'd like to make in your sexual routine; wait until you are relaxed and close and then share your Love Map exercise (as outlined below).
- Touching only when it leads to sex develops resentment, so increase your nonsexual touching.

- Assuming your spouse should know how to sexually stimulate you and then being angry when he or she doesn't is a common trap. Break this cycle by taking turns switching roles. Make love to your spouse exactly the way you'd most enjoy having your spouse make love to you. Then reverse the process.

## Remove Sexual Secrets

Secrets are perpetuated whenever you withhold relevant information about your sexuality or passively allow your spouse to believe misinformation. Common sexual secrets include faked orgasm, foreplay preferences, and intimacy wishes. Keeping such secrets builds walls that isolate relationships. Secrets also contribute to low sexual desire and performance problems.

Sexual desire is strongly affected by the quality of the marital relationship. If there are pending conflicts, unmet needs, or unresolved fears, a spouse may voluntarily turn off sexually.

## Share Preferences through Love Maps

Drawing from the suggestions we've given you for improving sexual intimacy, complete the following "Love Map" and share it with your partner.

**LOVE MAP**
### And they shall become one flesh. (Gen. 2:24)

**1. Background.** Four of the major hindrances to sexual intimacy are addressed in this exercise. Consider these hindrances before you develop your love map.

    **A. Lack of Openness/Communication.** Sex is *not* an easy subject to discuss; little experience or role modeling leaves many couples feeling resentment and frustration. Sexual intimacy can't be a guessing game; two physically different people with differing personalities, backgrounds, preferences, and hangups must gradually learn to talk more openly about sexual oneness.

B. **Unhealthy Preoccupation with Getting rather than Giving.** Tragically many of us (especially men) grew up with the mind-set that sex is something to be taken, earned, or manipulated; the art of giving oneself to another person is therefore foreign and awkward to us. Try changing how you speak of sex. Instead of saying, "Can we have sex?" or "Let's do it!" say, "I really look forward to us being together."

C. **Boredom—Lack of Creativity/Freshness.** "Sameness" produces complacency and feelings of obligation and duty while creativity communicates initiative, desire, and anticipation. Change the atmosphere and vary your routine; trade off pleasuring each other; creatively be together other than in the bed.

D. **Lack of Anticipation and Expectancy.** As he (or she) thinks in his (or her) heart, so is he (or she) (Prov. 23:7). We repeat: Your mind is your most important sexual resource; learning to mentally anticipate lovemaking with your spouse builds excitement, creativity, and desire.

**2. Complete Your Love Map.** Each spouse uses the spaces below to complete this statement: From my point of view, a perfect sexually intimate time with my spouse would include the following:

1.                          7.
2.                          8.
3.                          9.
4.                          10.
5.                          11.
6.                          12.

(Include personally meaningful items related to timing, location, clothing, and romantic preparations, as well as personal preferences concerning initiative, foreplay, positions, and "after-play.")

**3. Marriage Intimacy.** The freedom to share all of oneself with another person . . . body, soul, and spirit.

1. Pick a private time and place and exchange your love maps.
2. Discuss them as much as you feel comfortable doing. (You'll grow more at ease as you repeat the exercise.)
3. Clarify and answer questions as appropriate.
4. "Free" your spouse to fulfill as much of your love map as he or she is now comfortable with; don't insist, get pushy, or love conditionally!

**4. Give to One Another.** Schedule two times of intimacy to fulfill both love maps.

1. Husband should first "give" to fulfill his wife's love map, with a subsequent time for the wife to "give."
2. Schedule a time for this so you both can anticipate it.
3. Throughout the day spend moments anticipating the pleasures of the two of you becoming one.
4. Freely share all of yourself with each other.

**5. Reflect, Experiment, and Repeat the Exercise.**
1. Return to Step 2, Complete Your Love Map, and repeat this exercise, composing an entirely new love map to delight both your spouse and yourself! Have fun!

# CHAPTER 15

# Maintain Intimacy
# Throughout the Life Cycle

YOU, YOUR MARRIAGE, and your family have embarked on a journey. Just as an infant develops over time from a passive, fragile newborn into an overactive toddler or a peer-conscious teen, so your marriage and family develop through recognizable stages. Awareness of these stages and the challenges they present can serve as important warning signs for what lies ahead, allowing you time for planning and preparation. This element of preventative counsel can be extremely helpful in your journey toward deepening marital and family intimacy.[1]

Each family is a small group with a recognizable beginning. We can trace its development as it expands with the birth of children and later loses members as children grow and leave the nest, and finally, as it is reduced to a single widowed spouse.

Families face their greatest marital stress and the potential for crisis at the transition points from one stage to the next. As a couple moves from the honeymoon stage into the childbearing stage, they will need to reestablish their marriage as a priority in order to maintain intimacy. Failure to complete certain developmental challenges at each stage can hinder their closeness and cause their relationship to deteriorate. Our goal in this chapter is to highlight the challenges of each stage and give practical encouragement toward a more intimate journey.

## THE FOUR STAGES OF MARRIAGE

The four stages of marriage can be described as:

**Stage 1, New Love:** The honeymoon begins as two individuals start blending their lives. (The average time before newly married couples have children is two years.)

**Stage 2, Shared Love:** The first child arrives . . . and love must now be shared. (The average time for families to have children up to age thirteen is thirteen years.)

**Stage 3, Mature Love:** The first child becomes a teen . . . and love had better be mature! (The average time for this stage—until the last child is "launched"—is fifteen years.)

**Stage 4, Renewed Love:** The last child is launched into the real world . . . and love can now be renewed. (Empty nest . . . average time is twenty-eight years.)

Keep in mind that some married couples don't fit neatly into the family life-cycle timetable. They marry earlier or later than the national norms. They bear their children earlier, later, or over a longer period of years than is typical. They, or their children, may have exceptional abilities or disabilities that markedly affect their family life. One or more family members may be away in institutions or on government or corporate business, thereby altering the usual family expectations and experience.

Broken and rebuilt families resulting from divorce and remarriage will also vary markedly from the typical life cycle. In fact, as increasing divorce rates, delayed marriage, and alternatives to marriage become long-term trends, the proportion of adults experiencing a typical family life cycle will decline significantly.

A clear-cut sequence of stages in the family life cycle occurs only in a family with one child. Families with more than one child will experience several years of overlap at various stages. A family grows through a given stage with its oldest child and, in a sense, repeats that stage as subsequent children come along.

Generally, when a couple marry, each person demands little but receives much. Under the influence of very intense feelings, each responds to the other's needs. But in time this changes; as life's demands grow more pressing each partner focuses on his or her own needs, and conflict results. Curiously, the very characteristics that are most appealing initially and that draw a couple together inevitably become sources of major irritation later. Simply adding children to the system creates additional complexity and potential for misunderstanding and conflict as well.

In the nuclear family there are a number of positions: husband-father, wife-mother, son-brother, and daughter-sister. To each position are attached *roles*, or behavior expectations, of the person filling that position. In a given family, the man has a different role to play as husband to his wife, as father of a preschool son, and as father of a teenage daughter. The stress of changing hats from husband to father and from wife to mother creates considerable pressure on marital priorities.

To experience more of God's abundance throughout the family life cycle, couples must give particular attention to the partner's intimacy needs during transition from one stage to the next. For example, when the Stage 1 couple has their first child and enters Stage 2 the husband often experiences feelings of rejection and insecurity and needs his wife's attention and reassurance. On the other hand, the wife and new mother feels overwhelmed and unappreciated and needs practical support and expressed appreciation from her husband.

The developmental challenges of each of the four stages of marriage are listed in Table 15.1, and the general expectations of each stage are discussed in the following sections. Remember that the intimacy ingredients, outlined in Chapter 6, are critical for sustaining closeness during the transitions from one stage to another.

## Stage 1, New Love

No doubt about it. Kathy and Clint were in love. Nuzzling each other, cooing and kissing, whispering sweet endearments, these newlyweds were lost in their own little world, hardly aware the rest of the world was watching with a knowing little smile. "Just give 'em time; they'll wake up to reality. The honeymoon can't go on forever!"

## Table 15.1
# The Four Stages of Marriage

| *Stages of Marriage* | *Developmental Challenges* |
| --- | --- |
| **Stage 1, New Love** <br> . . . the journey begins | • Freedom from power struggles <br> • Freedom from expectations <br> • Freedom from in-law control <br> • Freedom to establish identity <br> • Freedom to confess and forgive <br> • Freedom to enjoy sexual oneness |
| **Stage 2, Shared Love** <br> . . . the children arrive | • Freedom from wrong priorities <br> • Freedom from hidden agendas <br> • Freedom from doubting God's provision <br> • Freedom to accept imperfections <br> • Freedom to give and not take <br> • Freedom to balance one another |
| **Stage 3, Mature Love** <br> . . . teenagers are here | • Freedom from adolescent control <br> • Freedom from losing personal identity <br> • Freedom from unhealed childhood pain <br> • Freedom to prioritize "us" <br> • Freedom to enjoy kids <br> • Freedom to deal with inevitable loss |
| **Stage 4, Renewed Love** <br> . . . the "nest" empties | • Freedom from fearing growing old <br> • Freedom from fearing the empty nest |

- Freedom from fearing intimacy
- Freedom to enjoy life as it is
- Freedom to build new dreams
- Freedom to be friends with kids and grandkids

"Right. He'll wake up and smell the coffee—and just wait'll he tastes hers!"

"She thinks he's Prince Charming. But wait'll she has to polish his armor and feed his horse!"

True enough, research shows the time prior to having children is the period of highest marriage satisfaction for most couples. They have more free time to get to know each other. With no children to occupy nonworking hours, they can spend time alone together or with other couples so they're usually quite happy. But soon something strange happens. The magic begins to fade; the rosy glow of romance begins to dim. This happened with Kathy and Clint. After just two months of marriage, they noticed a disconcerting change in their relationship.

"Our dates used to be so much fun," she said wistfully. "Every outing was an adventure. Clint thought of the most original ideas and the most fantastic restaurants. He made me feel like a princess—opening doors, taking my coat, always so gallant and attentive. I'd be floating on clouds for days after one of our dates, and I'd spend hours alone in my room just dreaming of Clint.

"But these days we hardly ever go out except to work or to a fast-food restaurant. Clint says we've got to save our money for a house someday. He even wants to make a budget! And instead of going home to my room to dream of Clint, we go home together to our cramped one-bedroom apartment, and I go around picking up his socks while he watches TV. It seems that's all he wants to do. I don't understand it. He never watched TV when we were going together!"

Clint agreed marriage wasn't quite what he expected either. "Kathy used to go along with anything I suggested," he said. "She was so agreeable I used to worry maybe she didn't have a mind of her own. Well, no more! She's plenty quick to give me a piece of it every chance she gets. My mom used to let me toss my stuff around and watch TV when I got home from work or a date. If Mom didn't have a problem with my habits, why should Kathy? She acts like it's a crime when I leave my socks on the floor or want to watch a couple of hours of TV before bedtime. We got along better when I could drop her off at her house after a date. Now there's no break. We go home together and we're always in each other's face. Why should I feel like I have to perform in my own home? Can't she understand I just want to kick back and relax?''

Clint and Kathy were facing the harsh reality of married life. While dating, they were on their best behavior, always conscious of the impression they were making. They rarely saw each other on their home turf, letting down their guard and simply being themselves. Now that they're married, they expect each other to fit in naturally with their way of doing things and the lifestyle they grew up with. They don't stop to realize they came from two different backgrounds and two distinct families with dissimilar behavior, roles, and communication patterns. Kathy wasn't around to notice Clint's sloppiness or penchant for TV; he wasn't around to notice how fastidious she was or how bossy she could be when she wanted her own way. For both Clint and Kathy, the honeymoon is under attack!

The honeymoon phase can last anywhere from one minute to one year, but it usually lasts from three to six months. During this time, disagreements over the guiding principles of the marriage are glossed over. Each person feels a little upset that things aren't being done "correctly" but puts aside his or her feelings to maintain harmony.

Gradually differences mount. One day one person objects, and the couple clashes over what the rules are, who determines the rules, and how the rules will be negotiated. This first disagreement produces disillusionment, but if the couple works together, they can meld the rules of two families of origin into the rules of their unique marriage. By confronting the challenges of their "new love" stage, they can lay a solid foundation of security, closeness, and trust that will prepare them for the next stage of their relationship.

To evaluate how well your marriage has "negotiated" Stage 1, take this self-assessment test, checking those statements that are true:

_____ In-laws don't control our schedule, finances, or decisions.

_____ We don't have recurring power struggles over who "wins" in daily decisions.

_____ I am not repeatedly hurt by my spouse's not measuring up to my expectations.

_____ We have established our identity as a couple by sharing common interests, developing couple friends, and creating our own traditions.

_____ We tend to quickly confess and genuinely forgive each other for inevitable hurts.

_____ We have established a mutually satisfying sexual relationship.

Now count the number of items you checked and assess your score:

0-2 items checked = major concern
3-4 items checked = needs improvement
5-6 items checked = good

After taking this test, Clint and Kathy realized they would need to implement some practical guidelines to help them gain freedom from power struggles, unrealistic expectations, and in-law control so they could experience the freedom to establish their couple identity, confess and forgive, and enjoy sexual oneness. These are some of the guiding principles they established for their marriage:

We will make significant decisions only in oneness; if we don't agree, we'll wait and pray until oneness comes.

We are prepared to give up expected roles we thought our spouse would assume based on our family of origin.

We will establish at least one family tradition that doesn't involve either family of origin.

We will begin speaking of "our" home, possessions, and finances—not "my" and "mine."

We will not rationalize our wrongs but admit them, remembering this is a sign of maturity.

When we part in the morning and reunite in the evening, we will practice being as affectionate as we were before marriage.

We will express our love to each other without waiting for the other to speak up first.

We'll encourage conversations about our feelings, fears, dreams, and hurts just as we did while dating—and we'll practice listening and caring!

We'll face the challenge of developing a common budget and joint finances.

We'll consider what our partner missed when he or she was growing up and we'll concentrate on meeting those needs.

## Stage 2, Shared Love

When Clint and Kathy have their first child, they'll enter Stage 2 of their marriage, Shared Love. No longer will they have the luxury of being absorbed only in each other; now another little being will hungrily demand their love and attention. That child will require huge amounts of care and time, not to mention patience and sacrifice. Schedules and priorities will have to be rearranged, potentially disrupting the delicate balance of intimacy between husband and wife.

If you've just had your first child, you're probably experiencing the stresses and strains of just such an adjustment. If you're a new mother, your most common complaint is exhaustion. You're probably trying to do everything you did before while taking care of your infant's demands as well. If you're a new father, your most common complaint is that you feel neglected by your wife. Both of you probably have noticed a decrease in intimacy. No longer can you spontaneously eat out or drive to a nearby resort for a weekend alone. Camping and hiking are out. Vacations are anything but relaxing. Even walking around the block to talk about your day requires the planning and preparation of a major move.

With all your new parenting responsibilities, it's easy to see how your marriage can take a backseat. You're so busy with the baby you hardly realize what's happening. You just know you don't feel as close to your mate as you used to. This is a particularly vulnerable time for husbands. Feeling left out, they may be tempted to become involved in other relationships. So it's important for both partners to make their marriage a priority by recapturing their Stage 1 romance.

But that's only the beginning. As your newborn grows older, usually during his or her second year, you'll realize the child has a will of his or her own—which differs markedly from the will of you parents! You'll have to decide when and how to discipline him or her.

As fallen human beings, we all dislike discipline. It's an emotional issue with a family history—actually two family histories. As a child, each parent was disciplined differently for different reasons, and each parent has strong feelings about the way his or her parents meted out correction and discipline. You'll find the attitudes and feelings you developed about discipline as a youngster will carry over into your behavior with your own children. If you and your spouse can't agree, you'll stumble into still another area of potential marriage conflict.

Each age poses a new threat to family harmony. The "terrible twos" are usually more terrible for the parents than for the child; at age five or six your youngster enters school, and his or her behavior is suddenly on public display. Authorities will judge your child-rearing abilities by your child's deportment. If Junior terrorizes his teacher, alienates his peers, and bullies smaller children on the playground, you may feel like a failure. You may argue that one of you is too lenient or one is too rigid. Your child's problems become problems of the marriage.

Rearing children during their school years is difficult because both parents are often busy with their own careers while juggling parental responsibilities. When you're both bombarded from every side by the demands of colleagues, clients, the P.T.A., extracurricular activities, Scouts, church functions, civic and community responsibilities, not to mention relatives, neighbors, and friends, no wonder there's so little time for intimacy with your spouse!

To evaluate how well your marriage has "negotiated" Stage 2, take the following self-assessment test, checking those statements that are true:

_____ We have recognized and overcome some of the hidden agendas or expectations we each brought from our childhood.

_____ Neither work pressures nor the children's needs prevent us from routinely setting aside special times just for us.

_____ I've ceased any doubting over my spouse's being God's special provision just for me.

_____ My partner's peculiar imperfections are not stealing my joy in marriage.

_____ We focus more on giving to each other than on being preoccupied with what we're getting.

_____ I've come to see many of my shortcomings and how my spouse balances me with his or her strengths.

Now count the number of items you checked and assess your score:
0–2 items checked = major concern
3–4 items checked = needs improvement
5–6 items checked = good

Jimmy and Marla Carlton were in Stage 2 of their marriage relationship since their children, Jeffy and Anna, were not yet teenagers. The Carltons did well in their self-assessment test, although Marla admitted the results would have been vastly different just a few short months earlier. "I never would have thought God had anything to do with bringing Jimmy and me together—just the opposite, in fact. Both Jimmy and I were obsessed with what we were *getting* from each other, which wasn't much, believe me. We were like vultures, both feeding off each other until there was nothing left. Thank God we've learned how to really love each other."

"Amen!" said Jimmy with a knowing wink at Marla. "Our marriage is still a long way from paradise, but it's the closest thing to heaven on earth I'll ever know."

Marla leaned over and gave him an impulsive kiss. "You ol' sweet talker!"

Having progressed successfully through months of counseling, the Carltons were clearly ready to face the challenges their future held. They were setting both short-term and long-range goals to free themselves from wrong priorities, hidden agendas, and possible doubts of God's provision. They were in the process of liberating themselves to accept their partner's imperfections, to give rather than to take, and to balance each other in their strengths and weaknesses.

These are some of the resolutions they set for themselves:

We will practice mutual confession and forgiveness on a day-to-day basis so hurts won't build up between us.

We will learn to look beneath our marital conflicts for unhealed growing-up pain.

We will focus on our partner's strengths of character, gifts, and talents and often express appreciation for them.

We will list our partner's "imperfections" and then note how each one is merely a *strength* needing some tempering or refinement.

We will carefully observe our responses to disappointments and irritations in dealing with our partner, remembering that if we stop giving, our love becomes conditional.

We will practice deferring to our partner's leadership in areas where he or she is obviously more gifted or insightful.

We will remember to give our spouse special little gifts, love notes, and "I-was-thinking-of-you" phone calls.

We will save any criticisms or concerns about parenting decisions until we can deal with them privately.

We will read together and discuss some good books on parenting.

Especially when it comes to our children, our policy will be, "Don't sweat the small stuff."

"Jimmy needs that last one more than I do," said Marla. "The kids can really get on his nerves. But I've got to watch that I don't override his authority by siding with the kids. The last time Jimmy disciplined Jeffy and I started to defend him, I just bit my tongue and kept quiet. Right, Jimmy?"

"Right, Babe. And did you notice how Jeff looked at you to see if you were going to defend him? When you didn't say a word he went and did what he was told. I felt real good about that."

"I did too," said Marla. "Usually with the kids it's divide and conquer. Pit Mom against Dad. No wonder they got away with murder. But no more. We're presenting a united front from now on."

"We're united in more ways than one," said Jimmy slyly. "It's like the good ol' days around our house. Only better!"

"He means we're dating again," said Marla. "Romancing each other like a couple of starry-eyed kids! Who'd believe it? In fact, Jimmy's promised to take me to a Billy Ray Cyrus concert. "I loved that hit of his, 'Achy Breaky Heart.' And I love it when Jimmy sings it to me."

Jimmy flashed a self-conscious smile. "You can probably guess from what Marla says, I'm back to singing. Not full-time, of course. I can't afford to give up my job with the insurance company. But I've put together a little band—some of the guys I knew years ago—and we're doing weekend gigs. It makes me feel alive again. I didn't realize how much I missed performing."

"He's good," said Marla. "Better than he used to be. I wouldn't be surprised if he lands a record contract one of these days."

"I'm not counting on that, but if it came along, I'd grab it up fast." Jimmy said with a grin. "I'm getting my old confidence back, thanks to Marla . . . and the good Lord."

She reached over and gave his knee a squeeze. "It works both ways, Honeybear. I know you love me and that makes me feel good."

"And when Marla feels good, we all feel good," said Jimmy.

Marla flashed the proverbial Cheshire grin. Her face glowed as brightly as her burnished locks. "It's like we finally figured out this love thing. Even the kids are different, not so hyper and on edge."

"Not to say we're suddenly the 'Brady Bunch,'" Jimmy added quickly. "And believe me, Marla's not Donna Reed and I'm not

'Father Knows Best,' but then again, we're not the Bickersons anymore either. We honestly like being together."

Marla nodded, giving a jaunty toss of her red hair. "Would you believe it? We're enjoying being a family. I think we're ready to tackle whatever's ahead!"

## Stage 3, Mature Love

It's a good thing Jimmy and Marla Carlton feel ready to tackle their future because what lies ahead of them is Stage 3, Mature Love, and with it the attack of the erratic, impulsive, unpredictable adolescent. Watch out, folks!

When the first child enters adolescence, numerous changes occur within the family, challenging a couple's love to mature. Fortunately, God gave parents twelve or more years to prepare for the arrival of teenagers!

During this stage, the adolescent's increasing independence forces the family to reevaluate its rules and allow more responsibility. It probably goes without saying, teenagers usually consider themselves more ready for independence than their parents do. Parents can lessen conflict by giving their teenager independence gradually before he or she demands it. That way, he or she gains freedom while the parents retain some control over dispensing privileges and necessary discipline.

Sometimes teenagers' demand for freedom can spark conflict between their parents, especially if the parents already struggle with unresolved hurts. One parent may be ready to grant the youngster freedom while the other, perhaps out of fear or insecurity, may choose to tighten the reins.

Not only are teenagers more difficult to control, they may not be as easy to love. While younger children, especially infants and preschoolers, are cute and spontaneous and freely show their love with smiles, laughter, hugs, and kisses, teenagers may suddenly turn silent and become withdrawn. They have often mastered the art of "looks that kill"; they don't want to be hugged, and they're anything but verbally appreciative! In a dozen ways every day they will probably test your love to the limits.

As adolescents wrestle with their own concerns—body changes, sexual identity, and appearance—their parents may be facing their own midlife crises. Mom may be experiencing menopause; Dad may feel that his own manhood is slipping as he sees his son approaching his sexual prime. While Junior mulls over his future career, his parents may be reevaluating their own careers. Dad may be at a precarious crossroads, forced to make significant occupational changes or even facing the painful reality of a career downturn or a job loss. Even though he is in his prime earning years, the expenses of a family with adolescents can be a hefty strain, especially when college expenses mount.

Often at the same time one child is entering adolescence, the last child is just beginning kindergarten. With all the children in school, many mothers enter or return to the work force, causing still more changes in the household. With Mom no longer available to handle as many chores, other family members must pitch in and help if their daily routine is to continue smoothly. If no one picks up the slack, the entire family grows disgruntled.

Add to these sources of stress anxiety over aging, disappointment over unfulfilled dreams, and the pain over family losses as a couple's own parents and siblings age and die. Torn between rebellious teenagers and sick or aging parents, many couples in this "sandwich" generation find themselves overwhelmed by circumstances and at odds with each other. In desperation, they may head for divorce court.

In short, adolescence is a time when family rules are challenged, when family structure is changed, when intimacy patterns are disrupted, and when individual concerns over sexual identity and career identity are paramount for both children and adults. Is it any wonder adolescence is a time of lower marriage satisfaction for both husbands and wives than most other times of life?

But take heart. If your marriage relationship has been growing through the years into deeper intimacy, these external pressures can actually draw you even closer together as a couple.

If your marriage fits into the Mature Love stage, take the following self-assessment test, checking those statements that are true for you:

_____ Each of us has established a fulfilling life and ministry through our unique gifts, talents, hobbies, etc.

_____ We work well together as a team in dealing with our kids so they can't manipulate us, pitting us against one another.

_____ Individually, we have come to recognize the imperfections in our growing-up years; we've felt the feelings those years generated, and we've received understanding and comfort from each other. Usually we no longer need to discuss our hurts from the past and they rarely affect our relationship today.

_____ We both freely give special time and priority to our marriage without complaining.

_____ Our kids are becoming our friends as we release them to live their own lives.

_____ We have addressed the loss of our children, jobs, or parents by deepening our couple relationships and sharing our feelings with each other.

Now count the number of items you checked and assess your score:
  0–2 items checked = major concern
  3–4 items checked = needs improvement
  5–6 items checked = good

If you scored poorly on this test, you may realize you need to gain freedom from your adolescent's controlling manipulation as well as to gain respite from the loss of your personal identity and unhealed childhood pain. Only then can you as a couple be free to make "us" a priority, to enjoy the kids, and to deal with your inescapable losses. You may wish to adopt some of the following resolutions to help you achieve family health and harmony:

We will remember that this adolescent period is a balance between freedom and responsibility; we'll trust our teens in new areas, and as they act responsibly we'll trust them with more freedom.

We will seize our rare "alone" moments with each other as a time to be quiet, hold each other, cuddle, and communicate that we enjoy each other.

Individually we will look underneath our rages and fears to see if some of our pain is contributing to our struggle with our teenagers.

We will escape with each other at least once each quarter for a night away to refocus, relax, and rekindle romance.

We will hug our teens and tell them we love them even if they don't show love back, knowing they need our love even if it's not "cool" to admit it.

We will grieve our losses together, giving comfort and support, not pretending we don't hurt, and not intellectualizing or giving advice. Instead, we will weep with those who weep.

We will practice honest apologies when we've been impatient, intolerant, insensitive, or unkind to our spouse or children.

We will begin talking about life "beyond the children," developing goals and plans for the empty nest.

We will avoid overly self-reliant, independent living by involving each other from time to time in our favorite activities, hobbies, or diversions.

We will pray often together at critical times of decision or pain, trusting one another and our children to the Lord.

## Stage 4, Renewed Love

As draining, turbulent, and stressful as those adolescent years may be, the day will come when your home rings with a peculiar silence. You will look around in surprise and the rooms will be empty. No more blaring CDs or MTV, no teens running through the house or up and down stairs with mohawks or spiked hair or whatever the most recent radical style happens to be. Suddenly the telephone sits idle, no longer an appendage on some teenager's ear. Just when you thought your house was the hub of the entire teenage civilized world, now no one comes near. Not only have your own teens disappeared, but also all your children's friends who used to exhaust you with their chatter and laughter and howls and hysteria—they're all gone too. And you feel—well, relieved. And lonely. And a little at loose ends. You look at your mate as if to say, *What do we do now?*

As disconcerted as you may feel, you're not alone. You are simply in Stage 4, Renewed Love, statistically by far the longest of all the stages of a marriage. You've returned to where you began twenty or thirty years earlier, and for better or worse it's just the two of you again! Over the next decade or so, you'll probably see your adult children marry and you'll probably become grandparents—a state of bliss touted by some as the next best thing to sliced bread.

In general, the empty-nest years have the potential of being the happiest years of your married life because career demands are usually lower and children occupy far less attention when they're out on their own. If you can reestablish your relationship roles and rekindle romance, you'll find you have a strong base of mutual support to help you cope with the inevitable transitions occurring in your remaining years.

But with the nest empty, you may find yourselves facing some difficult adjustments as a couple. One or both parents may be experiencing the emotional trauma of having the children leave home. Some couples divorce at this point, claiming they just stayed together for the kids. Conflicts that were displaced onto the children while they were home suddenly must be faced, and a couple may be unwilling or unable to resolve them.

During this stage you will need to redefine your relationship with each other in many ways. When one or both of you retire, you'll face significant changes in your time schedule. Eight to ten hours a day previously spent at work now need to be filled; alas, you suddenly have more time together than you know what to do with. Two very different routines need to be meshed without sacrificing either person's occasional need for privacy or autonomy. You may be forced to survive on the often inadequate financial income you receive from social security, retirement, and personal savings. You may find yourselves confronting unresolved power struggles as you make decisions about activities, friends, travel, and future plans.

Questions, questions—you've got lots and lots of questions! "Should we take that long-dreamed-of cruise to Alaska or save our money for a rainy day?" "Should we sell the house and move into that retirement community or fix the leaky roof and stay put?" "Should we tighten our belts and stash something away for the next generation or splurge on a few luxuries we've always wanted?" "Should we gad about and make new friends among our senior neighbors or lock the doors and settle into our easy chairs for a season of watching TV?"

And don't forget! Even though your children are out of the house, they may not be out of your lives. When one marries, he or she brings into the family circle a whole new set of relatives—spouse, in-laws, and an assortment of other kith and kin. If your adult child has successfully left you emotionally and financially as he or she begins a new, independent home, then you can establish new levels of friendship and shared interests. But that's a big "if." Chances are there are still tricky little areas where neither of you has quite let go.

For parents who have already let their adult child go, the transition to being a grandparent is relatively easy. However, if you've kept tight control of your child even after he or she is married, you may find yourselves caught up irrevocably in the tangled affairs of your son or daughter's family. Parents need to accept their status as advisers and peers to their offspring rather than trying to run their children's lives. Especially dangerous—a real can of worms, in fact!—is taking sides with grandchildren against their parents. It's the quickest way to be on everyone's hit list.

One of the biggest struggles during retirement years is satisfying the need for a new vision or purpose in living. The Bible reminds us, "where there is no vision, the people perish" (Prov. 29:18 KJV). Stage 4 couples need a fresh vision! Our social system is structured so that senior citizens are sometimes considered helpless or treated as useless appendages on a productive society.

But today's generation of senior adults is shattering the old myths and proving they can be as progressive and productive as their offspring. Those golden years can quite literally open the door to golden opportunities. With work loads and family responsibilities greatly reduced, mature couples have time to meet each other's needs for intimacy. Romance can burn as brightly as ever. Old friendships can be renewed, leisure activities pursued, and ministry opportunities explored. Some couples may even resurrect old dreams and seek out new careers, trying the things they always had a secret yen to do. Grandma Moses, untrained in art, began painting her colorful primitive masterpieces in her seventies. What have you and your mate always wanted to do if you could simply throw caution to the wind and follow your dreams? Maybe it's time to get started.

If you and your spouse are in or approaching Stage 4, take this self-assessment test, checking those statements that are true for you:

_____ I am not so preoccupied with age and health that I can't enjoy life.

_____ My spouse and I have a close relationship so that our children leaving the nest doesn't pose a threat.

_____ My spouse and I guard our intimacy by being careful not to lead lives that are too separate and independent.

_____ I am able to find the simple joy of being alive today.

_____ My spouse and I are able to be friends with our grown children.

_____ My spouse and I are able to wake up with a fresh vision for the day and set goals for the rest of our life together.

Now count the number of items you checked and assess your score:
   0–2 items checked = major concern
   3–4 items checked = needs improvement
   5–6 items checked = good

If you find you didn't score well on this little test, you may want to adopt some of the following resolutions to help you gain freedom from the fears of growing old, facing the empty nest, or experiencing intimacy. These principles will liberate you to enjoy life as it is, build new dreams, and become friends with your children and grandchildren.

We will rekindle our "first love" by taking a second honeymoon, going on a cruise, treating ourselves to a resort, spa, or other romantic getaway.

We will read together and discuss Christian books on keeping our romance and sex life vibrant and growing, and we'll dare to break out of our routine to be silly and experiment.

We will talk openly of new dreams, fond remembrances, and recurring fears, freely reassuring and supporting each other.

We will make separate lists of "things I still want to do that I've never done" and we'll help each other accomplish some of these goals.

We will seek counsel and assistance in finalizing a financial plan that gives us freedom for the years ahead.

We will initiate contact and schedule time alone with each of our children.

We will discuss and plan how we can fulfill our role as grandparents and schedule times to spend with our grandchildren.

We will remember some of our hobbies and common interests from earlier years and try them again together.

We will give each other freedom and encouragement to pursue individual goals, hobbies, and interests.

We will seek new opportunities of ministering, deepening our faith, giving, and service, and support each other in these endeavors.

## WHAT FALLING IN LOVE WAS MEANT TO BE

The last time we saw Jimmy and Marla Carlton they were performing a mini-concert in their church on a Sunday evening. They sang a medley of songs—some country, some spiritual—their rich, melodic voices blending like sugar and cream. Sure enough, they would have given Billy Ray Cyrus and Loretta Lynn a run for their money. Standing arm in arm on stage with eyes only for each other, Jimmy and Marla never looked happier, especially when they sang a little love song they'd written for each other. It wasn't great music, but the lyrics—and the sentiment—were unmistakably theirs:

> Little darlin', come sing with me.
> In God's abundance we'll live free.
>   Earth, moon, sun, sky, and sea,
>   His limitless love
>   Is ours to share.
>   Our sweet Jesus
>   Taught us to care,
>   And opened our hearts to the mystery—
>   What falling in love was meant to be!

As you close the pages of this book, we trust that you, like Jimmy and Marla, have a new understanding of what falling in love was meant to be. We hope you and your partner feel encouraged and inspired to reach out in love to each other in ways you never have before. We urge you to let Christ rekindle your passion, stirring those smoldering embers (or cold chunks of coal!) into ardent flames. Let yourselves fall in love with each other all over again. And fall in love with Jesus. Bask in His love. Savor it. Share it. Let it warm you and comfort you and fill you until it spills over to those you love.

Be tender with each other. Treasure what you have. Thank God for each other. Jesus wants the best for you. He wants to hold the two of you in His arms and soothe the hurts and help you heal each other's battle scars and childhood wounds. Let Him bless you. He loves you so! He's waiting to share Himself with you. He's been waiting a long time.

Think of it! You don't have to look any longer for the intimacy you've searched a lifetime for. It's there. In Christ. And in your mate. It's been there all along, yours to enjoy with Christ and to share with one another. And now you know how to begin.

Don't be afraid.

It's a glorious journey.

# Appendix
# Principles of Intimacy Therapy

1. Intimacy Therapy views man from a Judeo-Christian world view as being created in God's image and having existence in three dimensions—spirit, soul, and body. These dimensions give rise to various human functions: The *Body* functions through the five senses and we are "world conscious"; the *Soul* functions through our thoughts, feelings, and choices and we are "self-conscious"; the *Spirit* functions through conscience, intuition, and worship and we are "God conscious."

2. Intimacy Therapy sees man as being motivated to seek intimacy with God and intimacy through meaningful relationships ordained by God within marriage, within the family, and within the church (the body of Christ).

3. Intimacy Therapy views fulfillment and abundance in life as coming through personal intimacy with Jesus Christ and in intimate relationships with meaningful others ordained by Him.

4. Intimacy Therapy views problems in living (i.e., pathology) and marital and family conflict in the context of unmet intimacy needs that result in unhealthy thinking, unhealed emotions, and unproductive behaviors.

5. Intimacy Therapy views this pattern of unmet needs, unhealthy thinking, unhealed emotions, and unproductive behaviors as the major hindrances to intimacy and thus the focus of therapeutic intervention.

6. Intimacy Therapy seeks to address the personal, relational, and intergenerational origins of the intimacy hindrances noted above. Thus, in marriage counseling a premise of Genesis 2:24 would be: to *leave* father and mother, *cleave* to one another, and *become* one flesh. In other words, since "leaving" precedes "cleaving," one would expect intergenerational issues to hinder the relational issues involved in marital "cleaving."

7. Intimacy Therapy seeks to enhance intimacy by meeting intimacy needs within four major ingredients or intimacy processes: affectionate caring, vulnerable communication, joint accomplishment, and mutual giving. These intimacy processes become linked to one another in a repeated spiral over the family life cycle.

8. Intimacy Therapy views the family life cycle as bringing predictable challenges to relational intimacy—and with those challenges comes the need to repeat the "spiral" of intimacy ingredients, beginning with affectionate caring. Thus, the marital stage of mutual giving is challenged by the addition of children to return to affectionate caring, followed by vulnerable communication, joint accomplishment, and again, by mutual giving.

9. Intimacy Therapy draws on emotionally focused therapies as an addition to cognitive and behavioral techniques. The "empathetic comforting of identified hurts and needs" is a pivotal element in the affectionate-caring ingredient of intimacy. Because a fundamental breakdown or hindrance to intimacy results from a lack of empathetic comfort, this connection serves as the beginning point of Intimacy Therapy.

10. Intimacy Therapy, in a "staged" approach to marriage counseling, addresses in Stage 1, initial *assessment* (or self-inventory) of the individuals, the marriage relationship, and intergenerational dynamics. In Stage 2 it addresses increased *stability* of the marriage relationship as a basis for improved functioning and additional therapeutic intervention. In Stage 3 it addresses the *leave-cleave* issues of intergenerational significance that contribute to personal problems in living and marital discord. In Stage 4 it addresses the *becoming-one disciplines* that help ensure relational intimacy, personal maturity, and positive mental health.

11. Intimacy Therapy views the counselor as playing a God-ordained role within the body of Christ to assist and encourage others along a journey toward experiencing life "abundantly" (John 10:10). Specifically, the counselor's role is four-fold within the framework of eliminating hindrances and enhancing intimacy. He or she is to assist the couple by:

| **Eliminating Hindrances** | **Enhancing Intimacy** |
|---|---|
| a. Identifying and interrupting unproductive behaviors | Modeling and reinforcing productive behaviors |
| b. Resolving unhealed emotions | Experiencing positive emotions |
| c. Identifying and countering unhealthy thinking | Internalizing healthy thinking |
| d. Identifying unmet intimacy needs | Modeling and encouraging the meeting of intimacy needs |

# Endnotes

**Chapter 1. Marriage Intimacy: Elusive Dream or Obtainable Reality?**

1. Erikson, E. H. *Childhood and Society,* rev. ed. (New York: Norton, 1963), 263.

2. Rubenstein, C. M. and P. Shaver, *In Search of Intimacy* (New York: Delacorte Press, 1982), 21.

3. Medved, Michael from a lecture given at Hillsdale College, Hillsdale, Michigan, in March 1992, based on his book *Hollywood vs. America* (New York: HarperCollins and Zondervan, 1992), as quoted in Imprimis, vol. 21, no. 11 (November 1992): 2–3.

4. Veroff, J. E. Douvan, and R. A. Kulka, *The Inner American* (New York: Basic Books, 1981), 537.

**Chapter 3. Intimacy Needs: Is It Okay to Have Them?**

1. Narramore, Bruce. *Your Child's Hidden Needs* (Old Tappan, NJ: Revell, 1987), 219.

2. Maslow, A. H. *Motivation and Personality.* (New York: Harper & Row, 1970), 320.

3. Meier, Paul. *Christian Child-Rearing and Personality* (Grand Rapids, MI: Baker Book House, 1977), 222.

**Chapter 4. Intimacy Needs: What Are They?**

1. Carter, Les. *Broken Vows* (Nashville, TN: Thomas Nelson Publishers, 1990), 251.

2. Getz, Gene. *Loving One Another* (Wheaton, IL: Victor Books, 1980), 143.

**Chapter 5. Loving Your Spouse: Body, Mind, and Spirit**

1. Sproul, R. C. *The Intimate Marriage* (Wheaton, IL: Tyndale, 1986), 127.

2. Worthington, Everett. *Marriage Counseling—A Christian Approach to Counseling Couples* (Downers Grove, IL: InterVarsity Press, 1989), 371.

## Chapter 7. Block the Robbers of Intimacy

1. Greene, Bernard. *A Clinical Approach to Marital Problems* (Springfield, IL: Charles Thomas, 1970), 32, 37.

2. Hite, Shere. *The Hite Report on Male Sexuality* (New York: Alfred A. Knof, 1981).

3. "How Common is Pastoral Indiscretion?" *Leadership* (Winter, 1988), 12–13.

4. Jenkins, Jerry. *Loving Your Marriage Enough to Protect It* (Chicago: Moody Press, 1993).

## Chapter 8. Think Straight

1. Thurman, Chris. *The Lies We Believe* (Nashville, TN: Thomas Nelson Publishers, 1989), 206.

2. Thurman, Chris. *The Twelve Best Kept Secrets for Living an Emotionally Healthy Life* (Nashville, TN: Thomas Nelson Publishers, 1993).

## Chapter 9. Forgive Each Other

1. Minirth, Frank, Paul Meier, and Robert Hemfelt. *Love Is a Choice.* (Nashville, TN: Thomas Nelson Publishers, 1989), 275.

## Chapter 11. Leave Your Childhood Home

1. Hemfelt, Robert and Paul Warren. *Kids Who Carry Our Pain* (Nashville, TN: Thomas Nelson Publishers, 1990).

2. Lewis, Jerry M. *How's Your Family?* (New York: Brunner/Mazel, 1989), 192.

3. Kingsley, Davis. "The Sociology of Parent-Child Conflict," *American Sociological Review 5* (August 1940), 523–35.

4. Dobson, James. *Dr. Dobson Answers Your Questions* (Wheaton, IL: Tyndale, 1982), 515.

## Chapter 12. Mourn Your Childhood Hurts

1. Benner, David. *Healing Emotional Wounds* (Grand Rapids, MI: Baker, 1990).

2. Ferguson, David. "Healing Unhealed Emotional Pain," *Marriage & Family Intimacy Newsletter* (Austin, TX: Alpha Omega Publishing), July 1991.

## Chapter 13. Understand Who You Are

1. Crabb, Lawrence J. *The Marriage Builder* (Grand Rapids, MI: Zondervan, 1982), 143.

2. Swindoll, Charles. *The Grace Awakening* (Dallas: Word, 1990).

## Chapter 14. Practice Intimacy Disciplines

1. McMinn, Don. *Strategic Living* (Grand Rapids, MI: Baker, 1983), 183.

2. Wheat, Ed. *Love Life for Every Married Couple* (Grand Rapids, MI: Zondervan, 1978), 251.

## Chapter 15. Maintain Intimacy Throughout the Life Cycle

1. Minirth, Dr. Frank, Mary Alice Minirth, Dr. Robert Hemfelt, Susan Hemfelt, Dr. Brian Newman, and Dr. Deborah Newman. *Passages of Marriage* (Nashville, TN: Thomas Nelson Publishers, 1991), 335.